The Magazine

Málaga and Cádiz

Granada and Almería

Sevilla and Huelva

Walks & Tours

Practicalities

Appendix

Magical Moments

Be in the right place at the right time and experience magical moments you will never forget.

Granada's architectural splendour will never cease to amaze you

Do you enjoy long walks? Here, too, Andalucía offers the perfect setting, for instance along Cabo de Trafalgar

1

2

3

4

5

6

7

8

9

10

★★ TOP 10

Not to be missed! Our top hits – from the absolute No. 1 to No. 10 – help you plan your tour of the most important sights.

❶★★ Granada
Tales of 1001 Nights spring to mind inside the Alhambra, the Moors' last royal residence on Spanish soil. The Albaicín district is also part of their legacy (p. 80).

❷★★ Córdoba
The Mezquita, once the main mosque in Western Islam seats 25,000 worshippers, and is Spain's most eminent example of Moorish religious architecture (p. 116).

❸★★ Sevilla
The home town of Carmen and The Barber of Seville also impresses visitors with its Giralda, the largest Gothic church in the world, as well as the Alcázar, the Casa de Pilatos and the Plaza de España (p. 150).

❹★★ Ronda
One of the most imposing edifices in the town regarded as the cradle of bullfighting, Puente Nuevo offers an awesome view of the surrounding cliffs (p. 44).

❺★★ Úbeda
Affluent citizens once had magnificent palaces built here. The result is a unique and well-rounded city tribute to the Renaissance (p. 124).

❻★★ Carmona
A highlight of Carmona, apart from the beautiful town centre, is the Necrópolis Romana, Spain's most important Roman burial site (p. 164).

❼★★ Jerez de la Frontera
In the "world capital of sherry", the numerous wine cellars are as inviting as the Alcázar. The town is equally famous for its royal Andalucían School of Riding, where you can watch the horses "dance" (p. 48).

❽★★ Las Alpujarras
The magnificent mountain world of the Alpujarras with its steep valley and white villages offers a tremendous range of possibilities for mountain sports (p. 93).

❾★★ Parque Nacional de Doñana
The park ranks among the most beautiful nature reserves in Europe and offers migrant birds a superb winter hideaway (p. 166).

❿★★ Costa del Sol
The "sun coast" between Málaga de Estepona is a paradise for those who enjoy partying all night and lazing on the beach all day (p. 51).

That Andalucían Feeling

Find out what makes this autonomous community in the south of Spain tick, experience its unique flair – just like the Andalucíans themselves.

Ir de Copas – Go out for a drink

Spaniards love strolling from bar to bar, in order to drink a *caña*, a freshly tapped beer, a glass of red wine or a *fino*, a dry sherry, as they tuck into a tasty tapa. They even have a special word for it: *tapear*. You should try it too; it is a fun, albeit small, evening-meal option. Look for the bar with the largest crowd! That is where you will find the best tapas, and you will soon get into conversation with the other guests. Top tapa towns are Almería, Córdoba, Granada, Málaga and Seville.

Fiestas

Seville's *Semana Santa* and *Feria de Abril*, Spain's two largest fiestas, offer an ideal way to get a feel for the Andalucían soul, with all its religious fervour and festive exuberance. Yet every village festival offers visitors a similar experience, because every Andalucían community organises an annual celebration for its patron saint. For many days during these *fiestas patronales*, homage is paid to the saints with church masses, processions and, in particular, good food, dancing, music and fireworks.

El Rocío

For 362 days in the year, El Rocío (p. 172) is a dusty little town with about 800 inhabitants. But over the Whitsun weekend, Andalucía's most famous pilgrimage takes place here, the Romería del Rocío. Thousands of pilgrims from all over Spain flock to the town, many in horse-drawn wagons. In festive garb (the women in colourful flamenco dresses), they accompany the procession behind the garland-festooned *Virgen del Rocio* (Virgin of the Dew) through the Parque Nacional Coto de Doñana. At night, there is a lot of dancing and alcohol flows freely. The final procession in El Rocío takes place to the ear-piercing accompaniment of

Tapas are one of Andalucía's culinary highlights. You must definitely succumb to temptation and try these little delicacies, preferably in a nice bar

Spanish dance culture: the love of flamenco brings all the generations together

The Moorish legacy is visible in many places in Andalucía – such as Seville

musical instruments and fire crackers.

Flamenco
Flamenco is typically Andalucían. Málaga, Ronda, Jerez de la Frontera, Cádiz (p. 58), Córdoba (p. 116) and Seville (p. 150) are regarded as main centres of this art. To avoid ending up in some "dive" with an inferior, run-of-the-mill show and extortionate prices, ask in the tourist office for reputable flamenco venues. The more authentic the presentation with the musicians, singers, dances and dancing, the more the Andalucían audience let's themselves be caught up in the spirit of the occasion! It is fun watching that, too.

Arab Legacy
The rich Moorish legacy is not only tangible in fascinating architectural highlights, such as the Alhambra in Granada or the Mezquita of Córdoba with all their opulence, you can also experience it in the Hammam Al Ándalus Arab Baths of Córdoba (p. 141) or in the restaurants of Granada, which serve traditional Arab meals.

Shopping
Zara, Mango, Desigual? Everyone had heard of these innovative Spanish fashion labels, which also have international chains. When you are looking for something a bit more flamboyant and out of the ordinary, then you should browse through the town and village shops; they sell traditional products such as leather, ceramics, basketwork, flamenco guitars and the like, some of which you can actually watch being made.

Mercados
Throughout Andalucía, the *mercadillos* (weekly markets) offer the best shopping experience, regardless whether in the large cities, the small villages by the Mediterranean or up in the mountains. On Saturdays – mainly in the morning – the stands around the churches and main squares bow under the weight of the fresh fruit and vegetables, smoked and fresh meat products, herbs, dried fruit, clothing and household goods. The roofed market halls (*mercados*) also provide a nice alternative. Here, too, the sales people are happy to chat to visitors, even with the help of pantomime gestures where necessary. Trying things is generally quite acceptable. Crabs, olives, best Iberian ham...

Corrida
These days, bullfighting also has a lot of opponents in Spain itself. Yet in Andalucía, especially in Ronda, Málaga, Jerez (p. 48), Córdoba (p. 116) und Seville (p. 150), you will still find keen supporters (*aficionados*) who regard the Corrida as part of their special cultural heritage and cherish it as an art form.

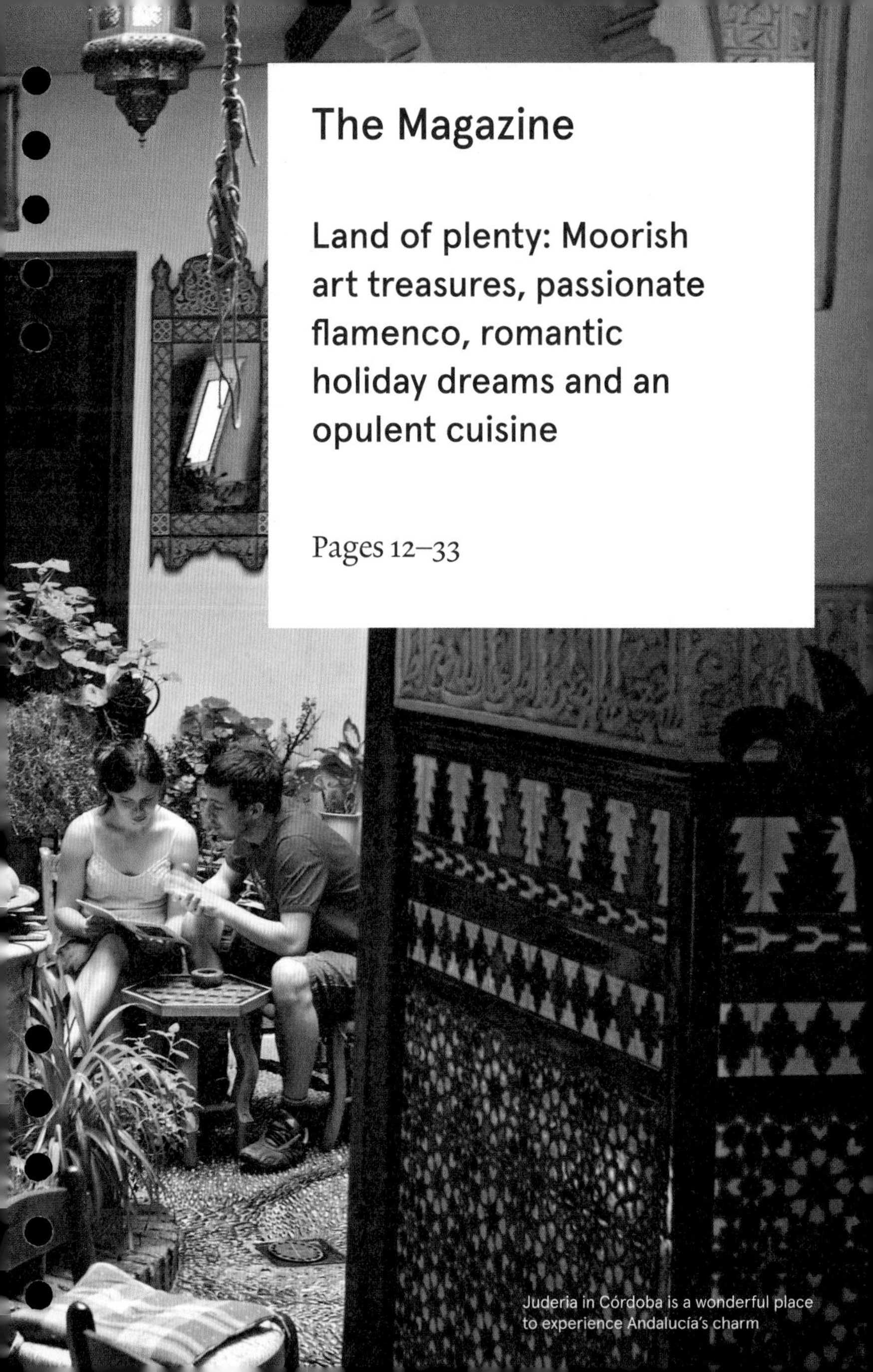

The Magazine

Land of plenty: Moorish art treasures, passionate flamenco, romantic holiday dreams and an opulent cuisine

Pages 12–33

Juderia in Córdoba is a wonderful place to experience Andalucía's charm

Come in! Restaurants in Granada's Albaicín district exude Arab flair.

Moorish Andalucía

Many different cultures have left their mark on Andalucía: the Phoenicians, Greeks Carthaginians, Celts, Romans and Visigoths. Yet the Moors undoubtedly had the most lasting influence. Under their reign, Al-Andalus experienced a golden age of the arts.

The name Moor derives from the word *amaurós* ("dark"), used by the Greeks and Romans to describe those Berber tribes living in North Africa who were converted to the Muslim faith by the Arabs in the 7th century and provided armed support during the conquest of the Iberian Peninsula. In AD711, the Arab commander Tariq Ibn Ziyad crossed the Strait of Gibraltar with an army of 7,000 men and landed near the town now known as Tarifa, the most southern settlement of the European mainland.

The invaders stayed for nearly 800 years. The legacy of their subtle and beautiful craftsmanship and their social and political skills is seen everywhere in Andalucía today, but especially in the starry fretwork and swirling arabesques of great buildings such as the Alhambra in Granada, the Mezquita in Córdoba and Seville's Giralda tower.

Water is Life

The Moors who came to what we now know as Andalucía found the kind of earthly paradise that they had only dreamt of in the desert wastes of their Moroccan home, the Maghrib. The key ingredient was plentiful water; it transformed arid lands into green oases and furnished Moorish palaces and modest homes alike with lush gardens enriched by the music of fountains and the glitter of pools.

The Moors had long called the land across the Straits of Gibraltar Al-Andalus. One suggested origin of the name relates to the Vandals

The intricate detail of the Myrtle Courtyard in the Alhambra in Granada makes it one of the most exquisite examples of the Moorish style

who occupied Spain and parts of North Africa during the 5th century. Another theory sees the etymology in the Visigothic "landa-hlauts" (which can be translated as "Lot Lands"), since the Visigoths drew lots for the various pieces of land. As the Moors advanced north, they used the name for the entire Spanish peninsula. Their invasion of France was stopped by the Loire at the Battle of Tours (732). This first victory of a Christian army over the Muslims at the Battle of Covadonga (722) saw the beginning of the Christian Reconquest from the north of Muslim-occupied areas. It took seven centuries to achieve, chiefly because the forces of Christian Spain were sparse, fragmented and often at odds with each other.

The reign of the Catholic monarchs, to whom these elaborate tombs are dedicated, ended Moorish dominion in Andalucía

A Golden Age

Initially undisturbed by the *Reconquista*, the Moors dug in their heels in the region now known as Andalucía. In this contracted Al-Andalus they tolerated other religions, and made wise agreements and concessions with Christian neighbours. Andalucía experienced a Golden Age under the Moors. Córdoba became the capital of Al-Andalus, and its rulers, or caliphs, rivalled those of Baghdad and Damascus for their wealth and accomplishments. In 756 the building of Córdoba's Great Mosque, the Mezquita, began, and over the next 200 years the city became enriched by trade in gold and silver, leather, silk, perfumes and spices, becoming Europe's leading centre of scientific and artistic achievement.

The Charm of the Moors' Al-Andalus

By the beginning of the 11th century, factionalism and internal rivalries brought an end to the Golden Age of the Córdoban caliphate, and Al-Andalus fragmented into a number of small independent Muslim

Artesonado or Azulejos?

Andalucía's architecture reflects its Islamic past. You'll frequently see the following terms used in literature about the region.

- Artesonado Intricate, coffered wooden ceiling.
- Azulejos Glazed ceramic tiles in vivid colours and designs.
- Mudéjar During the Christian Reconquest of Al-Andalus, many Muslims were expelled, but those with building and craft skills were allowed to stay. They were known by the name *mudéjar* (meaning "those permitted to remain"). From around about the twelfth century the word was applied to the architectural style that these craftspeople developed by merging Islamic and Christian forms.
- Muqarnas Masonry and plasterwork with stalactite effect.

kingdoms called *taifas*. The last such kingdom, the Kingdom of Granada, founded in 1238 by Mohammed Ibn al-Ahmar, a descendant of Beni Nasr, was able to hold out for some time. The kingdom stretched from Gibraltar to Almería, and its capital was the richest town on the peninsula and at the same time its cultural centre. With the Alhambra, built in the 14th century, the Nasrid dynasty left behind an outstanding monument to their reign. With the marriage of Isabel de Castilla and Fernando de Aragón (the "Catholic Monarchs") in 1469, the foundation stone was laid for the unification of the two large Spanish kingdoms. The couple was determined to banish all the Muslims. On 2 January 1492, the Catholic monarchs moved into Granada. The last Moorish ruler Boabdil fled to Africa. His departure marked the end of almost eight centuries of Islamic culture in southern Spain. The following expulsion of many hundreds of thousands of Moors and Jews meant a heavy setback for the further economic development and cultural life of Spain. Yet, as you travel through Andalucía, the persuasive magic of Moorish Al-Andalus is as gripping and captivating as it ever was.

Romantic Andalucía

Nineteenth-century visitors to Andalucía conjured up an image of the region as a seductive other world, a world of heat and passion, of scented orange groves, of raffish characters and mountain brigands, of licentious Don Juans and alluring Carmens.

It was an image that was self-perpetuating because many of these visitors exaggerated their stories to make them sound more romantic in what was easily portrayed as an exotic and even dangerous land. This had been the Al-Andalus of the Moors after all, a land where Europe gave way to Africa, an exciting alternative to what seemed the staid predictability of northern Europe.

The English writer Richard Ford described Spain as an escape to "racy

The Real Carmen

The image of scantily dressed female workers in the stifling heat of Seville's 19th-century tobacco factory excited the prurient rather than the romantic interest of more than one male traveller. "Most of them were young, and some were very pretty." said Théophile Gautier for example in his *Un Voyage en Espagne* (1843), adding: "The extreme carelessness of their dress enables us to appreciate their charms at ease."

George Dennis was far less charming (*A Summer in Andalusia*, 1839) "I have never beheld such an assemblage of ugliness." In truth the women worked in dreadful conditions, which no visitor paying any attention could fail to observe.

Carmen has also left her mark on romantic Andalucía – and as a muse inspired art such as this

Andalucía's 19th-century *bandoleros* lived in remote areas, including the Serranía de Ronda

freshness" from the "dull uniformity" of Europe. Ford wrote superbly of the Andalucía of his day. He first came to Spain in 1830 and over the next few years produced his epic *Handbook for Travellers in Spain and Readers at Home*, published in 1845 and still revered as one of the finest evocations of Spain ever written – exhaustive, witty and opinionated. Washington Irving came to Spain to work for the American Legation in Madrid in 1826, and in 1828 set off on a tour of Andalucía. He lived for some time in the semi-derelict Alhambra and there wrote *The Conquest of Granada* before beginning his famous work *The Alhambra: A Series of Tales*. The book mixes romantic stories of the Alhambra's Moorish past with vivid portrayals of the palace's decaying grandeur.

It triggered movements in Spain and in northern Europe that led to the Alhambra's preservation, and fuelled interest in the palace.

George Bizet's opera Carmen is also inextricably linked to the region's romantic image. First performed in 1875, the popular opera still features on the annual venue of the world's theatres. The music composed by Bizet (who actually never set a foot inside Spain) represented a revolutionary break with opera tradition of that time while the short story by Prosper Mérimée on which it was based fulfilled all the clichés: Carmen, a gypsy heroine of sultry good looks who worked in Seville's tobacco factory, a notorious bandit from the Ronda mountains, and a dashing bullfighter, all three locked into a passionate story of love, betrayal and death. Carmen's male counterpart was the fictional Don Juan – a legendary figure who became the definition of the lady-killer per se. In turn, the Don Juan legend was immortalised by subsequent adaptations, not least by Mozart's opera *Don Giovanni*. The visitor's image of the passionate lover and seducer shines as brightly as the Andalucían sun – a romantic fantasy that has little to do with reality.

Begging for Bandits

Andalucían bandits were all the rage among 19th-century travellers, who arrived in the region with their heads filled with the imaginative tales of previous visitors. There were certainly lawless *bandoleros* in the Sierras of Andalucía, but records show that foreigners were generally left in peace, even if some of them obviously cherished the idea of a romantic adventure. The French novelist Alexandre Dumas is said to have sent money to an Andalucían bandit chief in return for a promise that he and his party would be held up as they crossed wild country – with the proviso that no harm would be done to them. And the Danish writer Hans Christian Andersen expressed great disappointment that he passed unchallenged through the hills of the Sierra Morena.

The Bullfight – Art, Sport or Outrage?

To the *aficionado*, bullfighting is an art rather than a sport. Bullfight reviews come under the arts pages in Spanish newspapers, with the *corrida* still receiving the same superlatives as stage and ballet productions.

The classic setting of the bullfight is Andalucía, although of course *toreros* also stride out to face the beast in all of Spain's major towns, in some countries in Latin America and in the south of France. While Madrid can boast the largest arena, Plaza de Toros, it is Andalucía's Ronda that is one of the oldest. It is thus not very surprising

Lady in Lights

There were several accomplished female bullfighters prior to 1908, when a ban was placed on them becoming *toreras*. One such was Martina García, who took part in her last bullfight in 1880 at the age of 66. When the ban was lifted after the death of General Franco (on 20 November 1975 in Madrid), one woman who donned the *traje de luces*, the bullfighter's glittering costume, was Cristina Sánchez. She outshone many of her male peers and at one memorable *corrida* killed all six bulls. Sánchez retired early in 1999, on the grounds that she was finding difficulty in securing top-level fights because so many big-name male bullfighters refused to share the bill with her.

that the most famous *toreros* were and are Andalucíans: Manolete, Lagartijo, Joselito, Paquirri und El Cordobés – some of whom lost their lives in the arena. Their involuntary four-legged opponents, the *toros bravos*, those half-wild creatures bursting with energy, are for the main part the product of Anadalucían breeders and are only bred for this one purpose.

Battle of Life or Death

For some Spaniards, giving up bullfighting would be like giving up a piece of their deeply entrenched culture, although even in Andalucía, too, bullfighting is no longer accepted in the way it was, and it is facing growing opposition. Nonetheless, there are still plenty of opportunities to see bullfighting in Andalucía. Doing so, however, means supporting bullfighting –every spectator should be aware of this fact. The season runs from Easter to October. The major bullrings, such as Seville's Maestranza (p. 177), are the places to experience the atmosphere of the bullfight at its most intense; and it is in the main rings that you are likely to see the best *matadores* confronting the biggest and fiercest Andalucían fighting bulls. Even the smallest villages try to stage a *corrida* at least once a year. In Spain, the objective is not just to break the bull's spirit, because the fight still ends with the death of the bull – or, much less frequently, with the death of the *torero*.

Dirty Tricks

Opponents of bullfighting condemn the spectacle outright, because the bulls in the ring are made to suffer. But even enthusiasts argue that the modern *corrida* has become debased, not least by such practices as shaving the tips of a bull's horns to reduce its accuracy and sensitivity to movement. There are hints of worse practices being inflicted on "dangerous" bulls, before they are released into the ring, in order to reduce their potential lethality. *Aficionados* complain that this no longer has anything to do with the so-called *arte de lidiar*, the true art of good bullfighting.

Matadors such as Salvador Vega, shown here during a bullfight in Málaga, see their profession as an artistic – but at the same time gory – ritual.

Fire in the Blood

Flamenco is the soul music of Andalucía, a fusion of voice, guitar and dance that rarely fails to set the blood tingling. There is nothing quite like the raw, deep singing (*cante jondo*), the hand-clapping (*palmas*) and the rippling guitar that accompany the staccato footwork and sinuous movements of the flamenco dancer.

Not "only" music, dance and song: flamenco is an expression of one's attitude to life

The origin of flamenco is as varied as the history of Andalucía itself. Moorish influences and allusions to Byzantine liturgical music have been discovered in it as have elements of medieval romances. The only thing really known is that the *gitanos* (Romani) of Andalucía had the greatest influence on this art form; even today, the best flamenco artists come from this ethnic group, which call themselves *calé* (from Romani *kalo*: "black") and are a subgroup of the Romani. About 200 years ago, they began the original form

Finding Flamenco

Ask for details of flamenco *tablaos* and *peñas* at tourist offices. Hotels often have information about flamenco shows, but these may be "variety" performances or stylised cabaret, with a meal as part of the bill. There is accessible flamenco at the following venues: Tablao Cardenal and La Bulería (Córdoba, p. 141), Peña la Platería (Granada, p. 107), Teatro Miguel de Cervantes (Málaga, p. 71), Museo Lara (Ronda, p. 71), La Taberna Flamenca (Jerez de la Frontera, p. 71), La Cava (Cádiz, p. 71), Museo del Baile Flamenco, Los Gallos and El Tamboril (Seville, p. 177).

of today's flamenco. Like the song and the guitar playing, the dance has since developed into an extremely demanding art form. There are flamenco schools in practically every town of Andalucía. In Seville alone there are more than 30. Some offer day and weekly courses and are thus suitable for tourists who just want to get a taste of what it involves (www.sevillaflamenco.com; www.flamenco-carmendetorres.com).

Flamenco Secret

The finest flamenco singers are said to possess *duende* – the soul, the "ghost", the inspirational gift that transforms an ordinary performance into something sublime. Before achieving *duende*, singers may wait for hours, during which they massage their vocal chords with endless smoking and glassfuls of the fiery liqueur *aguardiente*, a combination that would render most people speechless, if not songless. In its purest form flamenco is *cante jondo* (deep song), especially when performed by the best *cantadores* (singers), whose scorched voices express real grief, yet with a triumphant reaffirmation of the human spirit. For most visitors to Andalucía, however, it is the magical combination of *el cante* with *el toque*, the guitar, and *el baile*, the dance, that gives flamenco its appeal.

Flamenco artiste Eva Yerbabuena knows how to inject real passion into her dance

Emotional Depth in Dance and Song

A distinction is made in flamenco between about 30 different kinds of song, not all of which are suited to dance. They have their origin in the Andalucían provinces. The *Buleria* comes from Jerez, for example, the *Alegría* from Cádiz and the *Malagueña* is mainly sung in Málaga. What all these forms have in common, however, is the emotional depth of the music and the song. The songs are about the fears and anxieties of everyday life, about happiness and grief and, of course, predominantly love. Full of metaphorical allusions, the words are as clear as they are haunting. Emotions are also expressed in the dance. The staccato of the boots symbolises anger and pride, the graceful movements of hands and fingers indicate seduction and tenderness. Just as the aim is for the audience to become one with the feelings of the singer and for a frisson to take hold of some that is released in the choral "*Olé*" at the end of the song, the audience is also expected to really "feel" the movements of the dancers. That is when the lines between song and dance are crossed and the flamenco has found its "demons", according to the writer Federico Garcia Lorca.

Experts will tell you that the real thing emerges spontaneously, and usually in the early hours of the morning, in hidden-away bars and in semi-private all-night parties called *juergas*. The next best thing to an impromptu flamenco event are *tablaos*, performances of "classical" flamenco by trained artistes. Flamenco clubs and associations called *peñas* are also open to visits. Perhaps the best experience for a visitor to Andalucía is to come across spontaneous flamenco at a village *fiesta*. You'll hear it before you see it, and you'll never forget it.

Famous Flamenco Names

Carmen Amaya (1913–63), was born in the poor district of Somorrostro in Barcelona (today Vila Olímpica) and started dancing at the age of seven. In 1929 she made her debut in Paris, which launched her career as one of the best flamenco dancers of all times.

Manolo Caracol (Manolo the Snail, 1909–73), a gypsy from the Seville province. He began his career aged just 11, at a flamenco event in the Alhambra of Granada staged by the Spanish composer Manuel de Falla, the poet Federico García Lorca and the guitarist Andrés Segovia.

Camarón de la Isla (the Shrimp of the Island, 1950–92), was the son of a blacksmith from the Isla del León/San Fernando in the province of Cádiz. He made his first appearance as a singer at the age of eight, but even then the experts realised that the youngster was on the path to a top career as a *cantador*.

Paco de Lucía (1947–2014), born in Algeciras and originally christened Francisco Sánchez Gómez, was one of the most important flamenco guitarists of the present day. Blessed with a grandiose technique, he was both a fascinating solo guitarist and superb accompanist for flamenco singers. As a cross-border musician, he also worked with jazz greats such as Al DiMeola, Larry Corryell and John McLaughlin. He also wrote the music for Carlos Saura's film *Carmen*.

Diego Ramón Jiménez Salazar (known as El Cigala, born 1968), the son of a *gitano* family from Madrid won his first flamenco contest at the age of 12. The CD Lágrimas Negras (2002) recorded with Bebo Valdés (1918–2013) was an international hit.

Joaquín Cortés, born in 1969 in Córdoba became a soloist for the Spanish National Ballet at the age of 15 and founded his own ballet company in 1992 with which he has successfully performed all around the world. He is also known for his work with pop stars such as Jennifer Lopez und Alicia Keys.

Estrella Morente (born. 1980) into a musical family from the Province of Granada, is one of a young generation of *cantatores*, who has even managed to get inveterate rock stars like Lenny Kravitz enthusiastic about flamenco.

Liquid Gold

In Andalucía, you don't simply drink sherry, you experience the entire sherry culture that goes with it – as befits one of the world's most exquisite wines.

A law stipulates that white wine can only be labelled as "sherry" if it is produced within the "Sherry Triangle", the area of land that lies in the northwestern part of Cádiz province between the towns of Jerez de la Frontera, Sanlúcar de Barrameda and El Puerto de Santa María. The Phoenicians began to cultivate wine in the area around Jerez 3,000 years ago. Romans, Moors and Spaniards continued the tradition. At the end of the 15th century, the first regulations came into force concerning the growing and harvesting of vines. It is said that Ferdinand Magellan's circumnavigation in 1519 was only successful because he had more sherry than (easily perishable) water on board. In 1587 during his attack on Cádiz, Sir Francis Drake seized 3,000 wineskins and took them back to England as part of his booty. Queen Elizabeth I liked the wine, and its popularity grew throughout her kingdom. From the 17th to 19th centuries, Irish and English businessmen founded major sherry dynasties such as Sandemann and Williams & Humbert.

What a wonderful bouquet – Experts test the taste and clarity of the sherry

Sherry is produced from three types of white grape: palomino, the basis of all sherry production, and muscat and Pedro Ximénez, both used in the blending of different types of sherry. The secret of sherry-making lies in the time-honoured system of fortifying the palomino grape with alcohol, then storing it in huge casks of American oak. The yeast retained in the wine creates a surface film called *velo de flor* (veil of flowers) which prevents oxidation. It is this "locking in" of the wine that preserves the pale colour of *fino*, the most popular sherry in Spain, and creates its dryness and bouquet. In the absence of *flor*, oxidation takes place, producing darker and fuller *amontillado* and *oloroso* sherries, which are often blended with the sweet wines made from muscat and Pedro Ximénez grapes to create pale, medium and cream sherries.

If you take a tour of one of the wine cellars (*bodegas*) of famous-name sherry empires such as Bodegas Tío Pepe, Domecq-Harveys, Sandeman and Williams & Humbert (p. 48), you'll see thousands of casks, in rows up to five casks high, where the sherry remains for between three and seven years. During this time, it is regularly blended with other wine until, as "liquid gold", it is finally bottled. The results of this blending are the delicious sherries of the officially denominated *Jerez-Xéres-Sherry y Manzanilla-Sanlúcar de Barrameda*. Its bouquet differs from the *fino* from Jerez, because in the coastal area around Sanlúcar the humidity is higher, which stabilizes the maturing process in the barrels.

Look out for one of the rare "sherry bulls"

Sherry Bullishness

On hilltops overlooking main roads all over Spain, you'll see huge metal silhouettes of fighting bulls. They were erected by the Osborne sherry company of El Puerto de Santa María from the 1950s onwards. When roadside advertising was banned in the late 1980s, Osborne removed its name from the bulls, but left the silhouettes – which are 14m (46ft) high and weigh 5t – in place. There was a national outcry when the authorities threatened to dismantle them, and 94 of the original 500 "sherry" bulls remain defiantly in place.

Land of Olives

Say Andalucía and most people will immediately think of Costa del Sol, Alhambra, Mezquita, flamenco and Carmen. Yet, anyone driving north of Granada soon lands in the middle of España Incognita: in the Jaen province, the home of Andalucían olive oil.

The olive tree is veiled in a sort of mystique; it gives life, can live several hundred years and still bear fruit like it did in its younger years. Some people dream of planting an olive tree. In the eastern Mediterranean area, the olive tree has been revered for centuries, its oil and fruit prized. Olive groves were sacred and carrying an olive

Around 2 million tonnes of oval fruits are harvested in Spain – the world's largest olive oil producer – each year. And 80% of the olive trees are in Andalucía.

branch was believed to protect the carrier from danger. At the Athenians' Olympic games, an olive branch was the highest award. Its wood was used for carving images of the gods. Over 2,000 years ago, the Romans brought the olive tree to their Spanish provinces and shipped the best oils to Rome. Olive oil served as an important foodstuff, but also as medicine, body lotion and for lighting, since oil lamps were popular for a long time before candles appeared.

In Rank and File

The olive trees stand atop the flat, rolling hills of Jaén province. Almost half of the annual harvest is exported. Abroad though few people know that most of the olives come from the Jaén province. When travelling between Jaén and Úbeda the only interruption to the row after row of olives tree is a pylon or two, so visitors soon work out that Jaén is the largest olive oil producer in the world – pure monoculture, yet nonetheless extremely efficient. In order to establish the exact number of trees for the subsidies from the EU, aerial shots were taken of the province. The figure is amazing: over 60 million! They need a lot of care, and at harvest time, there is little scope for daydreaming – even when, for example, the age-old trees near Martos are called "Romeo and Juliet", owing to the tender entwinement of the shimmering silver branches over the ochre-coloured grounds.

Star Chefs Swear by the Andalucían Olive Oil

The oval fruits of the tree are processed in modern factories into ordinary *Aceite de Oliva* and *Virgen Extra* while the crushed stones are used in the heating systems of quite a few health resorts. The "Region's Green Gold" is also used for cosmetics, in arts and crafts and, of course, in the kitchen. Even ice cream is made from it, although people tend to either like or hate the result.

The Piscual olive from Jaén province is particularly well known, and is a must in many local dishes, such as marinated partridge, pork tenderloin, roast lamb, dried cod or the garlicky *ajoatao* stew. Even Spain's star chefs, such as Ferran Adrià and Juan Mari Arzak from the distant Catalonia or the Basque region swear by the Andalucían oil.

A Very Special Experience...

Oil-tasting is an experience in itself. In the special *Catas de Aceite*, visitors can smell and taste the precious oil and then evaluate it. If the colour, taste and smell are first-class, the oil receives the top mark: *Aceite Virgin Extra!* To neutralise the palate between oils, you eat slices of apple and not bread.

Time for Tapas

Eat Andalucían and you eat tapas. These little dishes of food are a delicious accompaniment to a cold beer or a *copa de fino*, a glass of dry sherry.

In Andalucían bars, people come and go, order at their leisure, have a chat and generally don't tend to stay too long. When you order beer, sherry or wine, they come with two or three little dishes of tasty appetizers that are set out in a row in front of you. They can and should not be regarded as a full meal. The keyword is *tapear*: you stroll from bar to bar and try out a different delicacy each time, you will not only realise how much choice there is, but also have absolutely no problem skipping a main meal.

The literal meaning of *tapa* is "lid" or "cover", and its evolution as a culinary term is said to come from the old Andalucían habit of placing a small dish on a glass of sherry to protect it from flies and dust. Bar staff got into the habit of dropping morsels of bread and cheese and a couple of olives onto the dish and the custom grew. Today a good tapas bar will often

Tapas are served in a wide variety of simple and sophisticated styles. Whatever form they take, the choice is never easy – here, for example: shrimps or sardines?

Some Tasty Tapas

Different bars may serve them under slightly different names.

Fish and meat

- Gambas a la plancha: grilled prawns
- Puntillitas fritas: deep-fried baby squid
- Boquerones fritos: deep-fried anchovies
- Cazón en adobo: marinated and deep fried fish
- Croquetas: croquettes filled with meat or fish
- Jamón Serrano: fabled cured ham. Usually expensive
- Habas con jamón: broad beans and ham
- Lomo al Jerez: pork in sherry
- Flamenquin casero: sliced pork, egg and vegetables, rolled tightly in breadcrumb batter
- Pollo al ajillo: chicken in garlic
- Pimientos rellenos: stuffed peppers with tuna

Vegetarian

- Aceitunas: olives
- Ensalada mixta: mixed salad
- Revueltos: scrambled eggs
- Champiñones a la plancha: mushrooms with garlic
- Patatas ali-oli: diced potatoes in a garlic mayonnaise dressing
- Tortilla de patatas: potato omelette
- Arroz: rice

You are also spoilt for choice at Gallo Azul in Jerez de la Frontera...

have honey-coloured cured hams hanging from the ceiling, a row of stainless steel dishes filled with a selection of cold and hot tapas, a great choice of sherries and other drinks, and an atmosphere of enjoyment and good cheer. You can order them as a *ración* (whole dish) for several people or as a *media ración* (half a dish) for just one person. A tapa is generally served with the beer or white wine you have ordered on the café terrace. Some tapas bars have menus in several languages, but where the menu is in Spanish only, be careful; if you don't speak the language, you may end up playing tapas roulette. Choosing "blind" can bring enjoyable surprises, but it can also lead to the cruel reality of finding that the *criadillas* that you ordered, and that sounded so delicious, are actually fried testicles of pig. When in doubt, ask.

The Costa del Sol is not only blessed with the most sunshine, it offers sandy beaches, the blue ocean and its fair share of places to see

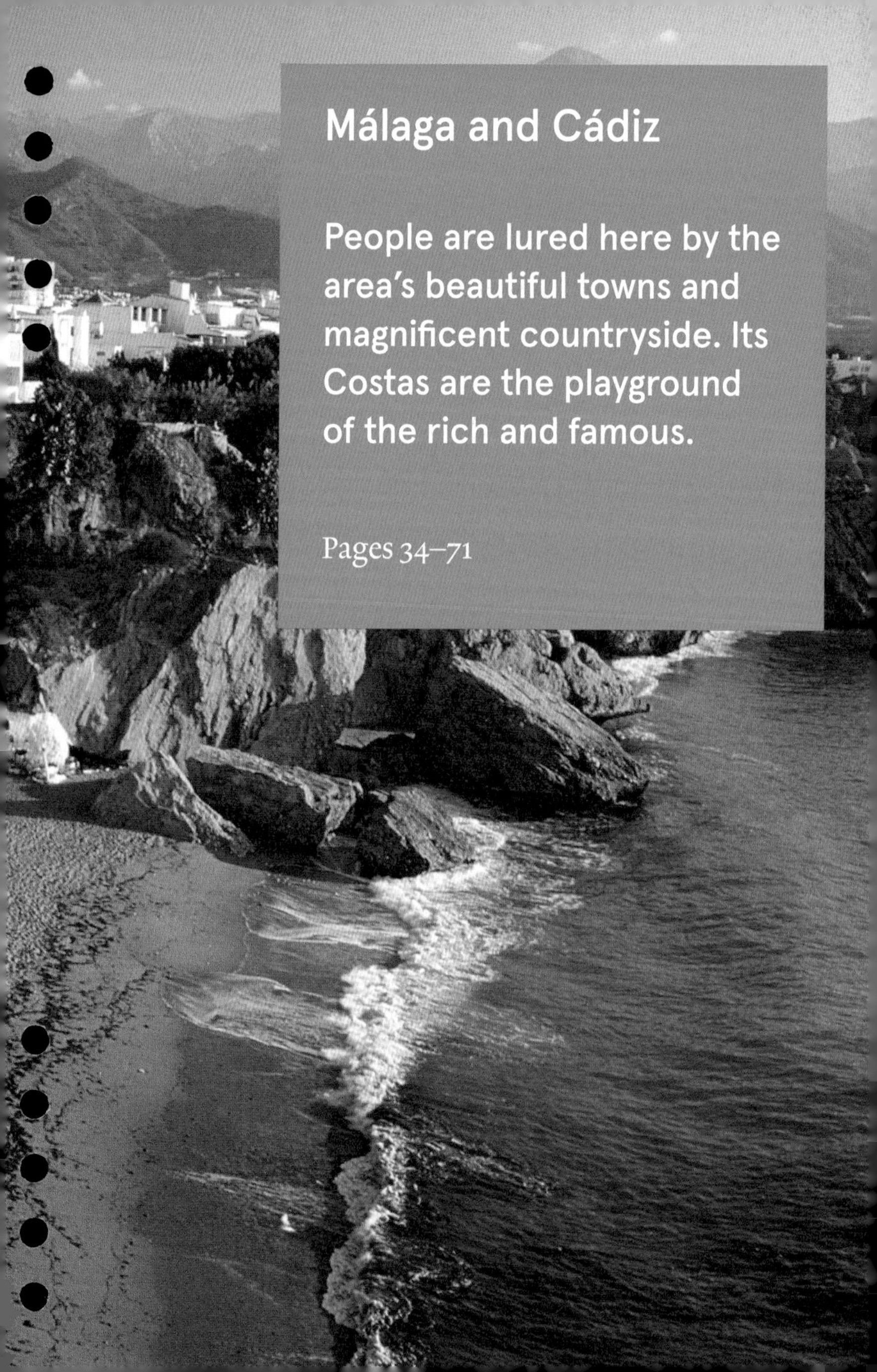

Málaga and Cádiz

People are lured here by the area’s beautiful towns and magnificent countryside. Its Costas are the playground of the rich and famous.

Pages 34–71

Getting Your Bearings

Málaga and Cádiz are Andalucía's most visited provinces, not only because of the popular appeal of Málaga's Costa del Sol, but for their spectacular landscapes, old Moorish villages and historic cities and towns.

Málaga province provides an ideal introduction to the extraordinary diversity of Andalucía. The vibrant, everyday life of its capital, Málaga, is a refreshing contrast to the conspicuous tourism of the neighbouring Costa del Sol's crowded resorts. North of Málaga and the Costa lie the forested valleys and rugged mountains of a different Andalucía, seen at its most dramatic in the bone-white limestone pinnacles and wooded ravines of the Parque Natural del Torcal near the historic town of Antequera. There is also dramatic scenery further west, in the Serranía de Ronda. The town of Ronda, for instance, actually appears to be hanging over the vast Río de Guadalevín gorge. To the south and west of Ronda villages of whitewashed houses known as the *pueblos blancos* (white towns) dot the mountains of the Sierra de Grazalema and the wooded hills of the area known as El Alcornocales.

TOP 10

❹ ★★ Ronda

❼ ★★ Jerez de la Frontera

❿ ★★ Costa del Sol

Don't Miss

⓫ Málaga

⓬ Cádiz

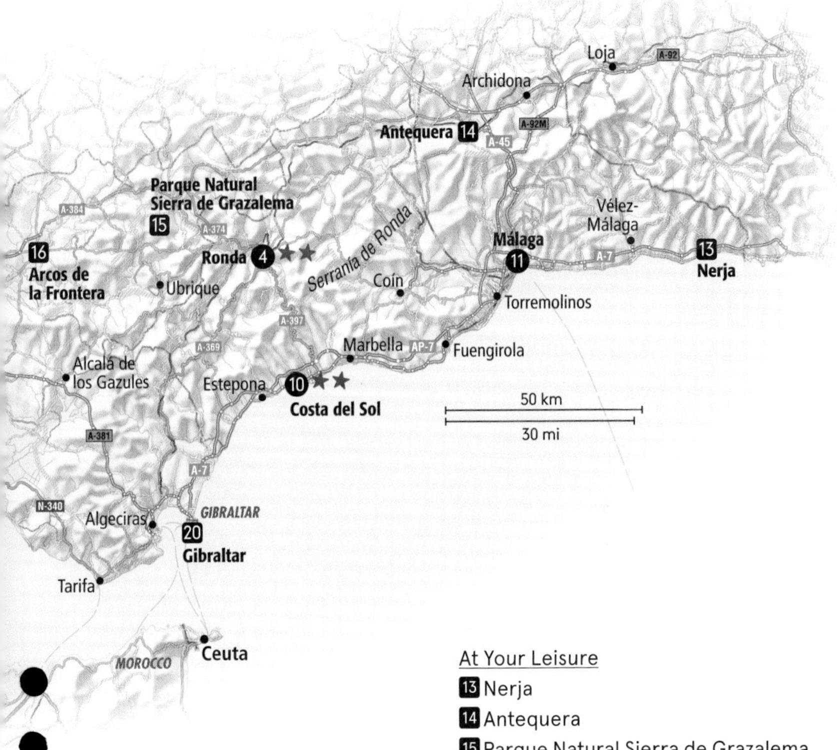

At Your Leisure

13 Nerja

14 Antequera

15 Parque Natural Sierra de Grazalema

16 Arcos de la Frontera

17 Sanlúcar de Barrameda

18 El Puerto de Santa María

19 Costa de la Luz (Cádiz)

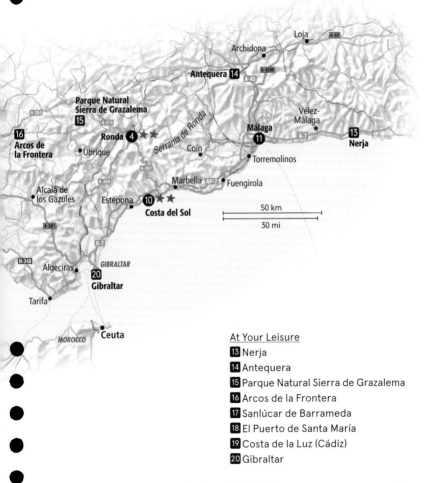

20 Gibraltar

My Day on the Squares of the White Town

Cádiz is perhaps the most remarkable town in Spain: a filigree isthmus in the middle of the Atlantic, tightly packed with houses, which are permeated by a tangled labyrinth of narrow streets. In between them, like small islands, are innumerable little squares. They will whisper their stories and history of the town whilst you take time to pause under the trees or on the terrace of a café.

9pm: Once wine, now tourists

The harbour of ⓬ Cádiz has always been a goods handling centre and transport hub. The Romans used to send their wine and pickled fish to Rome from here, then the treasures from the New World passed through, and now the cruise ships bring tourists. The best idea is to get a map of the town from the tourist information office in Paseo de Canalejas (p. 59) before setting off around the corner to Plaza de San Juan de Dios to find a nice café in which to order breakfast. This elongated square was once the most important market and trading place in Cádiz.

10:30am: Fragrant Flowers and an Elegant Post Office

Walk along Calle Pelota and you will reach the magnificent cathedral (p. 59). It flanks the Atlantic shore like a divine bulwark. The bottle-shaped

5pm: Vineyards, Mariners and the Madonna

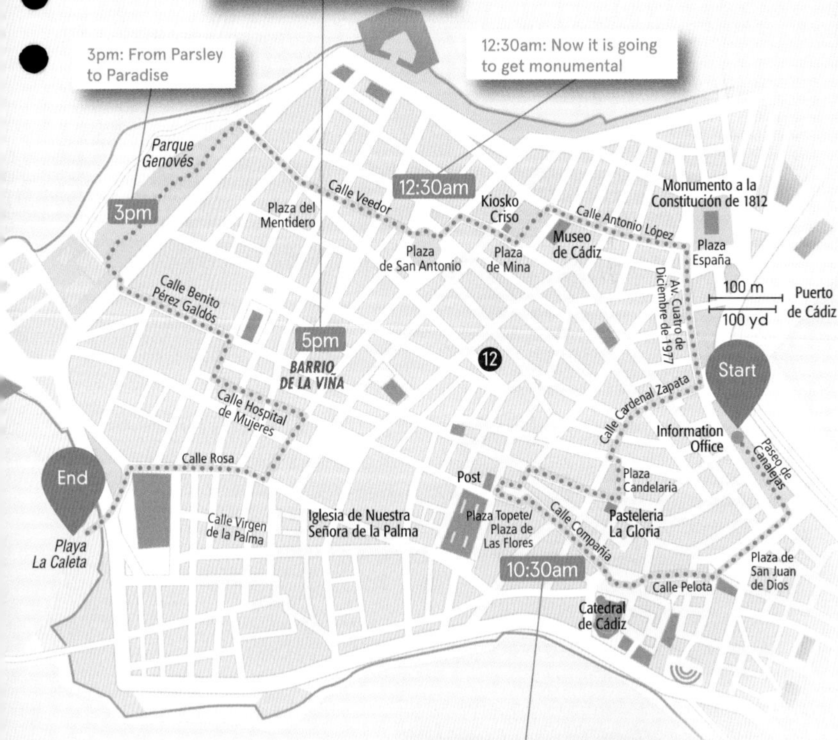

10:30am: Fragrant Flowers and an Elegant Post Office

Do you fancy the idea of breakfasting under palm trees? Then start your day with light refreshments on the charming Plaza de San Juan de Dios

Plaza Topete, better known as Plaza de las Flores (Square of Flowers), at the end of Calle Compañía, is one of the favourites places of the *Gaditandos*. They come here to buy flowers, to meet up in a café, or to celebrate carnival. Here, too, if you've still got some holiday letters you can send them in real style from the palatial post office, opened in 1930.

11am: Oasis in the middle of the town

Just northeast of the Plaza de las Flores is the Plaza de Candelaria. Only the name is a reminder of the monastery that existed here from the 16th to the end of the 19th century. It is worth popping into the Pastelería La Gloria to buy a little treat, which you can then enjoy sitting on a park bench in the shade of the trees.

12:30pm: Now it is going to get monumental

In the far north of the town you will find not one but three representative squares: in Plaza de España the marble monument in the shape of a parliamentary chamber commemorates the establishment of the First Constitution of Spain in 1812.

Afterwards admire the heaven-soaring and firmly rooted: walk on from the cathedral to the Plaza de Mina with its old kapok tree

Continuing along Calle Antonio López you will reach Plaza de Mina. Once the garden of a Franciscan convent, the square is now lined with 19th-century town houses, including the one in which the composer Manuel de Falla was born, and the Museum of Cádiz. Don't forget to look at the ancient kapok tree on the square. Afterwards, you may feel like having a snack in the Kiosko Criso, before walking on to Plaza de San Antonio. It was this rather sober-looking square that provided the stage for the proclamation of the constitution of Cádiz in 1812, and also for a number of bloody clashes during the liberal revolts of 1820.

2pm: The "Chat Corner"

The Cross of Truth (Cruz de la Verdad) once stood on the Plaza del

You must wander at least once through the pretty Parque Genovés and treat yourself to an enjoyable break in the "wine district" – and how about some fresh oysters?

Mentidero at the end of Calle Veedor. However, since the square was a popular meeting place for idlers whose gossip produced its fair share of fake news, people began to call it the square with the "Cross of Lies" (Cruz de las Mentiras), which is why it ultimately became the Plaza del Mentidero – the "Chat Corner". The café terraces under the shade of tall trees do indeed offer an inviting place to sit and chat.

3pm: From Parsley to Paradise

The Parque Genovés on the town's western bank was a restricted zone until well into the 18th century. Then ramblers advanced into the fallow land and affectionately dubbed it "Parsley Path". From the mid-19th-century Cádiz's most beautiful park developed around this delightful promenade (Paseo de las Delicias).

5pm: Vineyards, Mariners and the Madonna

Stretching out towards the south-west is the Barrio de la Viña – the vineyard district. Vines were actually cultivated here until the 18th century, then the seafarers

A day exploring the square of Cádiz must include Plaza del Mentidero, the "Chat Corner" of the white town (see below right)

settled here. It is regarded as the most authentic district in the town. In 1755 it was here, directly outside the Iglesia de Nuestra Señora de la Palma, that people believe the Mother of Christ stopped the tsunami caused by the large earthquake in Lisbon. She has been less successful with the Cádiz Carnival: that has its epicentre in the streets around Calle Virgen de la Palma. When you have had enough of the town's hustle and bustle, why not round off the day in the Playa La Caleta.

ⓘ

Pastelería La Gloria
✉ Plaza Candelaria, 9, 11005 Cádiz
☎ 09 56 28 34 55

Kiosko Criso
✉ Plaza de Mina, 2, 11004 Cádiz
☎ 06 26 67 42 54 ◷ Daily 10:45–9:15

❹★★ Ronda

Don't Miss	A leisurely stroll that always offers a definite edge
Why	The dizzying view alone merits a visit
When	In the early morning or late afternoon – just before or after the crowds
Time	Stay overnight to enjoy the town outside the very busy period
How	On foot
In Short	A bridge over a precipitous gorge, an attractive Old Town, pirate tales and an arena

Ronda is irresistible, not only because of its spectacular position above the Río Guadalevín's rocky gorge whose towering walls seem to be prised apart by a spectacular 18th-century bridge. The town has been popular with tourists since the 19th century, when it became an essential destination on the itinerary of travellers from northern Europe.

El Tajo is over 100m (109yd) deep and splits the town into two parts. Brown and white buildings cluster along the edges of the great cliffs like carved and painted extensions of the natural rock. The spectacular bridge, the Puente Nuevo, spans the gorge at its narrowest point and offers great views of El Tajo and the surrounding area from the Mirador de Ronda on the Paseo Blas Infante, right next to the bullring.

The Old Town

Ronda's most interesting sights lie on the south side of the gorge in the Ciudad Antigua, or Old Town, where you can discover beautiful squares, churches and Renaissance palaces as you thread your way through the side streets. At the southern end of the Old Town is the Plaza Duquesa de Parcent, a leafy square surrounded by handsome buildings and dominated by Iglesia de Santa María Mayor. The church stands on the site of a mosque, and Moorish features survive within the exquisite Gothic and baroque fabric of the building. The belfry crowns a fragment of an old minaret.

Impressive structure: Ronda's bridge over the gorge

Just around the corner from the church, along Calle Manuel Montero, is the 14th-century Palacio de Mondragón. Originally a Moorish palace, it was altered after the Reconquest, but some *mudéjar* (late Moorish) architecture survives: there are three small patios that in their decoration and style are superb examples of Islamic artistry. Take in the stupendous views from the garden terraces. Palacio de Mondragón doubles as the Municipal Museum and there are imaginative displays outlining Ronda's pre-Moorish history.

Nearby is the Casa de San Juan Bosco. The glory of this 19th-century mansion is its ornamental garden, with mosaics, fountains and clifftop views – a wonderful place of retreat.

Interested in learning some of the history? In Calle Armiñán, the main street of the Ciudad, is the Museo del Bandolero (Bandit Museum), which tells the story of the highwaymen who lived in the surrounding mountains in the 19th century.

Continue along Calle Marqués de Salvatierra to reach the medieval Puente Viejo and the Moorish Puente de San Miguel, with fantastic views. Close to the Puente de San Miguel are the Baños Arabes dating from the 13th and 14th centuries.

On the other side of Puente Viejo are the Jardines Ciudad de Cuenca. They offer a magnificent view down into the gorge.

The Mercadillo

Cross the Puente Nuevo into the Mercadillo district (which takes its name from the weekly market), the Ronda of smart hotels, restaurants, bars and souvenir shops. Ronda is regarded as the cradle of modern bullfighting. The Plaza de Toros inaugurated in 1785 is the second oldest and, with a diameter of 66m (216ft), largest bullring in Spain. An adjoining museum, Museo Taurino, within the handsome walls of the bullring is crammed with memorabilia of famous bullfighters and bulls and notable *aficionados*, such as American actor Orson Welles and writer Ernest Hemingway.

Arena with a rich past: Plaza de Toros

Opposite the bullring is the start of Ronda's main shopping street, the pedestrianised Carrera Espinel, flanked on either side by souvenir shops of varying quality, seductive delicatessens, and boutiques. Part-way up Espinel, on the left, is Plaza del Socorro with numerous restaurants, bars and cafés.

Smurfs in Andalucía?

Júzcar, *el pueblo pitufo*, the smurf village, 20km (12.5mi) south of Ronda, is quite a sensation. The houses in an idyllic tree-covered mountain setting were painted blue as part of an advertising campaign for the Hollywood film "The Smurfs" and have since become a tourist attraction in their own right.

INSIDER TIP For a spectacular view of Ronda's dramatic gorge and the Puente Nuevo, stop for a drink or snack at **Don Miguel** (Plaza de España 4; tel: 952 87 10 90; www.hoteldonmiguelronda.com), a classic Spanish restaurant.

---

211 D2

Tourist Information
Oficina Municipal de Turismo, Paseo de Blas Infante (OMT)
952 18 71 19
Oficina Comarcal de Turismo, Calle Espíritu Santo 37
952 87 07 392
www.turismoderonda.es

Parking
Underground car parks at the Plaza de la Merced and at the Plaza del Socorro (both next to Plaza de Toros), a public car park on Calle Lauría.

Iglesia de Santa María Mayor
Plaza Duquesa de Parcent
Mon–Sat 10–8, Sun 10–12:30, 2–8
€4.50

Palacio de Mondragón
Plaza de Mondragón, Calle Manuel Montero
952 87 08 18
www.museoderonda.es
Mon–Fri 10–7, Sat, Sun 10–3
€3.50

Casa Museo de San Juan Bosco
Calle Tenorio 20
600 27 51 25
www.casadonbosco.es
Daily 9:30–5:30 €2

Museo del Bandolero
Calle Armiñán 65
952 87 77 85
https://museobandolero.com
Summer 11–8:30, winter 11–7
€3.75

Baños Árabes
Calle San Miguel
Mo–Fr 10–7, Sa, So 10–3 €3.50

Plaza de Toros and Museo Taurino
Calle Virgen de la Paz
952 87 41 32
Daily 10–8 €7

❼★★ Jerez de la Frontera

Don't Miss	Three specialities in one sweep: sherry, horses and flamenco
Why	Authenticity is guaranteed here
When	Ideally, at the end of February/beginning of March, during the international Flamenco Festival
What Else	At the Royal Andalucían School of Equestrian Art – perfect elegance on four hooves
In Short	Don't leave before trying your new favourite sherry

Jerez is renowned as the sherry capital of the world and a centre for stylish equestrianism and flamenco. However, it also has enough fine plazas, fashionable shops, and lively bars and restaurants to make it one of Andalucía's most enjoyable provincial towns.

The Sherry Experience

Wine production in Jerez goes back to Phoenician times, when the rich chalky soil of surrounding Serit was found to be ideal for vine growing. The Romans carried on the tradition and called the settlement Seretium or rather Xeritium. The Moors adapted the name to Sheriss, which, in turn, became Jerez. After the conquest by Alfonso X in 1264 "de la Frontera" was added when Jerez became a border settlement of the Moorish kingdom of Granada. From the 18th and 19th century, the drink produced from fermented wine, and particularly popular in England, was called "sherry".

A tour of one or other of the *bodega*s is *de rigueur* and you'll find it an enjoyable experience, even if you do feel a little like a captive as liveried guides march you through vast wine stores or decant you briskly from "road trains" at each stage of the tour. A tasting session at the end is a satisfying lesson in the differences between the types of sherry. The city's *bodegas* include such famous names as Tío Pepe, Domecq-Harveys and Williams & Humbert, but the tours of the Tío Pepe and Domecq-Harveys *bodega*s are the most lavish. Both are like self-contained villages with lush gardens, covered patios and cobbled streets. At the Williams & Humbert *bodega* you get flamenco and a horse show too.

A walk through the enchanting gardens of Alcázar is a must (left).

Displays at the Real Escuela Andaluza del Arte Ecuestre show equestrian skills of the highest calibre (bottom)

Horses and More

Jerez's association with horses dates from the 18th century, when the monks of the nearby La Cartuja monastery began the selective breeding of Cartujano horses, which were noted for their elegant lines and obedience. The Jerez area is still the premier horse-breeding district of Spain. At the Real Escuela Andaluza del Arte Ecuestre (Royal Andalucían School of Equestrian Art) you can watch the Sinfonía a Caballo displays of choreographed equestrianism or visit the school's training area and stables. If you have a little more time at your disposal, pay a visit to the 12th-century Moorish Alcázar, a walled complex of enchanting gardens from 1001 nights. You enter the Alcázar through the Puerta de la Ciudad. Inside you will discover a well-preserved domed mosque with a restored mihrâb as well as Arab baths dating back to the 14th century. The Palacio de Villavicencio, renovated in the style of the Renaissance, has a camera obscura in its tower that offers a 360-degree view of the town through lenses and mirrors. Alcázar offers a good view of the rear of the Colegiata de San Salvador Cathedral, built in 1695, in the baroque style. Admire the free-standing belfry, the protruding buttresses built as protection against earthquakes, the dome as well as the beautiful baroque steps leading up to the main façade.

The acclaimed Centro Andaluz de Flamenco (Andalucían Centre for Flamenco) is also worth a visit if you are interested in Spain's iconic dance. The centre lies at the heart of the Barrio de Santiago, Jerez's old gypsy quarter, and is one of the acknowledged cradles of flamenco in its purest form. There is an audiovisual theatre, which screens excellent films of flamenco greats such as the late Manolo Caracol. If you visit the *barrio* in the morning you may hear the evocative clatter of heels and the ripple of guitar music echoing from local flamenco schools.

For the best of modern Jerez, explore the pedestrianised Calle Larga to the west of the main street, stopping at serene Plaza de la Asunción, known locally as Plaza San Dionisio after its handsome 15th-century church. The entire area is well supplied with excellent tapas bars.

INSIDER TIP At **La Maceta Bar** (Calle Lancería 27; tel: 629 63 13 63), a typical local bar but with more character than most, you can enjoy an ice-cold *fino* accompanied by pickled mussels or a more substantial *bocadillo* (sandwich). Sit *al fresco* or in the bar decorated with numerous sherry posters.

---

i

210 C2

Tourist Information
Plaza del Arenal
956 33 88 74
www.turismojerez.com

Alcázar
Alameda Vieja
956 14 99 55
Daily 9:30–2:30; July–Sep Mon–Fri until 5:30
€5, with Cámara Oscura €7

Real Escuela Andaluza del Arte Ecuestre
Avenida Duque de Abrantes
956 31 96 35 (reservations)
www.realescuela.org
Sinfonía a Caballo (riding displays): Dec–Feb Thu noon; March–Nov Tue, Thu noon: Aug–Oct also Friday and sometimes Monday and Saturday. Training sessions and stable visits: non-show days 10–1
€21–€27 (main show); €11 (training sessions). Book well ahead for the show (online).

Centro Andaluz de Flamenco
Palacio Pemartín, Plaza de San Juan, Barrio de Santiago
956 90 21 34
www.centroandaluzdeflamenco.es
Mon–Fri 9–2 Free

⑩★★ Costa del Sol

Don't Miss	Sunshine galore, beach fun and pretty little towns
Why	In Spain's most popular holiday region, summer dreams come true
When	In winter, to soak up a bit of sun
Time	Preferably for ever – but a few days will suffice to start with
How many	320 days of sun a year
In Short	The sun coast deserves its name

My yacht, my car... See and be seen in Puerto Banús

The tourist mecca on the coast stretching from Málaga to Estepona is regarded as Europe's largest holiday "playground". Until the 1950s hardly anyone strayed here, but then the tourist industry discovered the sun-kissed coasts and its exceptional beaches.

Estepona

The most westerly of the Costa del Sol's main resorts, the former fishing village Estepona, grew phenomenally with the arrival of mass tourism in the 1960s, although the pretty centre has been retained. The 2km (1.25mi) long seafront promenade is entirely urban, but sensible planning has created a pleasant *cordón sanitaire* of aromatic flower beds, palm trees and shrubs alongside Estepona's fine beach. The heart of the old town is the Plaza de las Flores, a small jasmine-scented square that evokes 19th-century Andalucía. There are numerous bars, cafés and restaurants in the town centre. The Orchidarium to the north of the Old Town is regarded as Spain's finest orchid collection, but Estepona's beach is the main attraction. At the west end of the resort are an old lighthouse, the fishing harbour, a yacht marina and – a few kilometres further west – Costa Natura, Spain's longest-established (1981) nudist beach. East from Estepona the ubiquitous *urbanizaciones*, the "fill-in" residential estates of the Costa del Sol, cling to either side of the highway as far as Marbella, the next main resort.

In the heart of Estepona

Marbella – Beautiful Sea and Much More

The Phoenicians first founded a settlement here called Salduba (Salt town). In 1485, the Catholic monarch Queen Isabel is said to have cried: "*Qué mar bella*!" when she saw the sea – which is how the town got its name. Marbella's promotion to in-place followed in 1953 when Prinz Alfonso von Hohenlohe founded the Marbella Club, which became the hub of the high society for many years. The town's generally subdued air by day is surprising, but you can expect lively nightlife, especially around the yacht harbour of Puerto Deportivo and in Plaza Puente Ronda in the carefully manicured Old Town, the Casco Antiguo. The Casco Antiguo has not been robbed entirely of its traditional character. At its heart is the Plaza de los Naranjos, surrounded as the name suggests by orange trees, which was created in the 15th century after the old Moorish quarter was demolished. The alleyways that radiate from the plaza are full of upmarket clothes shops and craft galleries. Just east of the square is Plaza de la Iglesia, where the handsome church of Nuestra Señora de la Encarnación rubs shoulders with Marbella's old town walls. Just around the corner Marbella's Museo del Grabado Contemporáneo (Museum of Lithographic Art), housed in a pleasant Renaissance building, contains work by Joan Miró and Picasso as well as contemporary Spanish graphics.

Playground of the rich and beautiful: Nikki Beach in Marbella (left).

Those who prefer less can relax in the park (below)

South of Plaza de los Naranjos the Old Town gives way to the busy through-road of Avenida Ramón y Cajal, on the other side of which lies the oasis of shade Parque de la Alameda with its big central fountain. From the far side of the plaza a broad esplanade descends to the seafront promenade past a succession of eccentric Salvador Dalí sculptures. Marbella's beach offers the inevitable mix of churned-up sand and seafront *chiringuitos* (fish restaurants), souvenir shops, bars and cafés.

Keep heading west along the seafront for 6km (3.75mi) to reach the marina resort of Puerto Banús, with pseudo-Moorish apartment blocks, floating gin palaces, expensive shops and restaurants, and a particularly well-to-do clientele.

Fuengirola and Torremolinos

About 25km (40mi) east of Marbella is Fuengirola, perhaps one of the least favoured of the Costa resorts because of the high-rise hotels that crowd the seafront. This said, Fuengirola is a wholeheartedly fun resort as well as a genuine Spanish working town. The long, narrow beach is packed with sunbeds hired out, for a king's ransom, by adjoining bars and restaurants.

Torremolinos, probably the most visited of the Costa resorts, is 20km (12.5mi) northeast of Fuengirola. The place is a mass of souvenir shops, bars, cafés and restaurants, although fragments of an older Torremolinos survive. At peak season the main streets of the resort are dense with people and the beaches are carpeted with sunbeds. Take a walk along the resort's delightful promenade, the Paseo Marítimo. It runs for about 6km (3.75mi), passing the pleasant beaches of La Carihuela and de Montemar, before reaching Benalmádena Costa's kitsch Arab harbour complex with layered terraces and whipped-cream domes. All the way along the Paseo Marítimo are tempting beachside *chiringuitos* sizzling with barbecued sardines and glittering with cool, beaded glasses.

In the mountains behind the Costa del Sol there are many attractive hill villages. Casares lies in the Sierra Bermeja about 18km (11mi) in and from Estepona, its whitewashed houses overlooked by a Moorish castle. The pretty village of Mijas lies 8km (5mi) north of Fuengirola. Although touristy and crowded during the day, it still retains much of its charm, and this is especially apparent when you walk through the town in the evening. There are regular bus services to both villages from the main resorts.

INSIDER TIP Splash out on an extortionately expensive drink at the famous **Sinatra Bar** (Casa E, Local 2, Puerto Banús; tel: 952 81 90 50) in Puerto Banús for a little celebrity spotting. This front-line bar is a traditional hang-out for the Marbella jet-set, and if you get tired of doing that, you can admire the luxury yachts, or do a little window shopping instead.

Estepona Tourist Information
211 D1 Plaza de las Flores
952 80 20 02
www.estepona.es/turismo

Marbella Tourist Information
211 D2 Plaza de los Naranjos & Glorieta de la Fontanilla
952 7 68 76 60
www.turismo.marbella.es

Fuengirola Tourist Information
211 E2 Avenida Jesús Santos Rein 6 952 37 42 57
www.fuengirola.es

Torremolinos Tourist Information
211 E2 Plaza de las Comunidades Autónomas
952 37 42 31
www.turismotorremolinos.es

⓫ Málaga

Don't Miss	An early evening walk through the meandering streets of the Old Town
Why	Picasso's birthplace is as inspiring as ever
When	In the Easter week when the Easter processions are taking place
Time	One or two days at least
In Short	Impressive architecture and lots of opportunities to indulge yourself

Andalucía's second-largest town at the foot of the Montes de Málaga is the economic and cultural centre of the Costa del Sol and enjoys 300 days of sunshine a year.

Málaga was founded by the Phoenicians who used it as a trading centre for salted fish, and this probably inspired the name of the town: the Phoenician *malak* derives from the word *malac,* the verb "to salt". Málaga is the second most important city of Andalucía, after Seville. It has a busy industrial harbour and a thriving financial sector. The Guadalmedina river divides the town into two districts: in the west, there is the new part of town with the main station and battalion of tower blocks, and in the east, the Old Town. Yet at its heart lie 19th-century streets and squares, crammed with bars and cafés as well as many shops and art and craft galleries. Scattered throughout are historic monuments that reflect Málaga's long history as a port and trading centre. A fine example is

Málaga is a wonderful town to stroll through – and for an enjoyable art interlude visit, for example, Museo Picasso (above)

Outstanding View: the Alcazaba in Málaga

the Moorish Alcazaba on the lower slopes of Monte Gibralfaro (Lighthouse Hill). Its name dates back to the time of the Romans, who had a lighthouse built on its summit.

The Sights

The building of Alcazaba fortress began on the Roman remains in the 11th century and saw substantial improvements under the Nasrid dynasty in the 13th/14th century which put it almost on a par with the Alhambra of Granada. After the demise of the Moors, the fortress fell into disrepair, and it was not until 1931 that serious reconstruction work began. Today, it is resplendent in its former glory. Alongside the entrance gateway are the impressive remains of a Roman theatre that once served as a quarry; numerous marble columns and capitals are embedded in the red brickwork of the palace's Moorish walls. As you climb higher into the Alcazaba, the views become spectacular.

The 14th-century Castillo de Gibralfaro (Gibralfaro Castle) stands on the summit of Monte Gibralfaro above the Alcazaba. There are magnificent views from the ramparts and there is a small military museum. It is a stiff uphill walk to the castle (head along the road to the right of the Alcazaba entrance), albeit by a surfaced path through pleasant gardens; but you can catch Bus No 35 from Avenida de Cervantes, or take a taxi, and then stroll back down with terrific views for company.

Near the Alcazaba is Málaga's cathedral, begun in 1582 and completed in 1783. It is known as La Manquita, "the one-armed old woman", because its west front has only one tower. Take a look into the light-infused interior with its almost 42m (138ft) high nave and the white and orange tiled floor. Adjoining Málaga's cathedral, the Iglesia del Sagrario has a splendid Gothic portal and a beautiful altarpiece.

Housed in the elegant 16th-century Palacio de Buenavista, the Museo Picasso is a superb celebration of Pablo Picasso. A permanent collection of Picasso's works is on display, plus temporary exhibitions by international artists.

The Casa Natal de Picasso in Plaza de la Merced (daily 9:30–5; €3) is well worth a visit

Soaking up the Atmosphere

Málaga is a wonderful city in which to wander. The pedestrian Calle Marqués de Larios, lined with smart shops and cafés, leads to lively Plaza de la Constitución at the heart of the Old Town. West of here, a tangle of narrow streets and squares is overlooked by tall, balconied buildings and historic churches. Offering a feast for your eyes and palate is Mercado Central Atarazanas, to the west of Calle Marqués de Larios. Similar to the famous Boquería in Barcelona, the market hall is full of stands selling fish, meat, fruit and vegetables.

INSIDER TIP There is only one place that you will find the true Malageño enjoying his afternoon coffee, a glass of wine or tapas and that is **El Pimpi** (Calle Granada, 62, Málaga, daily from 10am; tel: 952 22 54 03; www.elpimpi.com) a bar encompassing two floors between Calle Alcazabilla and Calle Granada.

---

211 E2

Tourist Information
Plaza de la Marina 11; Avenida de Cervantes 1 (OMT) 951 92 60 20
www.malagaturismo.com

Alcazaba
Calle Alcazabilla 952 22 72 30
Daily from 9am €2.20

Catedral
Calle Molina Larios 9 952 22 03 45
Mon–Fri 10–8 (April, May), 10–9 (June–Sep), 10–6:30 (Nov–March), Sat 10–6:30, Sun 2–6:30 €6

Iglesia del Sagrario
Calle Santa Maria, 22
Mon–Sat 10–noon

Museo Picasso
Calle San Augustín 952 12 76 00
www.museopicassomalaga.org
Daily. March–June, Sep, Oct 10–7, July, Aug until 8, Nov–Feb until 6 €9

Parking
Underground car parks are reached from the Alameda Principal and the Plaza de la Marina.

⓬ Cádiz

Don't Miss	Watching how the locals wander along the sea promenade
Why	Even at the height of the summer, the Atlantic brings you a nice cool breeze
When	During carnival, because in Andalucia there is nowhere wilder and more spectacular than here
In Short	This town is enchanting!

The harbour town sits atop limestone rock at the end of a 9km (5.5mi) long isthmus that stretches like a tongue into the bay on the Atlantic coast, its earlier wealth reflected in the great cathedral and other baroque buildings. Much of the pleasure of a visit comes from wandering through the narrow, cobbled streets and out to the brilliant sunlight of the seafront promenade.

A constant, cool breeze flows along the streets, making a visit agreeable even in the height of summer and creating a shimmering clear light that has earned the town the nickname *tazita de plata* ("little silver cup").

Although Cádiz was an important port for Phoenicians, Romans and Visigoths, it declined under Moorish control and what you see today dates essentially from the 18th century, when the Spanish-American gold and silver trade revived the city's fortunes. The Museo de Cádiz is a good place to start your exploration of the city. The museum, which is housed in a restored 18th-century mansion, is one of the best in Spain; the archaeological section includes superb Phoenician jewellery and glassware and a reconstruction of the wreck of a Roman trading vessel. The first floor contains the city's art treasures, including work by Murillo, Rubens and Zurbarán.

The city's narrow streets are linked by pleasing squares. Torre Tavira, one of Cádiz's ancient watchtowers and its Camera Obscura is well worth seeing. The Oratorio de San Felipe Neri has an oval interior which soars up to a sky-blue dome encircled by tiers of railed galleries; the view from the top is sensational. Of particular interest are the side chapels and Murillo's luminous painting that graces the high altar.

The "gilded dome" of the cathedral is a real eye-catcher (left) Cádiz also caters for keen shoppers (below)

The monumental, Catedral Nueva, built from 1722 to 1838, is Spain's only completely baroque cathedral. Its main front dominates the broad Plaza de la Catedral and its interior is a vast arena of baroque architecture, all in plain stone and marble. The cathedral's central, so-called "gilded" dome is in fact faced with yellow tiles rather than precious metal, but the effect is still glorious, especially when you see it from the seafront promenades.

INSIDER TIP There is always a lively atmosphere in **La Gorda te da de comer** ("The fat lady feeds you"; Marqués de Valdeiñigo 4) and the tapas are tasty and good value.

---

210 B2

Tourist Information
Avenida José León de Carranza
956 28 56 01 Paseo de Canalejas
956 24 10 01 www.turismo.cadiz.es

Parking
Visitors are advised not to drive through the heart of Cádiz. There are car parks on Plaza San Juan de Dias, adjacent to the railway station and on the nearby Cuesta de las Calesas. Parking is also possible along parts of the seafront.

Museo de Cádiz
Plaza de Mina 5 856 10 50 23
Mid-Sep to mid-June Tue–Sat 9–3, Sun 10–5; mid-June to mid-Sep Tue–Sun 9–3
free for EU passport holders

Oratorio de San Felipe Neri
Calle San José
662 64 22 33 Tue–Fri 10:30–2, 4:30–8, Sat 10–2, Sun 10–1; July, Aug Tue–Fri 10:30–2, 5:30–8:3, Sat 10–2, Sun 10–1 €3

Catedral Nueva
Plaza de la Catedral
956 28 61 54
Nov–March Mon–Sat 10–7, Sun 2–7; April–June, Sep, Oct Mon–Sat 10–8, Sun 2–8; July, Aug. Mon–Sat 10–8:30, Sun 2–8:30 €6

At Your Leisure

13 Nerja

Seaside Nerja, 56km (35mi) east of Málaga, makes a refreshing change from the Costa del Sol's main resorts. Nerja's best-known feature is the Balcón de Europa, a palm-fringed promenade overlooking the sea. The smallish beaches either side become crowded; the best and biggest beach is Burriana, east of the Balcón along the Paseo de los Carabineros.

About 3km (2mi) to the east of Nerja are the popular Cueva de Nerja. On the tour you will see fantastic stalactite formations and prehistoric rock paintings that are accentuated with light effects.

212 A1

Tourist Information
Carmen 1 (in the town hall)
952 52 15 31
https://turismo.nerja.es/

Cueva de Nerja
www.cuevadenerja.es
Daily 9:30–3:30, July–Aug until 6
€10

14 Antequera

Historic sights in Antequera range from prehistoric burial chambers to Moorish ruins and fine churches. Oldest of all are a remarkable group of Neolithic to Bronze Age burial chambers: the Menga and Viera dolmens, off Camino del Cementerio on the northeastern outskirts. In

Hikers' Heaven: Parque Natural del Torcal

the highest part of the town, above central Plaza San Sebastián, stands the Arco de Los Gigantes, a 16th-century gateway incorporating Roman sculpture in its stonework. The dignified Renaissance façade of the church of Santa María dominates the adjoining plaza, and above it are the vestigial ruins of the town's Moorish Alcazaba, now a pine-scented, terraced garden.

Just north of the Arco de Los Gigantes is the 17th-century church of Nuestra Señora del Carmen, its baroque altarpiece a feast of carved and painted figures. About 14km (9mi) south of Antequera is Parque Natural del Torcal, a striking natural landscape of tall limestone pinnacles and wooded ravines. In Lobo Park, you can visit the wolves and watch them in natural surroundings.

Running 33km (20mi) southwest of Antequera between the little towns of Ardales and Álora is what was, until its repair, perhaps the most dangerous trail in the world: El Caminito del Rey ("The King's Little Pathway"). The trail is 7.7km (5mi) long; it includes a spectacular 1.5km (1mi) long, narrow wooden walkway, which is anchored with metal fixtures into the vertical walls of the gorge at a height of 100m (328ft). This is not a walk for people who suffer from vertigo – some sections of the walkway have a glass base! If you want to walk along Caminito del Rey, you have to book early.

211 E2

Tourist Information
Plaza de San Sebastián 7
952 70 25 05
http://turismo.antequera.es

Menga and Viera Dolmens
Jan–March, mid-Sep–Dec Tue–Sat 9–6, Sun 10–3; April–June Tue–Sat 9–8, Sun 9–3; June to mid-Sep Tue–Sun 9–3
Free

Parque Natural del Torcal
www.torcaldeantequera.com/en/

Lobo Park
Ctra. Antequera – Álora – A. 343 –, Km 16 www.lobopark.com
Guided tours (1.5hrs.): daily 10, 11, 1, 3 and 4:30 €11

Caminito del Rey
www.caminitodelrey.info

15 Parque Natural Sierra de Grazalema

The Sierra de Grazalema is a range of craggy limestone peaks swathed in forests of oak and the rare Spanish fir, the pinsapo. Tortuous roads wind through the mountains and link villages such as Grazalema, Zahara de la Sierra with its clifftop castle and Benaocaz, classic examples of the *pueblos blancos*.

The entire Sierra is a wildlife reserve. There are many walking and cycling trails along which you can explore this district, and you can sample horse riding, cycling, rock climbing, canoeing, and even paragliding, with experienced guides and instructors (p. 71). You need to obtain a permit from the park information office at El Bosque office if you wish to enter certain areas such as the Garganta Verde and one of the main roosting sites of the magnificent griffin vulture.

211 D2

Tourist Information, El Bosque
Federico García Lorca 1
956 70 97 33

Tourist Information, Grazalema
Plaza Asomaderos 3
956 13 20 52

16 Arcos de la Frontera

Arcos de la Frontera tumbles downhill in a careless sprawl from the spectacular clifftop site of its old Moorish quarter. The Old Town's alleys surround the two main churches, San Pedro and Santa María de la Asunción. San Pedro is a quiet haven; the highlight of the late

A haven of peace: San Pedro in Arcos de la Frontera

Gothic interior is a fine 16th-century altarpiece. Santa María dominates the central square, Plaza del Cabildo, and has a splendid Renaissance façade and a richly decorative interior full of pleasant gloom and Gothic extravagance. As you take in the vista across the plain from the plaza's viewpoint, look for the kestrels that drift along the cliff face. Then descend to mix with the boisterous life of the bars and restaurants of the lower town.

210 C2
Plaza del Cabildo 956 70 22 64

17 Sanlúcar de Barrameda

Great seafood restaurants and dry Manzanilla wine, which has a different flavour from Jerez *fino* and is claimed to be of superior quality, are Sanlúcar de Barrameda's specialities. The town stands at the mouth of the Río Guadalquivir opposite the southern edge of the Doñana National Park, which is accessible from here by boat. The morning market in Calle Bretones, close to the main square, Plaza del Cabildo, is a colourful, raucous affair. Stroll uphill from the market for a look at Sanlúcar's town hall, located in the 19th-century Palacio de los Infantes de Orleans y Borbón, a showpiece of extravagant decoration in neo-Moorish style.

For the Manzanilla experience, visit the Bodegas Barbadillo in Calle Luis de Eguilaz or the Bodegas La Cigarrera in Plaza Madre de Dios near the market. The best fish restaurants are in the Bajo de Guía district by the river.

210 B2
Calzada Duquesa Isabel 956 36 61 10
www.sanlucarturismo.com

18 El Puerto de Santa María

The river port of El Puerto de Santa María is at the southernmost angle of the "Sherry Triangle", and has a reputation for excellent sherry and seafood. It is a useful base for exploring the region: Sanlúcar de Barrameda and Jerez de la Frontera (p. 48) are only about 20km (12.5mi) away – and accessible by car, bus or train, while Cádiz is 10km (6.25mi) across the estuary – about half an hour in a catamaran. One of the finest of El Puerto's many churches is the Iglesia Mayor Prioral in Plaza de España, and there are several ornate 18th-century palaces scattered around the town. Castillo de San Marcos is a 13th-century fortress built on the site of a mosque. The pedestrianised Calle Luna has a number of fun bars, and the waterfront area is full of life in the evenings. Sherry bodegas with famous names such as Osborne, Luis Caballero and Taberna Obregón, are open to visitors.

210 B2
Plaza del Castillo ☎ 956 48 37 15
www.turismoelpuerto.com

19 Costa de la Luz (Cádiz)

Costa de la Luz, which means the "Coast of Light", is far less developed than the Costa del Sol. There are excellent beaches at Los Caños de Meca on the famous Cape Trafalgar (where Nelson won his famous naval battle against Napoleon-led forces in 1805) and Zahara de los Atunes, where broad stretches of golden sand still offer you room to breathe. This is an Atlantic coast, however, and the sea can be chillier and choppier than on the Mediterranean coast. Inland from the coast the hilltop settlement of Vejer de la Frontera preserves its secretive Moorish character.

The beaches at breezy Tarifa, the most southerly town in Iberia, are a windsurfer's paradise. From Tarifa, the Rif Mountains of Morocco seem only a stone's throw away across the Strait of Gibraltar. You can take a one-day or two-day trip to Tangier from Tarifa; or try windsurfing, kitesurfing, join a dolphin- and whale-watching cruise, or take a diving trip with experts.

210 C1

Vejer de la Frontera Tourist Information
Avenida Los Remedios ☎ 956 45 17 36
www.turismovejer.com

Tarifa Tourist Information
Paseo de la Alameda s/n
☎ 956 68 09 93 www.tarifaweb.com; www.tarifaturismo.com

FIRMM (Dolphin- and Whale-Watching)
Calle Pedro Cortés 4, 11380 Tarifa
☎ 956 62 70 08 www.firmm.org

20 Gibraltar

A visit to Gibraltar, one of the UK's last remaining colonies, is like finding yourself in Britain at the heart of Mediterranean Spain. The Old Town

Kings of the Big Blue Sea

Swift as an arrow, specks of silvery grey cut through the blue water, shooting to the surface with such ease, only to dive again and pop up again a little further on. Who is actually watching whom? Anyone who has seen dolphins in their natural environment will not forget the experience in a hurry. At the southern point of the Iberian Peninsula you can enjoy their spectacular water dance out in the ocean. Book a boat tour and let yourself be mesmerised by these small yet great kings of the sea (p. 71).

(North Town) begins on the other side of the airport with Casemates Square. Towering above it in the east, you can see the ruins of Moorish Castle, which dates back to the 8th century and was rebuilt by the Almohads in the 14th century. The market and the harbour, constructed in 1309 and substantially extended in past years, are just to the northwest of the castle. Main Street, on which you will find most of the hotels, shops, pubs and public buildings, leads from Casemates Square to the post office and stock exchange with the adjoining town hall at the rear, and on to the Cathedral of Saint Mary the Crowned, once a mosque that underwent a Gothic facelift in 1502.

Following Bomb House Lane that leads off to the right, you come to the Gibraltar Museum, which apart from providing all sorts of facts about the town history also includes a 30m² (39yd²) model of "the Rock" from 1865 as well as the Moorish Baths. On Cathedral Square, you will find the Anglican Church of England (Cathedral of The Holy Trinity) built in 1821 in Moorish style. At the south end of Main Street, on the right-hand side, is the Governor's Palace (The Convent) built on the foundations of a 1531 Franciscan monastery.

An exciting cable-car ride whisks you to the Upper Rock, where you can visit the famous Barbary apes. Gibraltar's "apes" are a breed of tail-less monkey that have been brought over from Morocco. There is a myth that Gibraltar will cease to be British if the apes ever leave the Rock. Fears of this happening during World War II prompted British officials to import more of the animals.

See, too, the vast St Michael's Cave, venue for occasional musicals and dance shows, and the Upper Galleries or "Great Siege Tunnels", a vast labyrinth excavated for military defence in the 18th century. The Gibraltar tourist information offices are the best sources for information about tours, dolphin-watching trips and sightseeing cruises.

→ 211 D1

Tourist Information
✉ Cathedral Square ☎ 350 20 07 49 50
🌐 www.visitgibraltar.gi

Gibraltar Museum
✉ 18/20 Bomb House Lane
🕐 Mon–Fri 10–6, Sat 10–2

Cable Car
🕐 Daily 9:30–7:15, in winter until 5:15
🎟 £18.50

Gibraltar has more than its fair share of naughty little monkeys!

Where to... Stay

Expect to pay per double room per night

€ up to €60
€€ €60–€90
€€€ €90–€140
€€€€ over €140

COSTA DEL SOL

Hotel Humaina €€
Away from the clamour of Málaga's coast, this is the perfect place to relax. The location is idyllic, in the centre of a natural park but just 16km (10mi) from the city. terracotta tiles, ochre walls and balconies in most rooms. Food is prepared with organic vegetables grown in the garden.
211 E2 Carretera del Colmenar s/n, Las Montes de Málaga ☎ 952 64 10 25
www.hotelhumaina.es

La Fonda €€€
On a pretty pedestrian street in the centre of the relatively unspoilt town of Benalmádena, this hotel has a pretty rooftop terrace overlooking the Mediterranean and a wonderful outside pool. There are cool patios shaded by palms, pebbled floors and fountains, and the rooms are light and airy with terraces and views.
211 E2 Calle Santo Domingo 7, Benalmádena Pueblo ☎ 952 56 90 47
www.lafondabenalmadena.es

Larios €€€€
You get a top location in a swanky shopping street, yet from here it's just a short stroll to the cathedral and atmospheric old part of Málaga. Black-and-white tiles, soft beige furnishings and light wood make for an upbeat yet elegant look. There is a lovely rooftop terrace where you can enjoy a glass of wine after a busy day sightseeing.
199 F2 Marqués de Larios 2
☎ 952 22 22 00
www.room-matehotels.com

Chic: Hotel Larios

RONDA

Alavera de Los Baños €€€
Next to the 13th-century Baños Arabes (p. 46), this German-run small hotel was featured as a backdrop for the film classic *Carmen*. It has super views of the Serranía de Ronda uplands and the city walls, plus facilities like a reading room, library and lounge. In the pleasant dining room, there is an emphasis on organically grown foods.
211 D2 Calle Molino de Alarcón 2
☎ 952 87 91 43
www.alaveradelosbanos.com

JEREZ DE LA FRONTERA

Itaca Hotel Jerez €€
The hotel is located in a former 19th-century convent; the rooms are nonetheless equipped with the latest amenities. Breakfast is served in what was once the chapel, which is decorated with a statue from the cloister. The restaurant offers guests traditional Andalucían cuisine.
210 C2 Diego Fernández Herrera 1
☎ 956 35 04 62 www.itacajerez.com

CÁDIZ

Hostal Bahía €€
On a tree-lined pedestrian street just off the bustling Plaza de San Juan de Dios, this is a real winner with firm beds, smart bathrooms, TV, air conditioning and small balconies in most of the rooms. The lack of a dining room is compensated by the choice and proximity of bars and restaurants, including the excellent Mesón La Nueva Marina which is right next door (p. 73).
210 C2 Calle Plocia 5 ☎ 956 25 90 61
http://hostalbahiacadiz.com

Where to... Eat and Drink

Expect to pay for a three-course meal, incl. wine and service

€ up to €15

€€ €15–€40

€€€ over €40

COSTA DEL SOL

Antonio Martín €€–€€€

Seafood and fish at its best is on offer at this long-established, family-run restaurant located right on the sea front and with the benefit of a pleasant terrace. Everything from *gambas a la plancha* (grilled prawns) and *boquerones fritos* (deep-fried anchovies), to *merluza* (hake) and *pez espada* (swordfish) is on offer. The food and atmosphere make this is a very popular place with locals, and it draws celebrities too, so reservations are advised.

211 E2

Playa de la Malagueta

951 77 65 02 www.grupogorki.com

1–4, 8–10:30

Bar Lo Güeno €

Shoehorned into a deceptively small space, with extra seating space across the road, this well-loved traditional tapas bar is tucked down a side street near Calle Larios. The L-shaped wooden bar is crammed with a choice of tapas, including many Lo Güeno originals, like scallops au gratin (*vieira gratinada*) or skewered with monkfish and crayfish (*brochetita de rape y langostinos*). There is an excellent range of Rioja wines, and service is fast and good.

211 E2

Calle Marín García 12

952 22 30 48

www.logueno.es

Mon–Sat 1–4, 7 to late

La Méson Salina €€€

One of the best restaurants in town! Here you can order excellent meat dishes and fish, too. You should also try the chef's speciality: *Boquerones salineros* (sardines) and the Iberian ham. The service leaves nothing wanting and it is pure enjoyment

Typically Andalucían: braised oxtail

eating here. Also visit the *bodega* (wine bar). It stocks around 300 different wines – from over 40 denominations (Rioja, Rebera del Duero etc.).

211 E2

Avenida de Las Salinas 28, Fuengirola

952 47 18 06

www.mesonlasalina.com

Closed Wed

Restaurante Chinitas €€

Expect traditional Andaluz décor here, with paintings of bullfighters on the walls. The cuisine is predictably macho, with oxtail a speciality, plus *serrano* hams and calf sirloin. Several dishes include Málaga sweet wine, including *solomillo al vino de Málaga* (fillet steak in a wine sauce).

211 E2

El Moreno Monroy 4

952 21 09 72

Daily noon–midnight

Restaurante Frutos €€€

The restaurant serves very good fish and meat dishes and is regarded as a true classic in the region. The menu is very long. Many of the dishes are served in smaller portions so that you can try more than one. Another good point is the location which offers lots of parking spaces.

211 E2

Avenida Riviera 80, Torremolinos

952 37 20 21

www.restaurantefrutos.es

Daily 1–5, 8–midnight

Restaurante Santiago €€€

Opened half a century ago on the esplanade, Santiago's fish and fruits de mer dishes have made it one of Marbella's favourite restaurants, and it is very popular with prominent members of society. You can choose between reasonably priced tapas at the bar and or meals in normal-sized portions, which are more expensive. Attentive service and excellent wine list. Although it is located on the esplanade, you cannot see the sea from inside.

211 D2
Avenida Duque de Ahumada 5, Márbella
952 77 00 78
www.restaurantesantiago.com
Tue–Sun 8–11

RONDA

Pedro Romero €€

This restaurant decorated with bullfighting memorabilia (posters, bull's heads etc.) serves very good, grass-roots food. Its set menus offer a choice between three different starters, main courses and desserts, but it is also possible to eat à la carte. Among the hearty mountain dishes, specialities include partridge (*Perdíz*) and oxtail (*Rabo de Toro*). There is a large selection of wines and the employees are very friendly.

211 D2 Calle Virgen de la Paz 18
952 87 11 10
www.rpedroromero.com
Tue–Sun 1:30–3:30, 8:30–10:30, Sun lunch only

THE SHERRY TRIANGLE

Bar Juanito €€

This bar, which opened in the heart of Jerez de la Frontera in 1943, serves the best tapas – and has a wide selection to choose from. There is also an enormous choice of *finos* as well. Generally very full, there is unfortunately often quite a wait.

210 B2 Calle de Pescadería Vieja 8-10, Jerez de la Frontera
956 33 48 38
www.bar-juanito.com
Mon–Sat 1–4:30, 8–midnight

La Molinera €€

The restaurant belongs to Hotel Mesón de la Molinera, a former oil mill on the edge of Lake Arcos with a fantastic view of the Old Town of Arcos de la Frontera. On the menu are typical, fairly priced Andalucían specialities. Regardless of whether fish or meat, a drop of wine, sherry and brandy is an essential liquid in the ingredients.

198 C2 Avenida El Sombrero de Tres Picos, Arcos de la Frontera
956 70 80 02 www.mesondelamolinera.com Daily 1–4, 8–11

CÁDIZ

Atxuri €€€

At Atxuri, which opened in 1957, the menu is a combination of Basque and Andalucían cuisine. One highlight is the stockfish dish *Bacalao a la andaluza*. The fish served is always very fresh. Many people regard it as the best restaurant in town.

210 B2 Calle Plocia 15, Cádiz 956 25 36 13 www.atxuri.es Daily 1–4, until late. Closed 24, 25, 31 Dec and 1 Jan

El Aljibe €€

On the ground floor of the restaurant, you can buy simple but quite delicious tapas. On the first floor, refined meat and fish dishes are on offer. The lamb and seabass are popular choices. It is a nice atmosphere and the staff are friendly

210 B2 Calle Plocia 25, Cádiz
956 26 66 56 Daily 1–4, and 8 till late. Closed 24, 25, 31 Dec and 1 Jan

El Faro €€–€€€

El Faro, in the city's shabby, one-time fishermen's quarter, is deservedly famous. You can opt for seafood tapas at the bar or really splash out in the restaurant and choose from a whole variety of rice and fish dishes with wonderful ingredients, or the relatively pricey *menú del día*. The décor is understated Andalucían with ceramic wall tiles, marble and mahogany bar, and lots of photos of Cádiz past and present.

210 B2 Calle San Félix 15, Cádiz
956 21 10 68 www.elfarodecadiz.com
Daily 12:30–4, 8–11

Where to... Shop

MÁLAGA

Málaga's Calle Marqués de Larios is the heart of the city's fashion shopping. Try the branch of the smart Spanish fashion chain Mango (Larios 6; tel: 952 60 77 05), and Zara (C/ Liborio García 10; tel: 952 22 24 06) for ultra-chic clothes.

There is a more traditional shopping area in the streets around Plaza Flores, Plaza de Félix Sáenz and Calle Puerta del Mar and Calle Nueva, where you'll find shops of all kinds.

Málaga's branch of the department store chain of El Corte Inglés (Avenida de Andalucía 4–6) is enormous. It carries a big range of foreign-language newspapers and is a good source of maps and books. Another mammoth shopping centre is the Larios Centro with 153 shops.

In the Plaza Mayor shopping centre (Calle Alfonso Ponce de León; www.plazamayor.es) there are numerous fashion shops, such as C & A, Zara and Mango; you can stock up on groceries, the restaurants cater to creature comforts, and cinemas offer entertainment.

A perfect pair: sherry and ham

RONDA & SIERRA DE GRAZALEMA

Ronda (p. 44) has many souvenir shops, a good number in the town's main shopping street, Carrera Espinal. Scattered among them, however, are some excellent shops selling *productos artesanos*, local produce of all kinds. Look for Márquez (Espinel 13; tel: 952 87 29 86) for everything from cured meats to wine, herbs and honey. For more upmarket craftwork and souvenirs you'll find a sprinkling of outlets in Ronda's Old Town. In the mountains of the Sierra de Grazalema (p. 66), Artesanía Textil de Grazalema (factory: Carretera de Ronda, shop: Plaza de España; www.mantasdegrazalema.com) has a range of local clothing, carpets, pottery, and produce that includes cheeses, honey, and pears in wine.

Another pleasant place to browse in Grazalema is La Jara Cerámica Artesanal (Calle Agua 19; tel: 956 13 20 75) for quality craftwork and gifts. On the Grazalema to Zahara de la Sierra road, stop off at Molino El Vínculo Molino Alojamiento Rural (tel: 956 12 30 02) for a chance to buy some very fine olive oil, wine and cheeses, and/or to stay the night.

THE SHERRY TRIANGLE

Pedestrianised Calle Larga and its surrounding streets are where you'll find the best shopping in Jerez de la Frontera, with shops selling fashion, crafts, ceramics, leatherware and jewellery. If it's sherry you want, you'll find that, although every *bodega* sells its own product exclusively, La Casa del Jerez (The Sherry Shop, Divina Pastora 1; tel: 956 33 51 84; www.lacasadeljerez.com) stocks all brands and you can sample happily.

You can browse pretty ceramic products in Amaya Cerámica (Avenida de Blas Infante 16; www.ceramicaamaya.com).

The Manzanilla and sherry *bodegas* in El Puerto de Santa María (p. 63) and Sanlúcar de Barrameda (p. 62) all sell their own products. Some companies that manufacture sherry, for example Osborne und Terry, offer interesting tours.

For the area's food specialities, don't miss Sanlúcar's busy morning market off Plaza de

San Roque, or the fresh shellfish shop attached to the Romerijo fish restaurants in Ribera del Marisco, in El Puerto de Santa María.

CÁDIZ AND BEYOND

Cádiz has a superb Mercado, located just next to Plaza de las Flores with its colourful flower stalls. The pedestrianised Calle Francisco, Calle Rosario and Calle Ancha, together with their linking streets, form Cadiz's main shopping district, where there is a good mix of shops. Farther along the coast to the east, Gibraltar (p. 65) is famous for its VAT-free shopping, and the town's Main Street is packed with shops of every kind. Prices are cheaper than in Britain and northern Europe, but you won't necessarily find that special Andalucían gift or memento.

Gibraltar is a scenic highlight and shopping paradise rolled into one

COSTA DEL SOL

All the main resorts confront you with ranks of souvenir outlets: you can take your pick of everything from jewellery to leather accessories, with little variation in quality or prices. For big fashion names, such as Versace, Armani, Donna Karan, Gucci, go for the smart main shopping drag Ramón y Cajal and Casco Antiguo (Old Town) in Marbella, or the waterfront Muelle Ribera in nearby Puerto Banús. Just around the corner, it is less expensive to shop at El Corte Inglés (Calle Ramón Areces).

Markets in this prosperous area are always worth browsing through. There are often good antiques and objets d'art lurking among the pottery, clothing and kitsch buys in Puerto Banús's Saturday morning market at Centro Plaza in the Nueva Andalucía district, near the bullring, or – biggest and best of all – Fuengirola's Tuesday morning market on Avenida Jesús Santos Rein. Fresh fish from this south Andalucían town travels as *pescado fresco de Fuengirola* to kitchens throughout Spain. If flea markets are more your thing then don't miss the Saturday morning event in the same Fuengirola location. It is huge.

Where to... Go Out

Andalucía offers a huge variety of entertainment, from the club scene on the Costa del Sol and in the larger cities, to the more traditional cultural pursuits of flamenco, bullfighting and *fiestas*. The energetic can enjoy water sports in the coastal resorts and dry-land adventure in the mountainous interior.

PUBLICATIONS

The *Guía Marbella – Día y Noche*, a tourist magazine (www.guiamarbella.com), and the daily *Diario Sur* newspaper (www.diariosur.es), which has a useful entertainment section, are available from tourist offices. One or two publications, aimed at expat residents, carry useful information on current shows and events.

NIGHTLIFE

The club scene in Málaga province is at its most intense on the lively Costa del Sol. In Puerto Banús, the waterfront Sinatra Bar (Muelle Ribera 2; tel: 952 81 09 50) is a top spot for stars and celebrity wannabees.

In Marbella the hottest scene is in the seafront area of Puerto Deportivo with its massed discos and bars. Fuengirola is a relentless nightlife zone; for total clubbers there's Crazy Daisy (Martínez Catena 37) – experience midnight-to-dawn dancing.

The Palladium (Avenida Palma de Mallorca; tel: 952 38 42 89) in Torremolinos is also popular. Visit Marbella's Casino Marbella (Hotel H10, Plaza de Andalucía; tel: 952 81 40 00) for a stab at blackjack, roulette, poker, and slot machines in plenty.

Alternatively, try your luck at Casino Torrequebrada (Avenida del Sol s/n; tel: 952 57 73 00; www.torrquebrada.com), where you can start your evening's enter-tainment at the gaming tables and then move on to enjoy a show in the next door restaurant. Passports need to be shown at both casinos.

Málaga's nightlife is concentrated on the area to the northeast of the cathedral around Plaza de Uncibay and the nearby streets of Granada and Beatas. In Jerez de la Frontera, you'll find discos and music bars in Calle Divina Pastora and around. In Cádiz city, head for the streets round Plaza de España.

FLAMENCO

In Málaga there are regular flamenco shows at the Teatro Miguel de Cervantes (Calle Ramos Marín; tel: 952 22 41 09; www.teatro cervantes.com).

In Ronda there is flamenco at Museo Lara (Calle Armíñán 29, tel: 952 87 12 63). Jerez de la Frontera has a strong flamenco tradition (p. 24) and there are worthwhile flamenco shows at La Taberna Flamenca (Calle Angostillo de Santiago 3; tel: 649 38 39 78). In Cádiz try La Cava (Calle Antonio López; tel: 956 21 18 66; www.flamencolacava.com).

THEATRE

Theatre lovers will find excellent programmes of music, drama and dance at Málaga's Teatro Miguel de Cervantes (Calle Ramos Marín; tel: 952 22 41 09) and at Cádiz's Gran Teatro Falla (Plaza Fragela; tel: 956 22 08 28). Ask at tourist offices for current programmes.

BULLFIGHTING

Novilladas, fights with young bulls and novice bullfighters, take place along the entire Costa del Sol, usually on Sunday evenings. These are advertised, and hotels often have details. The bigger rings in Málaga, Ronda and Jerez stage major fights; booking is advised.

GOLF

Most courses are on the Costa del Sol. Many require a handicap certificate and forward booking is heavy. Estepona Golf, Estepona (Arroyo Vaquero, Carretera de Cádiz, Km 150; tel: 952 93 76 05; https://esteponagolf.com), and Golf Torrequebrada, Benalmádena Costa (Carretera de Cádiz, N340; tel: 952 44 27 42; www.golftorrequebrada.com) are moderately priced.

HORSE RIDING

On the Costa del Sol try the Escuela del Arte Ecuestre (Carretera Nacional 340, Km 159, Estepona; tel: 952 80 80 77). For a canter on the beach, try the Hurricane Hotel (Carretera Nacional 340, Km 78, Tarifa; tel: 956 68 49 19; http://hotelhurricane.com).

OUTDOOR ACTION

For hang-gliding and paragliding try Club Escuela de Parapente Abdalajís (Valle de Abdalajís; tel: 952 650 68 59 69). In the spectacular Sierra de Grazalema, Horizon (Calle Corrales Terceros 29; tel: 956 13 23 63; www.horizonaventura.co) in Grazalema (p. 61) offers caving, rock climbing, mountain biking and other sports.

WATER SPORTS

For scuba diving, contact Simply Diving (Carlota Alessandri 25, Torremolinos; tel: 600 50 65 26; www.simplydiving.com) or YellowSub Tarifa (Plaza del Mirador 1, Tarifa; tel: 956 68 06 80; www.divingtarifa.com).

For windsurfing try ION-Club (Hotel Hurricane, Carretera Cádiz–Málaga; tel: 956 68 49 19) near Tarifa. Arrange dolphin-watching trips through Dolphin Safari (Marina Bay Complex, Gibraltar; tel: 956 77 19 14; www.dolphinsafari.gi).

An unforgettable highlight of almost every Andalucían trip. Immerse yourself in its beauty and history!

Granada and Almería

The legendary Alhambra awaits you – and you will be equally overwhelmed by the region's fascinating natural surroundings.

Pages 72–107

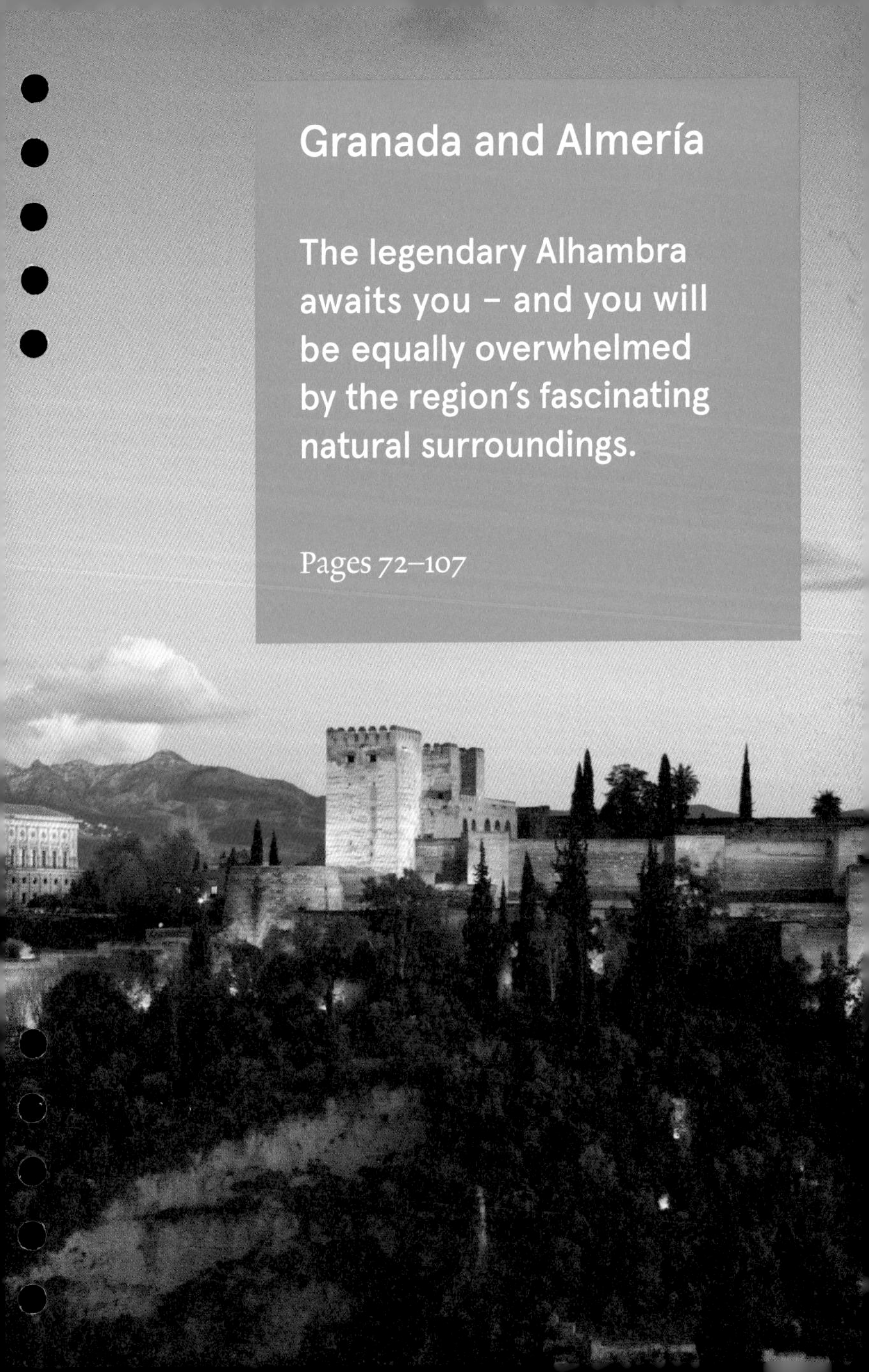

Getting Your Bearings

Andalucía's eastern provinces of Granada and Almería offer spectacular and diverse landscapes. In Granada, the mighty mountains of the Sierra Nevada range contrast with deeply wooded river valleys, while in Almería you'll find strange desert hills and arid coastal plains that seem more suited to North Africa than to Europe.

Such breathtaking diversity extends to the towns and cities of the region. Granada city's main treasure is the Alhambra Palace, one of the world's greatest palace complexes and the most hauntingly beautiful symbol of Moorish Andalucía. Granada also has a medieval quarter, the Albaicín, which seems more like a Moorish village in the heart of the Andalucían hills than a city enclave.

Granada has neither the exuberant sunny nature of Seville nor the easy-going atmosphere of Málaga and Cádiz. With its proximity to the rugged mountains of the Sierra Nevada, it is reminiscent of the Alpine foothills. Soaring to the southeast are the highest peaks in Spain, which then descend in great waves to the foothills of the beautiful Alpujarras, where the regional food and wine are particularly good.

In inland Almería province, parched desert buttes and gulches – Hollywood stand-ins for the Wild West – lie seared by the wind, while the arid, treeless coast offers strange lunar landscapes. The capital, Almería city, once surpassed Granada as a Moorish stronghold, and its formidable hilltop fortress, the Alcazaba, is a dramatic reminder of medieval Al-Andalus in its heyday.

TOP 10

❶ ★★ Granada

❽ ★★ Las Alpujarras

Don't Miss

㉑ Almería

At Your Leisure

22 Los Millares

23 Parque Natural Cabo de Gata-Níjar

24 Níjar

25 Mojácar

26 Sorbas

27 Mini Hollywood (Oasys)

28 Guadix

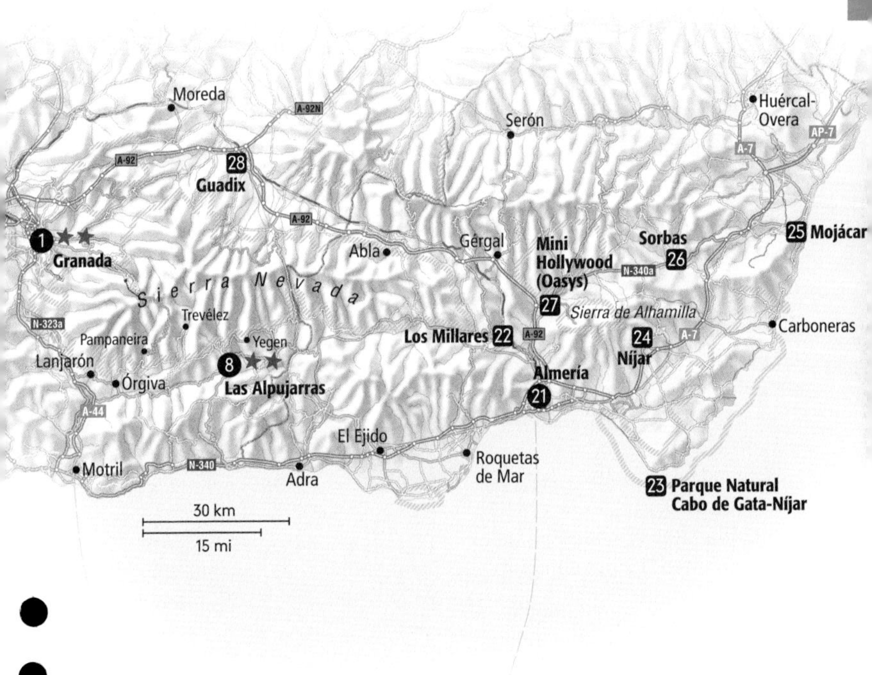

My Day With Beach and Gold Fever

Forget the problems of the world for a day as you spend a few hours on the beach, eat local delicacies at a seaside restaurant and also lap up some culture in the Cabo de Gata Nature Park. From Autumn to Spring it is possible to have western Europe's unique natural desert almost entirely to yourself.

9am: Breakfast with a View

San José awakes very gently. Here, from October to June, things move at a very leisurely pace. Start your day on the small village beach. With a bit of luck, Mesón El Pescador will have a table free on the promenade. The Andalucían breakfast, *Tostadas con Tomate y Aceite* – white bread crisply combined with a tomato, garlic and olive oil mixture, will taste twice as good accompanied by a view of the shimmering sea.

Would you like to see more of the sea? About 2km (1.25mi) to the south San José, one of Spain's most beautiful natural beaches awaits you. You have the choice: On foot it will take you about 30 minutes to get there, with the bike or car about 15 to 20 minutes along a rough gravel track.

11am: Pure Beach Delight

The Playa de Mónsul is Cabo de Gata's most well-known beach. Even more of a dream is the 1,500m (1mi) long Playa de Genoveves. At the end of the curved sandy cove, the white-chalk cliff of Morrón de

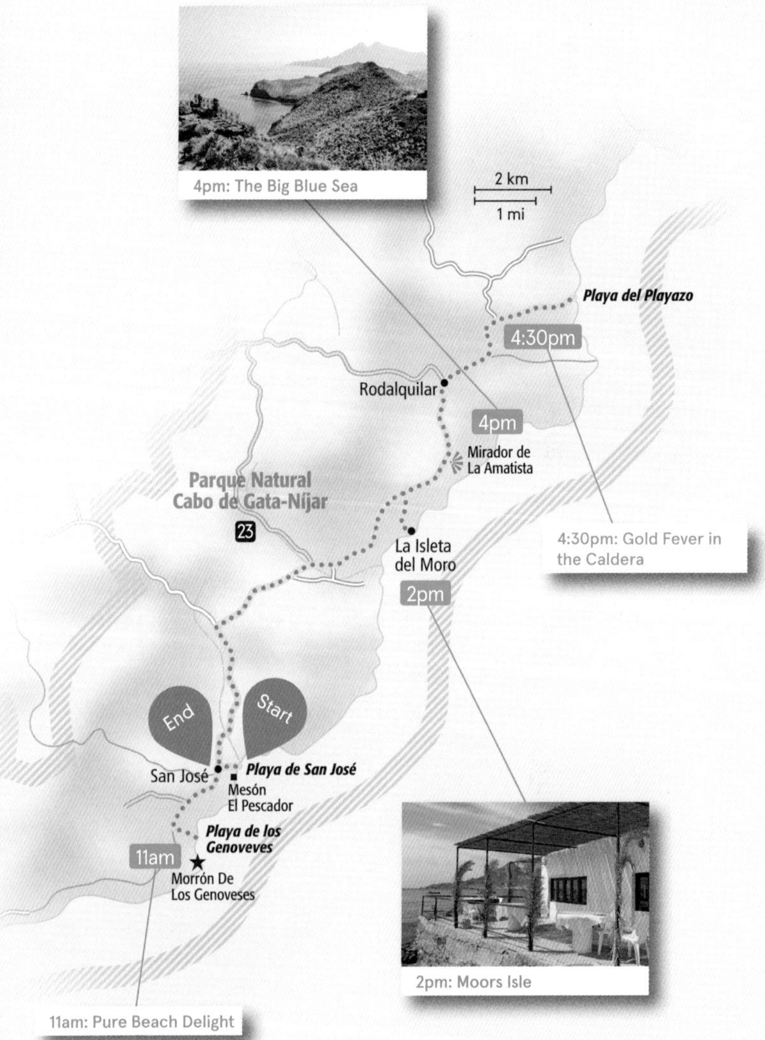
4pm: The Big Blue Sea
2 km
1 mi
Playa del Playazo
4:30pm
Rodalquilar
4pm
Mirador de La Amatista
Parque Natural Cabo de Gata-Níjar
23
La Isleta del Moro
4:30pm: Gold Fever in the Caldera
2pm
End
Start
San José
Playa de San José
Mesón El Pescador
Playa de los Genoveves
11am
Morrón De Los Genoveses
2pm: Moors Isle
11am: Pure Beach Delight

Start your day as the Andalucíans do with *tostadas*. Invigorated, you can then make your way to the dream Playa de Genoveves with its bizarrely beautiful coast

los Genoveves seems to dive into the sea like a whale. No buildings, no beach showers, or other tourist frills mutilate the coast. When the sea is calm, you won't be able to resist the clear, shallow water. Nude bathing is allowed.

2pm: Moors Isle

For lunch, reserve a table on the terrace of La Isleta del Moro 15km (9.5mi) further along the coast, a restaurant which takes its name from the fishing village in which it is located. This is one of the few charming gems in Spain, in which you can still enjoy fresh fish dishes in entirely authentic surroundings. You sit so close to the water that the fish could practically jump directly onto your plate. The name "Moors Isle" dates back to the time that lasted well into the 18th century when North African pirates controlled the little island.

4pm: The Big Blue Sea

After your meal, continue 5km (3mi) along the coast to Rodalquilar. Stop briefly at Mirador Las Amatistas to take a photo. Located high above the azure blue sea, this lookout point affords the most spectacular view of the rugged coastline, formed during a time of intense volcanic activity.

4:30pm: Gold Fever in the Caldera

Via a small pass, you can descend to Rodalquilar. As you enter the

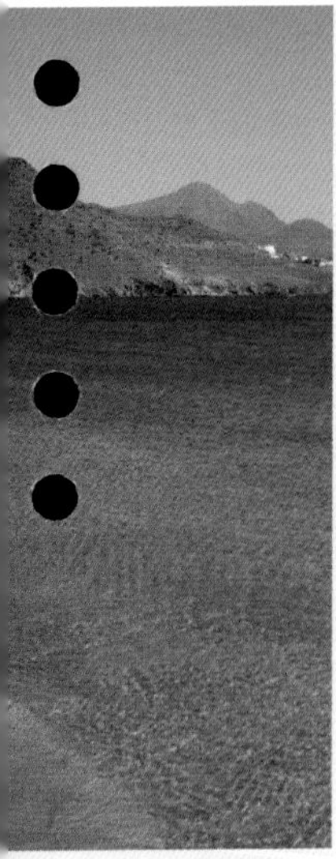

In Rodalquilar an abandoned mine awaits you (above) – you won't find any gold here, instead though a lovely little hamlet. And afterwards you can sit back and relax in San José (right)

village, you will see the derelict remains of a former workers' settlement. From 1883 until the mid-1960s people prospected for gold in the mine on the slopes above. After the mine was shut down, the number of inhabitants fell from 1400 to 75. From the old mine, you look down to the plain, which was once the bottom of a caldera. Stroll into the lovely little hamlet of snow-white houses and brightly coloured flowers and, afterwards, continue 4km (2.5mi) to the Playazo-Strand with its 18th-century fort.

7pm: Sundowner in a Tiny Harbour

Back in San José finish as you started: in one of the restaurants on the promenade – or look for a table along the tiny adjoining harbour.

Tip: Do the tour between Autumn and Spring when there are very few tourists about. Avoid the Easter week and the period between July and September if you can. During the summer months, the masses descend on the nature park and it is stiflingly hot.

Méson El Pescador
✉ Plaza Génova, 11, 04118 San José
☎ 950 38 04 82

Restaurante/Pensión La Isleta del Moro
✉ Calle Punta Barranco Negro, 59
☎ 950 389 713 and 950 389 764
🌐 www.pensionlaisletadelmoro.com

Bicycle hire
isub: ✉ C/Babor 3 🌐 www.isubsanjose.com or
Camping Tau (Easter–Sep)
✉ Camino de Cala Higuera, s/n,
04118 San José de Níjar 🌐 www.campingtau.com

❶ ★★ Granada

Don't Miss	Moorish culture par excellence, impressive churches and museums, and naturally: the incredible Alhambra
Why	To immerse yourself in Spain's Moorish soul
When	Straight away if possible!
Time	Leave yourself a bit more time!
What Else	Another visit to the Alhambra – after sunset
In Short	As beautiful as you had imagined it would be

Granada's Alhambra Palace is the greatest relic of Islamic Spain. As one of the most seductive monuments in the world, the Alhambra is a hard act to follow, but this compelling city has much else of beauty and interest, including the Albaicín (the old Moorish quarter), the Capilla Real (Royal Chapel) and cathedral, and some outstanding churches and museums. In the Old Town lies a leisurely world of colourful plazas and pedestrianised streets.

The former Moorish king's palace, a UNESCO World Heritage Site, is idyllically situated at the foot of the Sierra Nevada between two hills that slope steeply down to the fertile valley of the Río Genil. Albaicín, Granada's old quarter, is on the northern elevation; it is separated from the rest of the town by the deep ravine of the Río Darro, which flows into the Río

Phenomenal: The Alhambra is Granada's undisputed highlight

Yet if you only concentrate on the palace, you will miss a lot: the wonderful Old Town and the Arabian flair of many of the town's streets – for instance, the Arab Baths

Genil in the south of the city. Granada was ruled from Córdoba, and then from Seville, before emerging in the 1230s as the capital of the kingdom of the gifted Nasrid dynasty founded by Muhammad I ibn Yusuf ibn Nasr. In 1246, the Nasrids became vassals of the Christian kingdom of Castile, an arrangement that helped to ensure the survival of Granada as a Moorish kingdom until the late 15th century. A succession of Nasrid sultans did much over 200 years to create the Alhambra's most beautiful buildings and their exquisitely decorated chambers, scented patios and lush gardens. In 1492, the Catholic monarchs Fernando and Isabel "conquered" Granada and evicted Abur Abd Allah, known to the Spanish as Boabdil, the last Nasrid sultan.

Tourist Information offices
216 A/B1 Plaza del Carmen 9
902 40 50 45
216 B3 Real de la Alhambra, Cárcel Baja 3 958 24 71 28
216 C3 Santa Ana 2 958 57 52 04
http://en.granadatur.com

Parking
Access to the town centre is subject to strict regulations, so ignore your satnav and follow the traffic signs, otherwise you may have to pay a hefty fine. Hotel car parks have designated access routes. There are underground car parks in La Caleta (at the northwest end of Avenida de la Constitucíon near the railway station), in Plaza San Agustín (north of the cathedral) and one in Plaza Puerta Real (south of the central post office). There are car parks adjacent to the Alhambra ticket office.

The Alhambra

Within Alhambra's large hilltop complex are three main groups of buildings and gardens: the Alcazaba is the original fortress. To the east of the Alcazaba are the *palacios* (palaces): the Palacio Nazaríes, which served as the sultans' administrative, judicial and diplomatic headquarters as well as their private home; the Palacio de Carlos (Charles) V, an early 16th-century addition; and the Palacio de Generalife, the monarchs' summer palace and gardens, where they could escape from the pressures of court life.

The Lions' Courtyard at the Alhambra is a model example of the architectural expertise of the Moors

You have to book your ticket (ideally online) well in advance to be allowed to visit the Alhambra at all. Plan about three hours for your visit and wear comfortable shoes. Once you are in the complex, you can move around the grounds as you please. However, access to the Palacio Nazaríes is restricted, and you can only enter the building at the time designated on the admission ticket; if you arrive too late, the ticket is invalid. It is best to start your tour with the Alcazaba, the section at the western corner. From there you can work your way back via the Palacio Nazaríes and the Palacio de Carlos V to finish at the Generalife, a relaxing finale amid flowers and cooling fountains.

The Alcazaba

Built in the 13th century, the Alcazaba with its Torres Bermejas (red towers) is the oldest part of the Alhambra. The great tower at the western end is the Torre de la Vela, the Alhambra's belfry, from whose airy summit there are magnificent views over Granada, the Albaicín and the surrounding countryside known as the Vega. The poet García Lorca, a native of Granada, imagined the misty Vega as a bay of the sea, and once teased a friend by asking him if he had not seen boats bobbing below the Alhambra's towers.

On the southern edge of the Alcazaba are the lush, aromatic garden terraces of the Jardín de los Ardaves, a green oasis of elms and cypresses.

Palacio Real

The Palacio Nazaríes, a decorative treasure house of Islamic craftsmanship in brick, wood and stucco, is the crowning glory of the Alhambra. The entire complex reflects the subtle use of space, light and cool water that was the great gift of Islamic arts and crafts. You enter through a modest doorway and first come to the Mexuar (Audience Hall), where superb tiling and stucco work are a foretaste of what is to come.

Via a small patio and through the Cuarto Dorado (Golden Room) you enter the Patio de los Arrayanes (Patio of the Myrtles), a rectangular courtyard with a central pool, gently splashing fountains and a border of myrtle hedges. To the left, you walk through an arcade to the Sala de la Barca (Hall

The “Red Fortress”

The name Alhambra is derived from the Arabic word *Kala al-Hamra*, which means “Red Fortress”, the colour that its walls and towers radiate at sunset. Alhambra encompasses not only the Nasrid palace, but the entire complex, including the palace of Carlos V, the Alcazaba and the Generalife.

❶ Mexuar: The Mexuar was used for meetings and the public administration of justice. Carlos V had it turned into a chapel.
❷ Diwan or Serail: The royal palace proper where you will find the Patio de los Arrayanes with a water basin surrounded by myrtles.
❸ Harem: In the centre is the Patio de los Leones (Lion Courtyard) with the Lion Fountain.
❹ Patio de Mexuar: An impressive feature of this courtyard is its warm-coloured marble and azulejo cladding, especially in the Cuarto Dorado (the Golden Room).
❺ Torre de Comares and Sala de Embajadores The 45m (147ft) high Torre de Comares is the tallest tower in the fortress. Royal audiences took place on the ground floor in the Sala de Embajadores (Ambassadors’ Chamber). The ruler’s throne is opposite the entrance.
❻ Sala de la Barca: The name for this antechamber with its seven arcades derives either from the hull-like shape of the artesonado ceiling or from the Arabic word “baraka” (blessing).

❼ Sala de los Reyes: Of particular note are the three paintings from the 13th/14th century. Depicted on the middle one are the ten kings of the Nasrid dynasty (hence the name "Chamber of the Kings"). It is thought that they were done by Christian artists due to the less elaborate execution of the Muslim scenes.

❽ Peinador de la Reina: The "Queen's Dressing Room" is one of the most charming rooms: it was used by Isabel the Catholic and the wives of Carlos V and Felipe II.

❾ Torre de las Damas: More of an ornamental building than a fortress, it is one of the oldest structures in the Nasrid palace, erected at the beginning of the 14th century.

❿ Palace of Carlos V: Colonnaded square with a two-floor circular structure. The Museo de la Alhambra is on the ground floor and above it is the Museo Provincial de Bellas Artes.

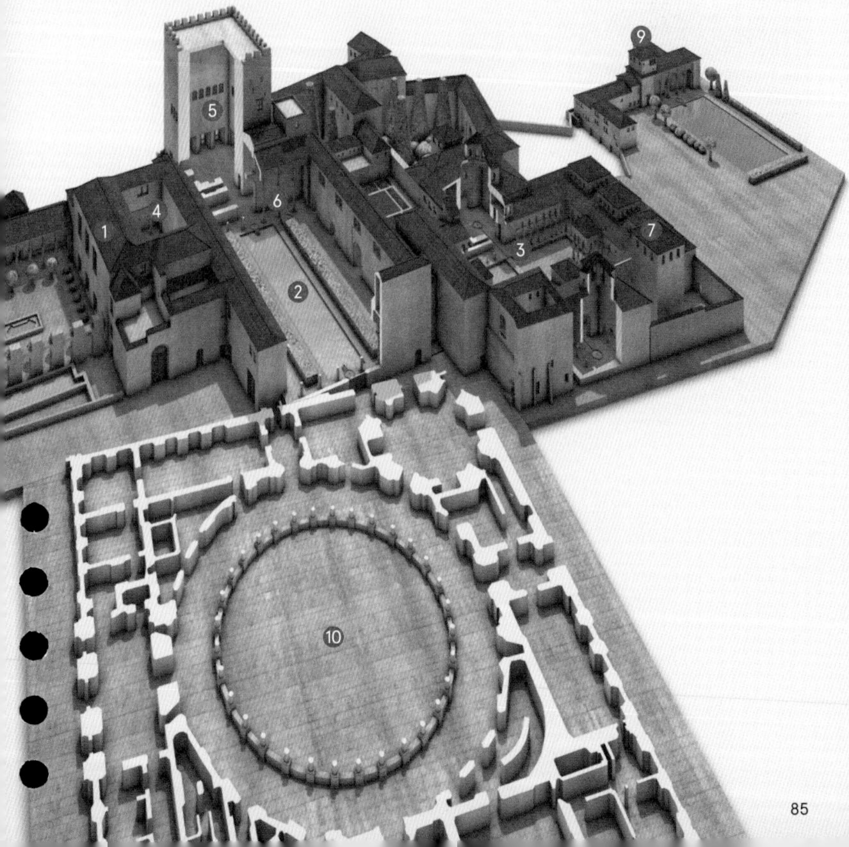

of the Boat), named for its boat-shaped ceiling, and the magnificent Salón de los Embajadores (Hall of the Ambassadors), in which there was a throne and was where the king received emissaries. The tiled and stuccoed walls soar to a ceiling dome that is a dazzling masterpiece of carved woodwork depicting the star-speckled heavens.

The next section was built as an inner sanctum for the sultans, and is where the rooms of the harem were located. The focus is the Patio de los Leones (Hall of the Lions), enclosed by marble-pillared arcades and with the famous fountain at its centre surrounded by 12 stone lions. Right of the patio is the beautiful Sala de los Abencerrajes. The ravishing dome, composed of a mass of tiny stalactites like starbursts, and the 16-sided ceiling frieze are reflected in a twelve-cornered marble fountain on the floor beneath it. The dark stains in the fountain bowl are said to represent the blood from the severed heads of 36 slaughtered knights, whose chief had coveted Sultan Abu al-Hassan's favourite concubine, Zoraya. Rust is probably the more likely source of the stains, but black deeds and acts of cruelty certainly did take place amid these exquisite surroundings.

Enchanting fountains in the Generalife

At the far end of the Patio de los Leones is a long narrow room, the Sala de los Reyes (Hall of the Kings), where recessed chambers retain paintings on their leather-covered ceilings. These are believed to depict tales of chivalry and are possibly the work of later Christian artists. The hall was used for summer entertainment, and the recesses may have served the same purpose as boxes at the theatre. To the left of the Lions' Fountain is the Sala de Dos Hermanas (Hall of the Two Sisters), named for two large slabs of marble in the chamber floor. The stuccowork on the room's roof is dazzling, like an explosion of shattered crystals. Beyond lies the romantic Sala de los Ajimeces (Hall of the Arched Windows), the private quarters of the sultan's favourite wife, where a gazebo overlooks a lush patio below.

Palacio de Carlos V

From the Sala de los Ajimeces a series of rooms and passageways leads into terraced gardens interspersed with patios and Moorish towers. You leave the gardens alongside the Renaissance Palacio de Carlos V, a quadratic intrusion by the Spanish monarch, who, from 1527, ripped out part of the Palacio Nazaríes to accommodate it. This is a building that would stand as a splendid structure in any other context. The core of the palace is a vast circular courtyard, open to the sky. It was used at one time as a bullring.

More austere than Islamic architecture: the Palacio de Carlos V

The surrounding rooms contain the Museo de la Alhambra with outstanding artefacts from the Islamic era, the finest of which is the great Jarrón de las Gacelas (Gazelle Vase), elegantly decorated in enamel.

The Generalife

On the Cerro del Sol (Hill of the Sun), at the eastern end of the Alhambra complex, is the luxurious Generalife, a world of cool fountains and pools, of garden patios and flower-filled terraces. The first green spaces were laid out in the 13th century, the interpretation of the name ranges from officer garden to fruit and vegetable garden. This was the extravagant pleasure palace of the Nasrids, where banquets and theatrical performances were staged. Today you can wander through the Patio de los Cipreses, a walled garden containing a cypress tree that is hundreds of years old, and dip your hands in the Camino de las Cascades.

---

217 D/E2
Calle Real de la Alhambra, s/n
958 02 79 71
Daily April to mid-Oct 8:30–8 (also floodlit visits Tue–Sat 10–11:30); mid-Oct–March 8:30–6, (also floodlit visits 8–9:30) Bus: Every 5 minutes from Plaza Isabel la Católica and Plaza Nueva
€14, senior citizens €9. You are strongly advised to pre-book your visit. Tickets can be reserved by phoning (tel: 034 858 95 36 16), or through the website: https://tickets.alhambra-patronato.es. Private individuals are only allowed to buy a maximum of 10 entrance tickets. More information available at www.alhambradegranada.org

The Albaicín

Granada's old Moorish quarter, the Albaicín, stands on the slopes of Sacromonte hill and faces the lofty Alhambra across the valley of the Río Darro. Its roughly cobbled streets and alleyways wriggle to and fro, punctuated by tall palm trees, between whitewashed walls splashed with bougainvillaea and geraniums. Scattered throughout are leafy plazas buzzing with local life. At sudden junctions you catch glimpses of the Alhambra painted against the backdrop of the Sierra Nevada.

The southern edge of the Albaicín is flanked by the Carrera del Darro, the narrow street that leads alongside the Río Darro, its line of buildings pierced at intervals by the steep and narrow alleyways that lead upwards into the heart of the Albaicín. In the Carrera del Darro, you'll find the 11th-century El Bañuelo (Arab Baths). You enter through a minuscule patio garden, an enchanting prelude to the brick-vaulted chambers of the baths themselves, with their starred and octagonal skylights. Nearby is Granada's excellent Museo Arqueológico (Archaeological Museum), with a fine collection of prehistoric, Phoenician, Roman, Visigothic and Moorish exhibits, housed in a Renaissance palace, the Casa de Castril. Its arcaded patio balcony has a view of the Alhambra above.

From the Mirador de San Nicolás, at the highest point of the district, you have the most beautiful view across the Albaicín and to the Alhambra, especially in the evening when the building is floodlit. To the north is the Plaza Larga, where everyday life is focused on surrounding shops and bars, and Plaza San Miguel el Bajo to the west; here amid whispering plane trees you can linger over drinks and tapas at the popular Bar Lara or Bar El Yunque. Nearby is another fine viewpoint, the Mirador de Cruz de Quirós. The eastern heights of Sacromonte hill contain the caves where a vibrant *gitano* community once lived. Now the former dwellings only house a few establishments offering expensive flamenco shows.

The Albaicín can be explored by a planned itinerary or by wandering at random. Heading downhill will usually

Wander along the side streets of Albaicín away from the clamour of the crowds

lead you back to central Granada. Don't wander in this area at night though, and watch for bag snatchers during the day.

217 D3

El Bañuelo
Carrera del Darro 31
958 22 97 38 Tue–Sat 10–2
Bus C1 (Plaza Nueva–Albaicín)
Free

Museo Arqueológico
Carrera del Darro 41
958 57 54 08
July, Aug Tue–Sun 93;
Sep–June Tue Sun 9–9, Sun 9–3
Bus C1 (Plaza Nueva–Albaicín)
€1.50

Capilla Real & Catedral

In the centre of modern Granada, just off the busy main Gran Vía de Colón, you'll find two important post-Moorish buildings, the catedral (cathedral) and adjoining Capilla Real (Royal Chapel).

The Capilla Real, built in late Gothic style and located on the south side of the cathedral was built over a 15-year period, from 1505 to 1521, under the direction of Enrique de Egas and destined as the resting place of the Catholic monarchs, Isabel and Fernando. The royal couple's original wish was to be buried in Toledo, but their conquest of the Moors encouraged them to build a burial chapel for themselves in Granada. The chapel is richly endowed with elegant columns and arches and superb altarpieces. A splendid grille encloses the lavish mausoleum of Isabel and Fernando, whose likenesses are depicted in Carrera marble. To its right are the figures of their daughter Joana ("the Mad") and her husband Felipe. Narrow steps descend to a crypt where the lead coffins of all four lie in grim display. Whether the remains within the coffins are those of the royal family is open to question, as they were vandalised by Napoleon's troops (always irreverent) during their short stay in the city during the Napoleonic Wars.

The Capilla Real is Granada's most beautiful sacred building from the Gothic period

The chapel's sacristy is an absolute joy and includes in its collection of royal artefacts Isabel's personal treasury of Italian and Flemish paintings.

Towering above the maze of houses in the town centre is the Catedral Santa María de la Encarnación, the first Renaissance church in Andalucía. It started out as a Gothic structure under the direction of Enrique de Egas in 1523, acquired lavish Plateresque elements when Diego de Siloé

Mighty and magnificent: Granada's cathedral is very impressive

took over in 1525 and was consecrated in 1561, although still not complete. In 1563, Juan de Orea was put in charge of continuing the work, which dragged on until 1703 when it was finally stopped without two of the towers foreseen in the plans being completed; even the tower that had been started did not reach its planned height. The 47m-(154ft)-high central dome gives the interior of the cathedral a wonderful airiness. There are impressive chapels to be seen in the side aisles as well as fine paintings and sculptures within the cathedral, several by the 17th-century Granada-born artist Alonso Cano, who worked on the cathedral's west façade.

To the southwest of the cathedral lies an area of narrow streets and attractive plazas that is worth exploring. On its east side, across the main thoroughfare of Calle Reyes Católicos to the Plaza del Carmen, is the entrance to the Alcaicería, a mock-Arab souk or arcade, crammed with souvenir shops. Just beyond is Calle Zacatín, a pedestrianised shopping street that leads into Plaza Bib-Rambla, a huge square ringed by tall buildings and well supplied with café-bars and restaurants and with a swathe of flower stalls. The streets beyond the plaza are the heart of Granada's shopping district.

Oasis of peace: Granada's Carthusian monastery

Monasterio de la Cartuja

Try to visit the Monasterio de la Cartuja (Carthusian Monastery) on the northern outskirts of the city, one of Spain's most extravagant baroque buildings. Started in 1506, the monastery was not finished until 300 years later. In 1835, the monks had to leave the monastery as a result of secularisation measures, and sections of it were destroyed. What remain are the cloister, refectory, church and sacristy. The lavish interior is a fine example of Churrigueresque (named after the Spanish architect and sculptor José Benito de Churriguera).

Parque de las Ciencias

A visit to the city's science park provides a modern, and futuristic, perspective of Granada. It is a treat for youngsters, who can get interactive with various hands-on installations, as well as a planetarium, a tropical butterfly house and a botanic garden; the BioDomo is dedicated to showing the biological diversity of our planet. The museum is 2km (1.25mi) from the centre but there are regular buses..

Capilla Real
216 B2 Oficios 3
958 22 92 39
Mon–Sat 10:15–1:30, Sun 11–6
Buses C1–C7 €5

Catedral
216 B3 Gran Vía de Colón 5
958 22 29 59 Mon–Sat 10–6:30, Sun 3–6 Buses C1–C7 €5

Monasterio de la Cartuja
216, off B5
Calle Real de Cartuja 958 16 19 32
Daily 10–8 (until 6 in winter), closed Sat 1–3
Buses U1, U2, N7 €5

Parque de las Ciencias
216, off A1
Avenida de la Ciencia 958 13 19 00
www.parqueciencias.com
Tue–Sat 10–9, Sun and public hols 10–3. Planetarium: hourly shows
Bus S5 Museum: €7, planetarium: €2.50

❽ ★★ Las Alpujarras

Don't Miss	An excursion to the mountains
Why	High peaks and white villages – Andalucían Switzerland
When	When you want an extra bit of fresh air
Time	As long as your feet can carry you
What Else	Forget about dieting – in the mountains, people eat hearty meals.
In Short	City breaks are not all that Andalucía has to offer

The Alpujarras, south of Granada and the Sierra Nevada, though slightly austere in places, have an attractive and very temperate mountain environment, which was discovered by writers and hikers at the beginning of the 20th century.

Moors settled in this region back in the 8th century and built up a lucrative silk business there in the 10th and 11th centuries. After losing Granada in 1492, the Moors retreated to the outlying villages until the majority were banished for good after several violent uprisings in 1569. Some Muslim families were allowed to stay, however, in order to help the new Christian settlers maintain the sophisticated irrigation systems and terraced gardens. The terraces are still used today for growing cereal crops, olives, citrus fruit and vegetables.

Gateway into Another World

The approach from Granada to the Western Alpujarras is through the spa town of Lanjarón. At the market town of Órgiva, 20km (12.5mi) east of Lanjarón, turn off north to follow the A-4132 that takes you into the heart of the formidable Poqueira Gorge. This is the best of the High Alpujarras. This was also clear to Chris Stewart: ex-drummer of the band Genesis, who set up as a small farmer near Órgiva.

The Poqueira Villages

The Poqueira Gorge, a broad but steep-sided valley, slices into the hills towards the second highest summit of the Sierra Nevada, Pico Veleta (3,398m/11,145ft), with the highest summit Mulhacén (3,481m/11,418ft) just out of sight to the east. The

Busquístar is located at an altitude of 1160m (3806ft) on the Rio Trevélez in the Alpujarras

white houses of a chain of three villages climb up the terraced slopes of the valley. The first village is Pampaneira, a compact jumble of houses that rises above the rugged old church of Santa Cruz in Plaza de la Libertad. On the square you'll find several bars and plenty of souvenir shops selling local pottery, rugs and blankets that reflect Pampaneira's popularity with coach parties.

Above Pampaneira is Bubión, the most tranquil and least visited of the Poqueira villages. On the corner of the small Plaza de la Iglesia is the Casa Alpujarreña, an outstanding museum of Alpujarran life. It occupies a traditional village house, left unchanged since its occupant moved away in the 1950s. On the way down to the square is the Taller del Telar (Weaver's Workshop), where fine woollen cloth is produced on a loom that belonged to the last master weaver of Granada. The cloth, of superb quality, comes in subtle colours; it is for sale, as are other artefacts such as textile lampshades.

The highest of the villages is Capileira. It is extremely popular and gets very crowded in summer. Away from the main road, however, you can wander between classic Alpujarran flat-roofed houses on narrow alleyways with covered roofs of twisted branches packed with clay. Then, as the lower houses of Capileira thin out, you can follow tracks that lead higher into the wooded gorge, where the Poqueira river gushes across polished boulders amid scented pinewoods.

Trevélez and Beyond

The road east from the Poqueira Gorge runs in delectable twists and turns along the great wooded shelf of hills and passes through the less visited villages of Pitres, Pórtugos and Busquístar, before turning north once more along the slopes of another deep valley to the town of Trevélez. Located at an altitude of 1,500m (4.920ft), Trevélez is one of the highest towns in Spain and is famed for its production of cured ham, *jamón serrano*. The houses of Trevélez climb the upper slopes of the valley in a succession of *barrios*, separate quarters that have quite distinct characters. The lowest of these, the *barrio bajo*, pays the price of Trevélez's popularity. Its main square is not much more than a large car-parking area with souvenir shops, cafés, restaurants and *jamón serrano* outlets. A steep zigzagging road leads up to middle Trevélez, the *barrio medio*, then continues to the upper village, the *barrio alto*, where traffic fades away and lanes grow narrower as they climb towards the steepening mountain slopes above. Continuing east from Trevélez takes you deeper into the Alpujarras, through a landscape of woods and streams, dense with chestnut, poplar, evergreen oak and pine. The road takes you past old Moorish settlements, such as Bérchules and Yegen, unspoiled villages that cling to the tumbling slopes of the hills and captivate with their slow pace of life and friendly inhabitants. Beyond Yegen the road continues east to the arid hills of Almería province.

INSIDER TIP At the entrance to Pampaneira, the flowery terrace of the **Casa Julio** offers a lovely place to sit (Avenida de la Alpujarra, 9; tel: 958 76 33 22; www.casa-julio.com). Across a narrow street with a water canal, you reach Plaza de la Libertad.

---

212 B2

Rustic Blue (Holiday Home Agency)
Bubión ☎ 958 76 33 81
www.rusticblue.com

Mancomunidad de Municipios de la Alpujarra Granadina (Association of Alpujarra villages)
Calle Obrador 6, Cádiar
www.alpujarraturistica.com

Casa Alpujarreña, Bubión
Plaza Iglesia
☎ 958 76 30 32
Wed–Mon 11–2,
Fri, Sat and public hols 11–2, 5–7

㉑ Almería

Don't Miss	A town that you should not miss
Why	The unpretentious sister of Seville & Co. is authentic and hospitable
When	To coincide with the Easter processions – less well-known, but just as poignant as in Seville
Time	As much as it takes to try all the tapas bars – or one or two…
What Else	The Archaeological Museum presents Early History in an exciting and entertaining way
In Short	Moorish, medieval, modern

According to an old Spanish proverb: *"Cuando Amería era Amería, Granada era su alquería"* ("When Almería was Almería, Granada was but a farmstead"). The Moors called the fantastic fortress towering above the town "al-Mariyat Bayyana", which depending on the context is translated as "fortress", "mirror of the sea" and also "salt coast". Below it, the Old Town, characterised by narrow streets and crumbling buildings, contrasts starkly with the busy shopping streets and recently refurbished boulevards of the modern districts. In Almería you move easily between Moorish and medieval Andalucía and the busy world of 21st-century Spain.

In the southeast of Andalucía, the wide open Gulf of Almería attracts visitors with its long beaches and its provincial capital's mix of modern flair and historic allure. The town's touristic highlight is the very beautifully restored Alcazaba, the largest Moorish fortress in Andalucía.

From the 8th century, Almería was the chief port of Al-Andalus and grew rich on two-way trade with North Africa and the eastern Mediterranean. The city fell to the Christians in 1490, and the break with North Africa led to a decline exacerbated by destructive earthquakes in the 16th century. By the 19th century, Almería was beginning to prosper once more. Today *plasticultura*, greenhouse farming, and increased tourism, have brought much development to the rather unspectacular but convivial and lively city.

The Alcazaba

The Alcazaba's 10th-century builders took advantage of the craggy edges of their hilltop site, and even today the restored walls and towers of the fortress look like natural extensions of the encircling cliffs. The approach ramp to the Alcazaba complex winds steeply up to the Puerta de la Justicia (Justice Gate), a perfect example of a Moorish entrance archway. The double horseshoe arch has a staggered inner gate that was designed to disorientate an attacker. Beyond is the Primer Recinto (First Precinct). Here, there is a cistern dating back to Moorish times, the garden has been arranged in the Moorish style. From here you climb gently to a cool oasis of trees that shades the high wall of the Segundo Recinto (Second Precinct). In this spacious, in part reconstructed areal, was the palace of the Moorish kings, the reception area and the personal chambers of the rulers. In the 16th century, the Christian castellan of Almería chose this section as a residence. Part of it was

Majestic and Moorish: The Alcazaba from Almeria still impresses its visitors.

View from Cerro de San Cristóbal, the peak near Alcazaba, on Almería

the Ermita de San Juan built in the Mudéjar style. The Tercer Recinto (Third Precinct) is the youngest section of the fortress. It contains the formidable inner fortress built by the Christian conquerors after 1492 on the site of a previous keep. From its walls there are breathtaking views to the sea. Immediately below the fortress lies the Barrio de Chanca, Almería's old cave district with the often brightly painted façades of the flat-roofed houses and of the cave dwellings that punctuate the rocky escarpments above them. The houses, and a few of the caves, are occupied by the poorest citizens of Almería.

Other Sights

The city's Catedral is a typical fortified church with four imposing corner towers, tower-like apses and battlements. Diego de Siloé built it after the earthquake of 1522 between 1524 and 1543 in place of the Friday Mosque. Less overbearing are the main entrance and the Puerta de los Perdones, both by Juan de Orea, with twin pillars, richly decorated with sculptural figures and crowned with the coat of arms of Carlos I. The exquisite choir stalls of carved walnut are also by de Orea (1558).

The Museo Arqueológico (Archaeological Museum) exhibits items from the Los Millares pre-Bronze Age site (Insider Info, p. 102), along with material from the Roman and Moorish periods. The Centro de Arte (Art Gallery; not far from the train and bus stations) exhibits traditional and contemporary art. Central Almería is divided by the Avenida Federico García Lorca (also Rambla de Belén), a wide boulevard that slopes down towards the harbour. To the west is the city's main street, the sleekly refurbished Paseo de Almería lined with shops, restaurants and café-bars. At its north end is Plaza Manuel Pérez García and Calle de las Tiendas. This takes you to the Plaza de la Constitución (Place of the Constitution), also called Plaza Vieja (Old Square). You can relax on the 17th-century square surrounded by arcades. Palm trees encircle a white monument, which commemorates the execution in 1824 of Almerians who defied the repressive rule of King Fernando VII.

INSIDER TIP For great *jamón* and fish tapas and meals, and a terrific selection of sherries, don't miss **Bodega las Botas** (Calle Fructuosa Pérez 3; tel: 950 23 42 39), a high-roofed bar with traditional upturned sherry barrels for tables.

---

212 B2

Tourist Information
Parque Nicolás Salmerón s/n
950 17 52 20
Plaza de la Constitución
950 21 05 38
www.turismodealmeria.org

Parking
There are underground car parks along the Rambla de Belén and off the main roundabout at the Rambla's southern end.

Alcazaba
Almanzor s/n
950 80 10 08
Mid-Sep–March Tue–Sat 9–6:30, Sun 10–5; April–May Tue–Sat 9–8, Sun 10–5; June to mid-Sep Mon–Sat 9–3:30, 6:30–10, Sun 10–5
Free to EU passport holders

Catedral
Plaza de la Catedral
April–June Mon–Sat 10–7, Sun 1:30–7; July–Sep Mon–Fri 10–8:30 (last admission 6:30), Sat 10–7, Sun 1:30–7; Oct–March Mon–Fri 10–6:30, Sat 10–2:30, 3:30–6:30, Sun 1:30–6:30 €5

Museo Arqueológico
Calle de Ronda 91 950 17 55 10
Tue 2–8:30, Wed–Sat 6–8:30, Sun 9–2:30
€1.50 (free to EU passport holders)

Centro de Arte – Museo de Almería
Plaza Carlos Cano s/n
950 26 96 80
June–Sep Tue–Sun 10–1, Fri, Sat 10–1, 5–8; Oct–May Tue–Sun 10:30–1:30, Fri, Sat 10:30–1:30, 6–9 Free

Grasping for the Stars

At Cabo de Gata in the east of Almeria, the landscape is not only as desolate as a desert, it is just as sparsely populated. The positive side: no light sources or air pollution blur the night's star-studded sky. On a clear night, drive along the Playa de Genoveves or the Playa de Mónsul and let the glittering firmament, stretching out high above the sea, work its magic on you. How small we are! From May to July stargazers can also see the wonderful Scorpius constellation in the south.

At Your Leisure

22 Los Millares

Los Millares, about 20 km (12 mi) north of Almería is well worth a visit. This very sophisticated complex is considered to be one of the most important European sites from the Copper Age (3200–2200BC). Besides the actual settlement, you can also see a necropolis covering an area of about 13ha (32 acres) with 80 (in part reconstructed) round burial chambers. Plan 1.5 to 2.5 hours for your visit. In summer, temperatures can be sweltering, so remember to take a hat, suncream and water with you.

212 C2

Enclave Arqueolócigo Los Millares
south of Santa Fé de Mondújar, access via Al-3409 or Al-3411 ☎ 677 90 34 04
Wed–Sun 10–2 Free

23 Parque Natural de Cabo de Gata-Níjar

This peninsula on the eastern side of the Gulf of Almería is the only natural desert in Europe, a landscape of long empty beaches and raw volcanic hills. On the southern tip of the peninsula stands a lonely lighthouse from where there are dramatic views of rugged cliffs and offshore pinnacles. Cabo de Gata's attractions lie in its natural beaches, its plant and bird life and the remoteness of the cliffs and lonely coves of the wild coast to the northeast of the cape. The most accessible beaches lie on the western shores of the Gulf of Almería alongside the road between the village of San Miguel de Cabo de Gata and the lighthouse. They are marred only by the occasional winds that blow up by midday. Just before the lighthouse, a narrow road, signed *Acceso Sendero Vela Blanca*, leads off left for 3km (2mi) to a final headland crowned by a radio station and by the old Moorish watchtower of Vela Blanca. You can reach the most beautiful beaches along the coast, Playa de Genoveves and Playa del Mónsul, via San José, the tourist centre of the nature park. The San José tourist sells wonderful handmade products by regional craftspeople.

The nature park is an area of special protection for plants and birds. Plants that can cope with the desert-like conditions include agaves with their tree-like flower stalks, and Europe's only indigenous palm, the dwarf fan palm. Behind the village of San Miguel de Cabo de Gata lies Las Salinas, a large area of salt marshes, where you may spot flamingos, avocets, storks and egrets among the many resident and migrant birds.

Wander along the sand dunes around San José

↠213 D1/2

Oficina de Información
✉Avenida de San José 27, San José
☎950 38 02 99
🌐www.cabodegata-nijar.com
🕐Daily 10–2, 5:30–8:30, closed Sun afternoon in winter

La Gallineta (€€–€€€)
✉Carretera de San José, El Pozo de los Frailes ☎950 38 05 01

Tourist Information
✉Centro de Información Parque Natural Cabo de Gata and Centro de Visitantes de Las Amoladeras

24 Níjar

The village of Níjar, centre of a ceramics industry dating from Moorish times, sits in the foothills of the Sierra de Alhamilla 30km (19mi) northeast of Almeria. Below is the arid plain of the Campo de Níjar, carpeted with the glistening sheets of *plasticultura* greenhouses. Níjar's potters specialise in vivid colours; you can buy their wares in the pottery and craft shops in main street, Avenida García Lorca. For excellent Níjar ceramics look for La Tienda de los Milagros on the western edge of town in Calle Pocico 9/Corner of Callejón del Artesano 1, which is slightly difficult to find. However, the main workshops and showroom are in the adjoining Barrio Alfarero, which leads off from the top of García Lorca. The craft shops also sell brightly coloured carpets and blankets. Beyond Avenida García Lorca is the Old Town with tree-lined Plaza la Glorieta and the 16th-century church of Santa María de la Anunciación, noted for its *mudéjar* ceiling.

↠213 D2 🌐www.nijar.es; www.latiendadelosmilagros.com

25 Mojácar

Mojácar is the main beach resort in Almería province and can become extremely busy in high season. If you want easily accessible beaches with modern conveniences, however, this is the place to find them. There are two Mojácars. The long, straggling coastal resort of Mojácar Playa makes the most of a narrow

The white houses of Mojácar Pueblo picturesquely enthroned on a hill

stretch of excellent beach alongside the rather busy main road. Side by side along the beachfront are numerous hotels, shops, cafés, restaurants and lively bars. Just 2km (1.25mi) inland is old Mojácar, known as Mojácar Pueblo, a settlement clustered round a rocky hilltop. The village can still charm in spite of the crowds of summer visitors who throng the souvenir shops.

↗ 213 D2
Tourist Information
✉ Plaza del Frontón, Mojácar
☎ 902 57 51 30 🌐 www.mojacar.es

26 Sorbas

The village of Sorbas, 40km (25mi) northeast of Almería, is noted for its pottery and you can visit workshops and salerooms in its Barrio Alfarero. To the east are the Cuevas de Sorbas, at the heart of the limestone hills. You can take two-hour guided trips through the cave systems. These are mildly adventurous, but even young children can cope with the occasional scrambling and clambering. Helmets and headlamps are supplied.

↗ 213 E2 🌐 www.sorbas.es

Cuevas de Sorbas
☎ 950 36 47 04 🌐 www.cuevasdesorbas.com. Booking a day ahead is advised.
🕐 Mon–Fri 10–2, 4–6, Sat, Sun 10–2
🎟 From €15 (depending on the route)

27 Mini Hollywood (Oasys)

The extraordinary Arizona-style "Badlands" of Tabernas to the north of Almería is where such Western classics as *The Magnificent Seven* and *The Good, the Bad and the Ugly* were filmed. The mock Wild West towns built for these movies amid drystone gulches and treeless wastes remain as tourist attractions. Mini Hollywood is the largest and is part of the "Oasys Theme Park" (Safari park, zoo and water park) – just off the Carretera Nacional, about 6km (3.75mi) west of Tabernas. Special cowboy shows are staged outside the sheriff's office. Youngsters love it, but adults may groan at the staginess of it all.

↗ 212 C2 ☎ 902 53 35 32
🌐 www.oasysparquetematico.com
🕐 July–Aug 10–9, otherwise shorter (Nov–March weekends only 10–6)
🍴 Restaurant and café (€–€€)
🎟 €22.50 (dogs are not admitted)

28 Guadix

The bustling episcopal seat, 60km (37mi) east of Granada, has earned acclaim for its remarkable cave dwellings that have been carved into the soft tufa rock. They have all the modern conveniences, and the windowless rooms maintain a constantly equable temperature. Many caves have whitewashed extensions and well-tended gardens. In the Cueva Museo (Cave Museum), a series of rooms have been preserved and furnished in traditional manner.

The main town is dominated by a Renaissance cathedral in sandstone. Opposite its main door, an archway leads to the attractive Renaissance square of Plaza de la Constitución, known also as Plaza Mayor. From the square, alleyways lead to a clutch of handsome Renaissance buildings in the upper town.

↗ 212 B2 🌐 www.guadix.es

Cueva Museo
✉ Plaza del Padre Poveda ☎ 958 66 55 69
🕐 Mon–Fri 10–12, 4–6, Sat 10–2 🎟 €2.60

Where to... Stay

Expect to pay per double room per night

€	up to €60
€€	€60–€90
€€€	€90–€140
€€€€	over €140

GRANADA

Casa del Aljarife €€€
The views of the Alhambra from this pension, set in a tiny square at the heart of the Albaicín, are splendid. The 17th-century house has been sensitively restored, and has a delightful shady central courtyard and rooftop terrace typical of the area. The rooms (there are just four) are small but have plenty of character with interesting angles and use of space.
216 C2
Placeta de la Cruz Verde 2, Albaicín
958 22 24 25
www.casadelaljarife.com

Hotel Los Tilos €€
This good-value, no-frills hotel has a comfortable, modern interior, and is about as central as you can get, overlooking a pleasant square where there is a daily flower market. Best of all is the fourth-floor terrace where you can sip a drink, read a book or just enjoy a fabulous panoramic view of the city skyline.
204 A2
Plaza de Bib-Rambla 4
958 26 67 51
www.hotellostilos.com

Tapas bars work their magic in Grenada, too.

LAS ALPUJARRAS

Las Terrazas €–€€€
There's a delightful homey feel to this *hostal* high up on the mountain, regardless whether in the simple but comfortable rooms or in one of the apartments. In summer you can enjoy the panoramic terrace and in winter you can snuggle round the fire.
2212 B2 Plaza del Sol 7, Bubión
958 76 30 34 www.terrazasalpujarra.com
Closed Jan

ALMERÍA

Hotel La Perla €–€€
The oldest hotel in town and still family-run, La Perla was favoured by the stars in Almería's "spaghetti western" days. It has been expanded to several more floors and modernised in a light and friendly style but still exudes a certain old-world charm. The rooms are pleasant – ask for one overlooking the plaza.
212 C2 Plaza del Carmen 7
950 23 88 77 www.hotellaperla.es

Where to... Eat and Drink

Expect to pay for a three-course meal, incl. wine and service

€	up to €15
€€	€15–€40
€€€	over €40

GRANADA

Chikito €
This used to be an artists' café, once frequented by the poet Federico García Lorca. Opened again in 1976, the Chikito is now one of the better restaurants in Granada. Andalucían meals are served here, as are tapas. As the evening progresses here, it becomes almost impossible to find a free seat in the bar. Most of the guests are locals. The owner is a great bullfighting fan as is obvious from the many photos on the wall.
216 B1 Plaza del Campillo Bajo 9
958 22 33 64
www.restaurantechikito.com

Cunini €€–€€€
This is one of the city's most famous *marisquerías*, and its fish and seafood specialities are delicious. Dishes include *caldereta de arroz, pescado y marisco* (rice, fish and seafood stew) and *pescaditos fritos* (fried fish). Located around the corner from the cathedral, there is an attractive outside terrace.
216 A2 Calle Pescadería 14
958 25 07 77
www.marisqueriacunini.com
Closed Sun and Mon evenings

La Gran Taberna €–€€
If you want a quiet drink, forget this typical town-centre tapas bar, especially if it's a football night. The tapas here are terrific. You can choose from a vast selection, including trout with cottage cheese, Roquefort with turnips, and goat's cheese canapés as well as the more standard selection.
216 C2
Plaza Nueva 12
958 22 88 46
Daily 9–3, 7–midnight

San Nicolás €€€
Head straight for a table on the outside terrace if you want to enjoy the fabulous views of the Alhambra (particularly recommended at sunset). The restaurant's décor is sumptuous and elegant, with exquisite marble, pale pistachio-coloured walls and linen-clad tables. The menu includes such nouvelle-Andaluz dishes as leg of pork filled with lavender and honey.
2217 D4
Calle San Nicolás 3, Albaicín
958 27 28 42
www.restaurantesannicolas.com
Tue–Sat noon–11, Sun noon–4

Via Colon €€
This entertaining café-bar stands between busy Gran Via de Colón and the quieter environs of Granada's cathedral. It's a bustling spot, especially at lunchtime, but there's a quieter outside terrace right under the cathedral walls. Inside, pride of place goes to a remarkable full-size sculpted angel that graces the end of the bar with some style. To eat, you'll find a range of tasty tapas and specialities such as scrambled eggs with green asparagus and prawns.
216 B3
Gran Via de Colón 13
958 22 07 52
www.restauranteviacolon.com
Daily 8am–midnight

LAS ALPUJARRAS

El Corral del Castaño €
This rustically furnished restaurant is located right in the centre on a pretty square. The entrance area alone is very inviting. Awaiting you inside is a large selection of delicious regional dishes. Both the waiters and the chef are very keen to please. All-round good value for money. The three-course menu is very recommendable.
212 B2
Plaza Calvario 16, Capileira
958 76 34 14
Daily 1–4, 8–10:30

Restaurante Iber €€
This family-run business near the church offers inexpensive regional dishes but also more exotic choices such as curry, dhal and couscous as well as plenty of vegetarian dishes. The atmosphere is lively and informal with swift and efficient service. Good wine selection.
212 B2
Calle Parra 1, Capileira
653 93 50 56

ALMERÍA

Casa Puga €€
This tavern in the centre of Almería has been in existence since 1870. Popular for tapas: its small fish and meat dishes are legendary – offering a large selection and great quality. Thus, it is not surprising that the restaurant is always full at lunchtime and in the evening. You can stand cosily at the bar or eat in the *Comedor*, dining room, at a small table next to the casks full of the house wine.
212 C2 Calle Jovellanos 7
950 23 15 30 www.barcasapuga.es
Mon–Sat noon–4, 8–midnight

Restaurante Valentín €€€
Valentín is one of Almería's best known restaurants, and one of several good places to eat located on this street. The speciality here is seafood with dishes like *cazuela de rape* (monkfish baked in a sauce of almonds and pine nuts) and *langosta* (lobster). The atmosphere is intimate and the interior typically Andalucían with dark wood, exposed brickwork and white paintwork. If you are celebrating then push the boat out with the excellent *menu degustación*.
212 C2 Calle Tenor Iribarne 19
950 26 44 75
www.restaurantevalentin.es Closed Mon and Sep

Torreluz Mediterráneo €€€
One of the city's most sophisticated restaurants, with elaborate brocade chairs, light brick walls and plenty of stained glass and gilt. The service is discreet and attentive and the dishes flavourful. Specialities include suckling pig (*cochinillo*) slowly roasted in a wood-burning oven, grilled meats, and fresh fish.
212 C2 Plaza Flores 1
950 28 14 25 www.torreluz.com/restaurante-mediterraneo
Mon–Sat 1:30–4, 8:30–midnight

Where to... Shop

Both Granada and Almería provinces have rich craftwork traditions, ranging from Granada's inlaid woodwork to the vividly coloured pottery of Níjar and the textiles and clothing of Las Alpujarras.

GRANADA CITY

Granada city's main shopping area is the streets between the arms of its two main thoroughfares, Calle Reyes Católicos and Gran Vía de Colón. In Reyes Católicos are a number of small, but very stylish fashion shops.

On the south side of the cathedral is the Alcaicería, a mock-Arab souk or arcade, crammed with souvenir shops full of crafts including brass and copperwork, embossed leather and pottery.

Nearby is the narrow, pedestrianised Zacatín with a good range of clothes and gift shops.

A Granada speciality is *taracea* (marquetry), and there are several shops selling it in Cuesta de Gomérez, the narrow street leading steeply uphill from Plaza Nueva to the Alhambra. The street also contains plenty of souvenir shops, as well as some of the best guitar-makers in Andalucía.

For the full range of shopping there's the department store El Corte Inglés between the Carrera de la Virgen and Acero del Darro, the broad continuation of Reyes Católicos.

One of the best food and drink shops in the city is the well-stocked Mantequería Castellano (Calle Almireceros 6; tel: 958 22 48 40) just off Gran Vía de Colón and opposite the cathedral.

In nearby Calderería Vieja and Calderería Nueva, on the webpage of the Albaicín, there are a number of shops selling "Arabic" spices, perfumes, food and souvenirs.

LAS ALPUJARRAS

In the High Alpujarras, shops in villages such as Pampaneira sell souvenirs, pottery and traditional *jarapas* (rugs and bedcovers). Worth seeking out in Pampaneira is Bodega La Moralea (Calle Verónica 12; tel: 958 76 32 25), which carries a vast stock of local food products and artefacts.

In Bubión go for Taller del Telar (Calle Trinidad; tel: 958 76 31 71; www.tallerdeltelar.com) for textiles and fabrics. For the *jamón serrano*, the cured ham of the region, Trevélez is the best bet.

ALMERÍA CITY AND PROVINCE

Almería city's main shopping area is Calle de las Tiendas and its surrounding alleyways. The morning market in Calle Aguilar de Campo, off Paseo de Almería, is lively and colourful.

For fine pottery, head for Níjar, where you can also buy brightly coloured *jarapas*. Look for La Tienda de los Milagros (Callejón del Artesano 1; tel: 950 36 03 59) for an imaginative approach to pottery.

Another good source of ceramics is Sorbas, where workshops in the Barrio

Alfarero (the Potter's Quarter) produce more functional wares than those of Níjar in such family-run workshops as Alfarería Juan Simón (San Roque 21; tel: 950 36 40 83).

In the tourist information centre at San José (Cabo de Gata), craftsmen offer pottery in individual and colourful design

Where to... Go Out

See www.granadatur.com for more information about events in Granada. The city's daily newspaper *Ideal* also has a useful entertainment section.

NIGHTLIFE

Many of the clubs and music bars in Granada cater to the city's lively student population. These inexpensive places are situated between the streets of Martínez de la Rosa and Pedro Antonio de Alarcon.

If you are looking for something a little more sophisticated, try Boom Boom Room (Cárcel Baja 10; tel: 958 22 40 01; http://boomboomroom.es) just off Gran Vía de Colón near the cathedral. It attracts a smarter set, and is consequently more expensive than many other places in the city.

The mainstream El Camborio (Camino del Sacromonte: tel: 958 22 12 15) is a less expensive alternative. Here you'll find several dance floors and a garden terrace with views of the Alhambra. Again, midnight is the earliest time for things to start happening.

Almería has some lively music bars in the Calle San Pedro area, and during the summer months disco-marquees are set up on the Paseo Marítimo to the east of the seaward end of the Rambla de Belén. These venues can be fairly noisy and youth-orientated, but Spanish youngsters are not ageist, so, whatever your age, you can join in.

DANCE

Granada's Teatro Alhambra (Calle de Molinos 56; tel: 958 02 80 00; www.teatroalhambra.com) stages flamenco, ballet and modern dance, as well as Spanish-language plays.

For night owls: El Camborio

There are a number of flamenco venues in Granada city. Bar Liberia (Duquesa 8; tel: 958 27 04 11), El Curro (Camino del Sacromonte 85; tel: 658 68 89 69), Peña la Platería (Placeta de Toqueros 7; tel: 958 22 77 12; www.laplateria.org), Pibe Peña Las Cuevas del Sacromonte (Camino del Sacromonte 41; tel: 620 18 26 63), Sala Vimaambi (Cuesta de San Gregorio 30; tel: 958 22 73 34; www.vimaambi.com).

OUTDOOR ACTIVITIES

The Sierra Nevada and Las Alpujarras have much to offer outdoor enthusiasts.

Las Alpujarras offers ideal walking conditions and, if you are experienced and well equipped, there's high-level walking on the Sierra Nevada peaks.

It is possible to book all kinds of guided activities in the mountains at Nevadensis (Plaza de la Libertad, Pampaneira; tel: 958 76 31 27; www.nevadensis.com).

For horse riding, contact Dallas Love (Bubión; tel: 608 45 38 02; www.spain-horse-riding.com) or Cabalgar Rutas Alternativas (Bubión; tel: 958 76 31 35, www.ridingandalucia.com), who organise anything from a few hours' riding to eight-day treks.

For adventure activities such as riding, rock climbing and paragliding, contact Nevadensis (above).

For water sports enthusiasts there are numerous places offering kayak and diving tours in the Cabo de Gata area, for instance Media Luna Aventura (San José; tel: 950 38 04 62; www.medialunaventura.com).

Admire the red and white arches of Córdoba's Mezquita
as you stride through its forest of columns

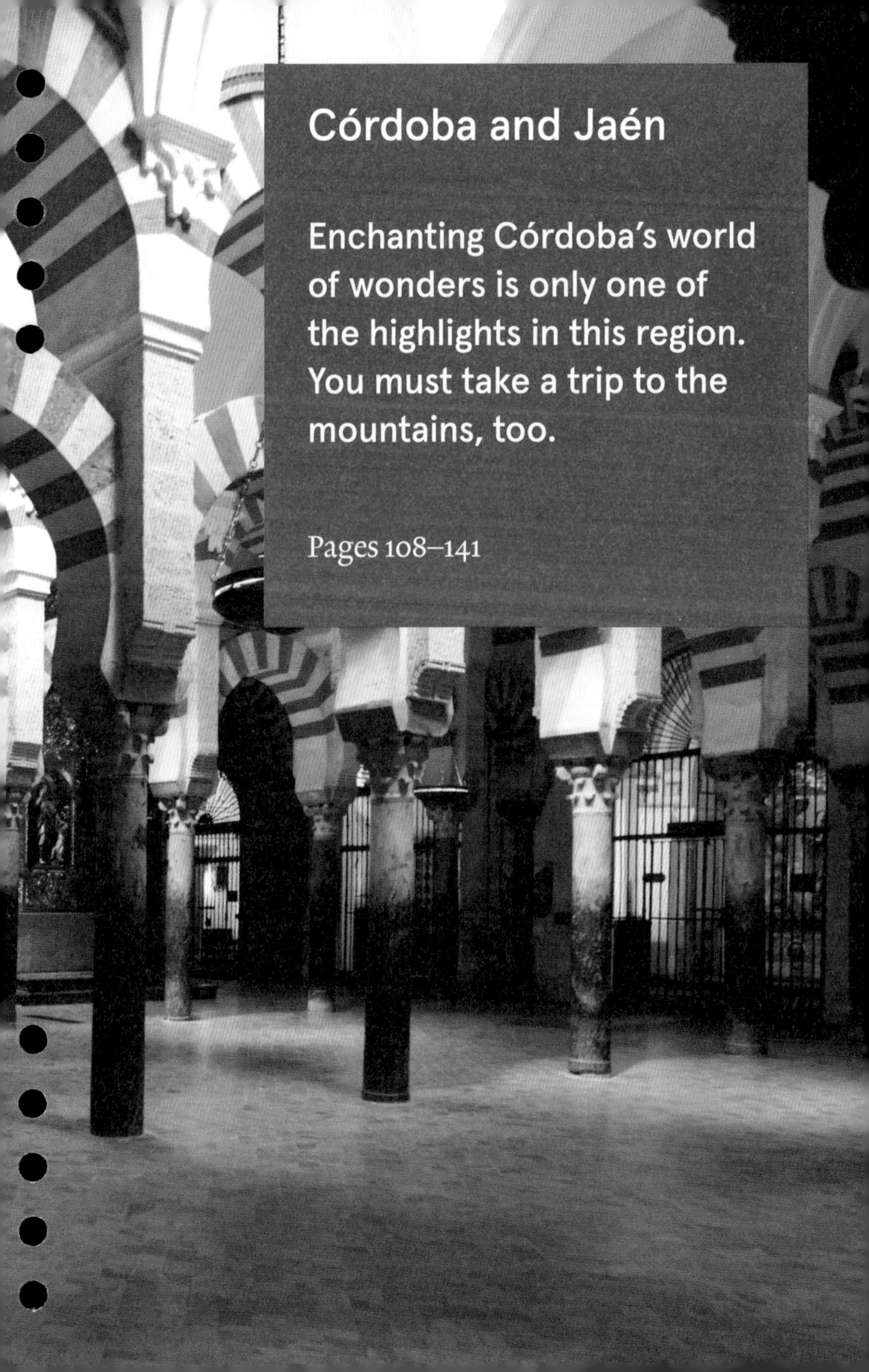

Córdoba and Jaén

Enchanting Córdoba's world of wonders is only one of the highlights in this region. You must take a trip to the mountains, too.

Pages 108–141

Getting Your Bearings

Art or nature? Ideally both, as can be seen here in the north of Andalucía. No other place has as many Renaissance buildings as Úbeda and Baeza in the Jaén province. And there is nowhere else with as many olive trees. The mountains in the northeast are wonderful havens for nature. Córdoba in the neighbouring province of the same name to the west was deemed the richest, largest, and most modern town of the Middle Ages.

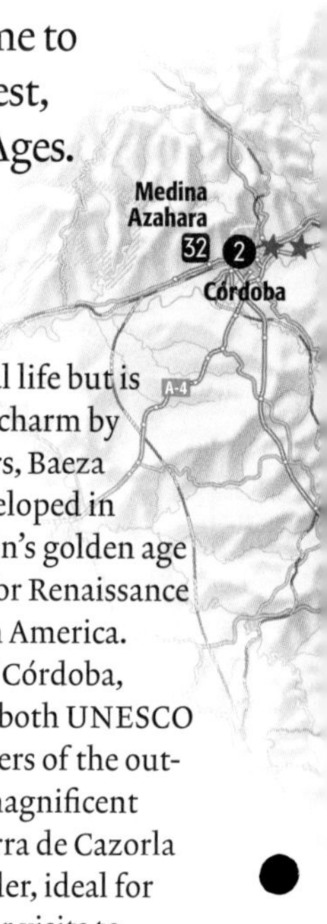

Today, the Mezquita, Europe's oldest mosque and the remains of the ancient city of Medina, recently added to UNESCO's list of World Heritage Sites, provide evidence of the area's glamorous past. Yet Córdoba also has many other attractions: quiet squares, flowering *patios* and a hinterland full of baroque glory.

The province of Jaén is quite visibly an olive-growing area, but also has a lot of other treasures to show visitors. Jaén city has a monumental cathedral and a bustling commercial and social life but is surpassed for overall charm by its smaller neighbours, Baeza and Úbeda. Both developed in the 16th century, Spain's golden age and became models for Renaissance art in Spain and Latin America. Like the Old Town of Córdoba, Úbeda and Baeza are both UNESCO heritage sites. For lovers of the outdoors, there are the magnificent mountains of the Sierra de Cazorla on Jaén's eastern border, ideal for woodland walks or for visits to isolated villages.

TOP 10
2 ★★ Córdoba
5 ★★ Úbeda

Don't Miss
29 Priego de Córdoba
30 Baeza
31 Parque Natural de Cazorla y Segura

At Your Leisure
32 Medina Azahara
33 Zuheros
34 Jaén
35 Baños de la Encina
36 Montoro

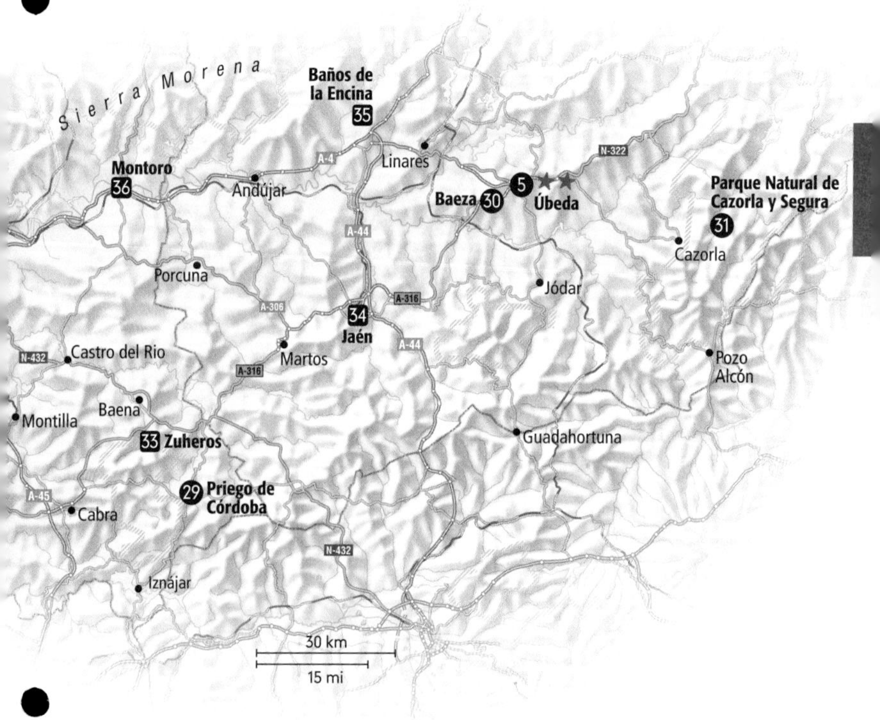

My Day with 1001 Delights

Meandering streets, brightly coloured flowers on snow-white facades, secluded patios and a rich Moorish heritage, Córdoba is the loveliest of the large Andalucían towns. While at home, cold, wet, sleet and snow dominate the weather forecast, you can revel here to your heart's delight in colours, fragrances and delights, as in the sensuous Al-Andalus of old.

8:30am: Savour the Morning
Admittedly, the fact that you can visit the Mezquita (p. 117) free of charge in the early morning hours is no longer an insider tip. Nonetheless, it is still worth getting up early. The low sun produces a very special atmosphere in the Patio de los Naranjos; before the crowds turn up, you can let the forest of columns work their magic and divine some of the real purpose of the world-famous building as a place of contemplation and reflection.

9:30am: A Feast for the Eyes
After so much culture in the morning, you have earned your breakfast – or even a hearty brunch? The ideal place for this is the Mercado Victoria. The light modern market hall is situated in the middle of the amiable park complex of the same name at the western edge of the Old Town. It is a fifteen-minute walk away: along the Calle Romero and Calle Almanzor and through the Puerta de Almodóvar on the southern edge of the park and then right to the market hall.

12:30am: 12 Patios in One Sweep

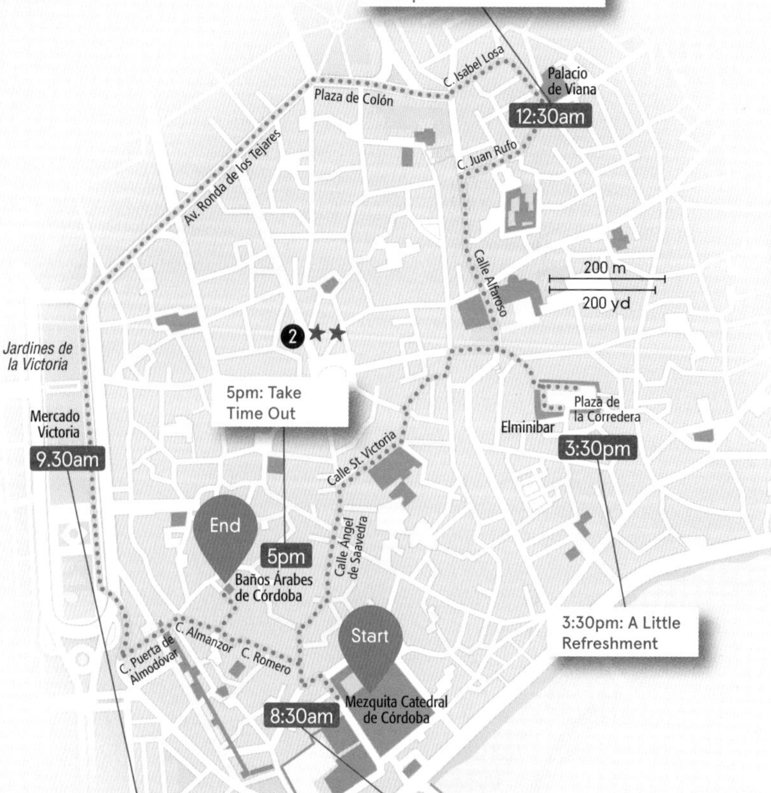

9:30am: A Feast for the Eyes

The young day greets you with the Mezquita in the morning light: Enjoy the quiet atmosphere before the crowds arrive. After a hearty breakfast, the sleepy patios of the Palacio de Viana await you

Now you have a difficult choice: You can breakfast quite traditionally in Panea with coffee or tea, croissants and sweet little pastries. Or spoil yourself with oysters and champagne in "Ostras & Mallorca? Perhaps you may also prefer, inspired by Al-Andalús, something a little heartier, with Moroccan aromas in "Bocaíto Andalusí? At the colourful fruit stand *Mil Sabores* you can take some pictures to show people at home (a bit of envy is guaranteed!) and some vitamin-rich food for the trip.

12:30am: 12 Patios in One Sweep

Córdoba is famous for its wonderful patios. One option is to take a painstaking tour through them in the Old Town. The more comfortable option is to visit 12 in one go at the Palacio de Viana. The stately palace can look back on a 500-year history. Since 2012 the magnificent courtyards have been open to visitors. You will not find a comparable variety of garden design in such a small area anywhere else in Córdoba. And every patio invites you in its own special way to stay for a while, be it in the shade of a little orange tree or next to a sparkling cascade.

3:30pm: A Little Refreshment

On the way back to the Old Town, it is worth stopping off in

Soak up some sun as you sip a coffee on the Plaza de la Corredera (top right). Finish off the day enjoying the sweet pleasure of doing nothing as you relax in Córdoba's enchanting Arab baths (bottom right)

the Plaza de la Corredera. It has a large selection of restaurants and tapas bar; try your luck in the tiny restaurant "Elminibar" in the southwest corner. Good food, nice service – what else could you wish for?

5pm: Take Time Out

The day had an early start, now it is time to relax. Unwind at the Baños Árabes de Córdoba. The stylish complex conjures up a dreamlike environment from 1001 nights – leave daily preoccupations and the winter at home.

Mercado Victoria
✉ Paseo de la Victoria
🌐 www.mercadovictoria.com
🕐 Mid-Sep to mid-June Sun–Thu 10am–1am, Fri, Sat 1am–2am; mid-June to mid-Sep Sun–Thu 10-midnight, Fri, Sat 10am–2am

Palacio de Viana
✉ Plaza de Don Gome 2
🌐 www.palaciodeviana.com
🕐 July–Aug Tue–Sun 9–3, Sep–June Tue–Sat 10–7, Sun 10–3 🎟 Patios: €5, incl. palace €8

Elminibar
✉ Plaza de la Corredera 39 ☎ 679 31 31 62

Baños Árabes de Córdoba
✉ Calle Almanzor 18
🌐 www.bañosarabesdecordoba.com
🕐 Sun–Fri 10–midnight, Sat 10am–2am
🎟 from €19 (bathing limited to 3 hours.)

❷ ★★ Córdoba

Don't Miss	Museums, galleries, boutiques and cafés
Why	Córdoba is the most attractive of the big towns
When	At the beginning of May for the Patios Festival to admire the floral displays normally hidden away in private courtyards
Time	For at least a day
In Short	Andalucían beauty with flair and a wealth of highlights

Andalucía's most important town after Seville sits perched on the gentle slopes of Sierra de Córdoba by the Rio Guadalquivir. With its narrow, winding streets, small squares and white-washed houses, often with patios so typical of the area, Córdoba can boast to having one of the largest historic centres of Europe and, on top of that, the fantastic Mezquita.

Even during the Old Iberian period, there was a settlement here in the bend of the Betis (Guadalquivir). "Córduba" ("elevation by the river") was elected capital of the province Hispania Ulterior Baetica in 171BC by the Roman General Claudio Marcelo. Under the Romans, Córdoba experienced its first economic and cultural success. In 4AD it became a diocesan town and eventually came under the Byzantine rule that ended the rampages of the Vandals. Occupied by the Moors in the 8th century, the city became the capital of Muslim Spain, and for 200 years a succession of gifted rulers turned it into a glittering rival to Baghdad and Damascus. In 1236, Córdoba fell to Christian forces. It was at the Spanish court here that Christopher Columbus first presented his plans in the 1480s. Granada's conquest and the expulsion of the Jews in the 15th century heralded Córdoba's decline, and it did not really recover until the 20th century; since 1984 Córdoba has been a UNESCO World Heritage Site; in 2012 the Fiesta de los Patios was added to its Intangible Cultural Heritage list.

ℹ

211 E4

Tourist Information
✉ Plaza del Triunfo (opposite Alcázar; Mon–Fri 9–7:30, Sat, Sun 9:30–3); Plaza de las Tendillas (daily 9–2, 5–7:30) and by the train station (daily 9–2, 4:30–7)
☎ 902 20 17 74
🌐 www.turismodecordoba.org

The Mezquita

Much of Islamic Córdoba survives and nowhere more triumphantly than in the Mezquita. Most of the Mezquita dates from between the 8th and 12th centuries. In beauty and magnitude, it can compete with the mosques of Mecca, Damascus, Cairo and Istanbul. The Christian cathedral in the middle, added in the 16th century after the Christian Reconquest, does not detract from this in any way.

Only the splendid carvings on the arched entrance gateways of the massive around 180m × 140m (590ft × 460ft) exterior walls hint at the marvels within. For hundreds of years, the Mezquita of Córdoba was the second largest mosque after Mecca covering an area of 23,400m² (252,000ft²).

Go through the Puerto del Perdón, beside the Torre del Alminar, into the Patio de los Naranjos (Courtyard of the Orange Trees), where Muslim worshippers once carried out their ritual ablutions. A stall in the courtyard (left of the Puerta del Perdón) sells entrance tickets. Once inside, thickets of pillars stretch away in all directions. Over 1,000 pillars – some plain, others multicoloured columns of marble, jasper and onyx – support arches composed of alternating stripes of red brick and white stone. The impression created is of great depth, intimacy and mysteriousness.

The Mezquita dominates Córdoba's skyline

Once the Main Mosque...

...of western Islam – one of the world's largest mosques, and now a cathedral (Mezquita Cathedral) is the most important example of Moorish religious architecture in Spain. While the exterior is fairly plain, the interior impresses with a "forest" of over 850 columns of jasper, onyx, marble and granite, which are arranged in double arcades.

❶ Maksûra: Originally the area where the caliphs prayed
❷ Cathedral: In 1523 Carlos V allowed Bishop Alonso Manrique to erect a cathedral in the centre of the Islamic prayer room. The mixture of Gothic and Renaissance styles look completely out of place in this architectural setting.
❸ Campanario (belfry): After the completion of the cathedral, work started from 1593 on transforming the minaret into a bell tower. The tower crowns a statue of the archangel Raphael, the town's patron saint.
❹ Wall: The building is surrounded by a wall, which in places reaches a height of 20m (65ft), complete with buttresses and the classic ornamental elements of Islam – red and while horseshoe arches, floral and geometric patterns and Kufic inscriptions.
❺ Water basins: The large basins were used for ritual washing before entering the courtyard to the public prayer hall.
❻ Muslim prayer room: More than 850 columns bear the arches with the alternating stripes of red and white arch bricks made of limestone and brick. In the Mezquita, there are no prescribed routes or directions; every position is its central point: For Muslims, Allah is near wherever he prays. At the time, daylight would have shone through the now walled entrances

and thousands of oil lamps were used to illuminate the room.

❼ Mihrâb Nuevo (New Mihrâb): Unsurpassed: the prayer niche of the Imam. Interestingly, the inner sanctum of the mosque does not point in the traditional east-southeast direction of Mecca, but actually faces south. The dome is made of marble and decorated with patterns, Koran verses and mosaics that are the work of Byzantine artists.

❽ Capilla del Cardenal: This is where the church treasure is kept: The most valuable pieces include a silver monstrance (1510–1516) and a processional cross from Enrique de Arfe, nine statues of saints, an ivory crucifix by Alonso Cano as well as Arabic manuscripts (9th/10th century).

❾ Arcades: Under the arcades on the north side, student and teachers met to expostulate. On the west of the tower, doctors provided advice, and on the east the *qadi* dispensed justice.

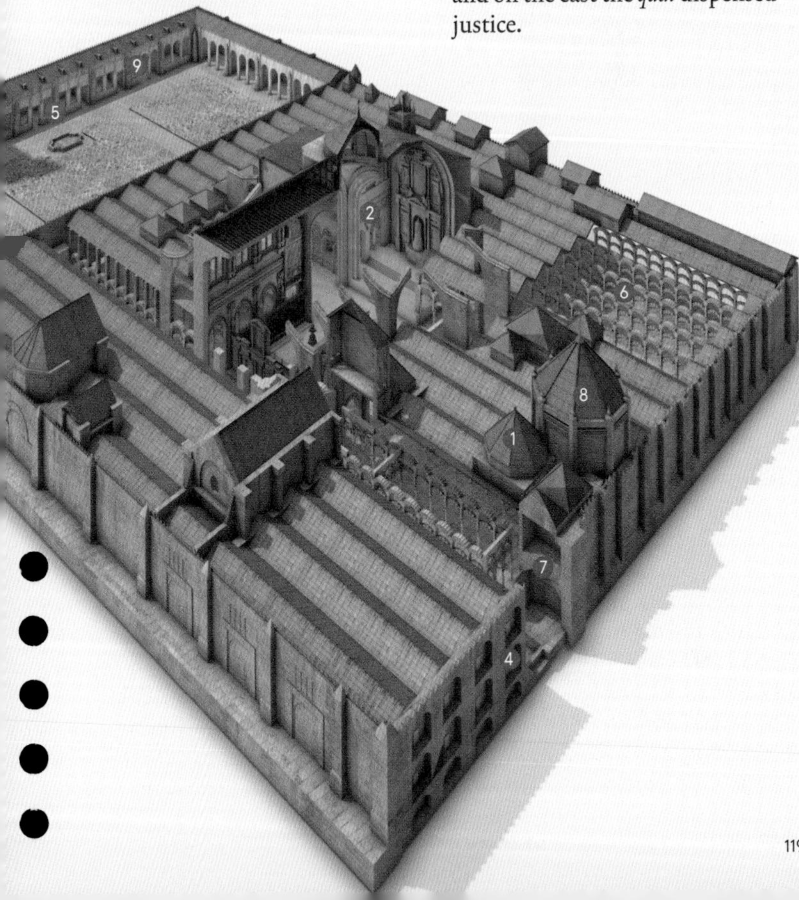

In Moorish times, light would have flooded in from the Patio de los Naranjos through open doorways. During the conversion to a Christian building, the arched doors were closed and side chapels added.

The finest example of Islamic design is on the far side of the building. At the end of the widest aisle is the *maksura* (where the ruling caliphs prayed), with the *mihrab* (prayer niche, which normally indicates the direction of Mecca). From behind the barrier that keeps the public at a distance, you can look through inside through the horseshoe-shaped arch. The dome in front of the *mihrab* is supported by intersecting ribs that form a star shape, a design that was copied by later Christian architects.

Floral patterns as opposed to images of worship adorn the walls of the mihrâb in the Mezquita

After the conquest of Córdoba by Fernando III de Castilla, the mosque was inaugurated as a cathedral in 1236. In the 14th century, the first architectural changes were made with the Capilla Real and the Capilla de Villaviciosa. The Cathedral in the centre of the Mezquita dates back to 1523. The invasive changes made to the Mezquita were condemned by the Emperor Carlos V; he had initially supported the idea but was horrified when he saw what had been done and accused the Archbishop of Córdoba of having "destroyed what was unique in the world".

It is true that the Cathedral inside the mosque does look out of place, but it does not really affect the overall effect in terms of the Mezquita as a whole. The choir and chapel have no enclosing walls so that there is a fluid transition to the Islamic columns around them. Looked at in isolation, their Gothic and Renaissance elements, the superbly carved choir stalls and slim, twisted pillars are just as beautiful.

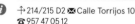

i 214/215 D2 Calle Torrijos 10
957 47 05 12
www.mezquita-catedraldecordoba.es
March–Oct Mon–Sat 10–7, Sun and public hols 8:30–11:30, 3–7; Nov–Feb Mon–Sat 10–6, Sun 8:30–11:30, 3–6
€10. Observation tower: every half an hour, €2. Mass: Mon–Sat 9:30, Sun noon and 1:30), when entrance to the rest of the Mezquita is free. A special highlight is a visit to the Mezquita at night (from 9:30pm, €18). Information: www.mezquita-catedraldecordoba.es or www.elalmadecordoba.com

The Judería and Alcázar

To the north of the Mezquita is the Judería, the old Jewish quarter. Narrow cobbled streets, whitewashed houses, plant-filled courtyards, and quiet, secluded squares create a unique atmosphere, which is best enjoyed well away from the tourist area directly adjoining the Mezquita.

Close to the Mezquita, the streets are awash with souvenir shops, but you can still find some enchanting corners such as the Calleja de las Flores, a narrow cul-de-sac bursting with flowers, and with walls that neatly frame the Mezquita's belfry. At the west border of the Judería, in Plaza Maimónides, you come to the Museo Taurino (Museum of Bullfighting).

To the left of the Museo Taurino is Calle Judíos, where there is a statue of Moses Maimonides, the great 12th-century Jewish philosopher and theologian, who was born in Córdoba. Further up the street is the small 14th-century synagogue (currently closed), sole Andalucían survivor of the Jewish expulsion in 1492. Nearby is a modern reconstruction of a Zoco, an Arab souk or market; craft shops and a bar overlook a charming patio. Calle Judíos leads to the Puerta de Almodóvar, a 14th-century gateway in Córdoba's ancient walls.

In Córdoba's Judería there are beautiful patios between the souvenir shops and restaurants

If you leave the labyrinth of little streets in Córdoba's Jewish quarter, you will immediately find the next attraction awaiting you, such as the Alcázar and its gardens

West of the Mezquita, on the banks of the river, stands the Alcázar de los Reyes Cristianos (Palace of the Christian Kings). It was built in the late 13th century by the Christian conquerors of Al-Andalus, and it is the same location on which the Romans, the Visigoths and the caliphs had their palaces. For many years it was the headquarters of the Inquisition and became a prison in the 19th century, though today its glorious gardens, filled with colourful flowers and shrubs and shimmering pools and fountains, give no hint of its grim past. The surviving buildings are somewhat stark, but contain superb Roman mosaics recovered from various parts of the city.

More Sights

North and west of the Mezquita, in an area far less visited than the Judería, is Córdoba's Museo Arqueológico (Archaeological Museum) in a Renaissance mansion, the Palacio de los Páez, on tree-shaded Plaza Jerónimo Páez. The palace displays prehistoric, Roman and Moorish exhibits. Highlights include Roman mosaics and an exquisite miniature of a bronze stag, found at the 10th-century palace-city of Medina Azahara 10km (6.25mi) west of Córdoba. Just inland from the river is Plaza del Potro (Square of the Colt), with a statue of a rearing horse on the central fountain. The plaza was once a livestock market surrounded by medieval brothels and drinking dens, the haunt of such Cordoban characters as the celebrated poet Luis de Góngora (1561–1627). On the plaza's western side is the old Posada del Potro Inn, mentioned in Cervantes's *Don Quijote*, and now the Centro Flamenco Fosforito. Diagonally opposite is the Hospital de la Caridad, housing the Museo de Bellas Artes (Museum of Fine Arts). The decorated ceilings of the ground-floor rooms are as fine as some of the paintings; the collection includes work by Zurbarán, Goya and Murillo. On the other side of the patio is a museum dedicated to Córdoban artist Julio Romero de Torres, most of whose paintings feature sultry nudes. To the south of the Mezquita the Puente Romano takes you to the other side of the Guadalquivir.

The heart of the modern city is Plaza de las Tendillas, where fountains spout sparkling jets of water from ground level. As you relax at a café table, you may hear the plaza's clock chiming flamenco phrases. From Plaza de las Tendillas, you can walk west down the shopping street of Conde de Gondomar to the pedestrianised Avenida del Gran Capitán.

INSIDER TIP Begin your evening with a sherry in **El Caballo Rojo** (Calle Cardenal Herreo 28; tel: 957 47 53 75; www.elcaballorojo.com), reputed to be the oldest restaurant in Córdoba.

Museo Taurino
214 C2 Plaza Maimónides
957 20 10 56
Summer: Tue–Sat 8.30–3, Sun 8:30–2:30; winter: Tue–Fri 8:30–8:45, Sat 8:30–4:30, Sun 8:30–2:30 €4

Sinagoga (Synagogue)
214 B2 Calle Judíos 20
957 20 29 28
Currently closed

Museo Arqueológico de Córdoba
215 D3 Plaza Jerónimo Páez 7
957 35 55 17
July, Aug Tue–Sun 9–3; Sep–June Tue–Sat 9–9
€1.50 (free with EU passport)

Alcázar de los Reyes Cristianos
214 A1
Plaza Campo Santo de los Mártires
957 20 17 16
Tue–Fri 8:30–8:45, Sat 8:304:30, Sun 8:30–2:30 4,50 €

Museo de Bellas Artes
215 E3 Plaza del Potro 1
957 10 36 59 July, Aug Tue–Sun 9–3 (Sep–June 9–9)
€1.50 (free with EU passport)

Museo Julio Romero de Torres
215 E3 Plaza del Potro 1
957 47 03 56
Tue–Sat 8:30–3, Sun 8:30–2:30
€4.50

❺ ★★ Úbeda

Don't Miss	A wonderfully homogeneous Old Town
Why	Because you get away from the crowds "on those hills"
When	If you can arrange it, the *Semana Santa*
Time	Half a day; those who can and wish to stay a bit longer
In Short	Wander through the town and admire the impressive architecture and traditional pottery

In medieval times Úbeda became synonymous with absent-mindedness, and the phrase "wandering across the hills of Úbeda" is still used to describe those who are forgetful. Its origins lie in a romantic tale. A young Christian knight missed a crucial battle; perhaps cold feet, a rendezvous – nobody knows. When asked by King Fernando III where he had been, he replied, "Sire. On those hills...".

Architectural Treasure Hunt

Famous son of the town: in 1949 Joaquín Sabina, Spain's most well-known songwriter was born here.

Úbeda hides an architectural treasure. Plaza de Vázquez de Molina on the southern edge of the town is an enclave of exquisite Renaissance buildings, claimed to be the finest such complex in Spain. Úbeda's leading families, the Cobos and the Molinas, who acquired great wealth from a 16th-century boom in textile production, employed the best architects and artists, who in the first half of the 16th century designed a masterpiece of Renaissance architecture, the single nave Sacra Capilla del Salvador (Chapel of the Holy Saviour) based on the plans of architect Diego de Siloé. The benefactor was the secretary of King Carlos I, Francisco de los Cobos, who is interred in the crypt. The chapel's main façade is decorated with relief work and flanked by two small round towers. Above the entrance, you can see allegorical presentations of belief and justice as well as the coat of arms of the Los Cobos and the Molinas. Enthroned above them is Christ the Saviour with Saint Peter and Saint Paul standing either side of him. In the chancel, behind an exquisite choir screen, the altarpiece bears a representation of the Christ figure. It is all that remains of the *Transfiguration of Christ* work by Alonso de

The most important event in the church year is the *Semana Santa*, the week before Easter. As here in Úbeda, it often starts with large processions

Berruguete which was damaged by fire during the civil war in 1936. The magnificently designed sacristy contains the church silver.

Other notable buildings in the plaza include the Palacio de las Cadenas (Palace of the Chains) designed with an elegant classical façade and now Úbeda's town hall. Directly opposite is the church of Santa María de las Reales Alcázares, whose Gothic cloister stands on the foundations of the mosque of Islamic Úbeda.

Just north of the plaza is the old market square, Plaza del Primero de Mayo, scene of bullfights and horrifying *autos da fé* (trials by fire) during the Inquisition. It contains the Old Town hall with elegant arcades, and the church of San Pablo with a fine Gothic portal.

Around the Calle de Valencia are the pottery works which produce the green-brown-black glazed Úbeda ceramics (p. 141). In the Pottery Museum Paco Tito at no. 22, you can admire typical everyday products; at the Melchor Tito workshop at no. 44, you can buy items directly from the manufacturer.

Just past the Sacra Capilla del Salvador, you come to the Plaza de Santa Lucía. From the lookout point there, you have a beautiful view over the olive groves to the mountains

The apse of the Sacra Capilla del Salvador is magnificently decorated

of Sierra de Cazorla. In the northwest, the former Hospital de Santiago, which dates back to the 16th century, now a cultural centre, has an inner courtyard which is particularly beautiful.

INSIDER TIP Take a step back in time and stop off for coffee at Úbeda's 16th-century *parador* on Plaza de Vázquez de Molina.

212 B4

Tourist Information
Avda Cristo Rey s/n 953 75 04 40
www.turismodeubeda.com

Sacra Capilla del Salvador
Plaza Vázquez de Molin
Mon–Sat 9:30–2, 4:30–7:30, Sun 11:30–2, 4:30–7:30 €5

Museo Alfarería Paco Tito
Valencia 22
953 75 140 96
Mo–Sat 8–2, 4–8, Sun 10–2
Free

Inner Courtyard of Hospital de Santiago
Calle Obispo Cobos 28
Daily 10–2, 5–9

㉙ Priego de Córdoba

Don't Miss	A refined church with baroque head-turning effect
Why	Small but wow!
When	When you want to have a nice relaxing afternoon
Time	A few hours
What Else	The view over the seemingly endless rows of olive trees from Mirador de Adarve
In Short	The flair of the fountain alone makes it worth a visit.

Priego de Córdoba is an idyllic mountain gem – enjoy the view

The quiet provincial town – a centre of the textile trade and olive oil production – is located in a breathtaking mountain landscape near the Sierra Subbética nature reserve. The town dates from at least Roman times and was fought over by Moorish and Christian forces during the 13th and 14th centuries. During the 17th and 18th century, silk manufacture brought affluence to the region, enabling the erection of lavishly decorated baroque churches and beautiful fountains. In the Moorish quarter, alleyways wind between whitewashed houses decked with flowers.

At the centre of Priego is the busy Plaza de Andalucía and adjoining Plaza de la Constitución, where the life of the town is gossiped over each morning. Historic Priego lies to the east of Plaza de Andalucía. Here, among other fine buildings, is the Iglesia de la Asunción (Church of the Ascension), Priego's most famous monument. A highlight of the church, which is plain white on the outside, is the Baroque Sagrario (Chapel of the Sanctuary). Francisco Javier Pedrejas, 1772–1784, used effusive stucco ornamentation to decorate this octagonal-shaped chapel with Biblical scenes. Apostle figures adorn the pillars, and in the centre are representations of church leaders.

A Fountain of Surprises

Water is a precious liquid commodity in Spain's sweltering south. That's what makes the huge baroque fountain complex in the small mountain village of Priego de Córdoba so surprising. With its grandiose proportions, it would not even look out of place at the Alhambra in Granada. In the evening, it is wonderful to sit next to the Fuente del Rey when the heat of the day slowly wanes, the birds twitter in the trees, the water gurgles, and slowly but surely the village comes back to life in the cool of the evening.

From the church, the Calle Real leads into the car-free Barrio de la Villa, where the white walls of the houses are hung with baskets of geraniums and draped with bougainvillaea. At the eastern edge of a public park, Mirador de Adarve affords great views of the surrounding countryside. Northwest of the *barrio* is the Iglesia de San Pedro (Church of St Peter), with a splendidly painted main altar. Just around the corner is the Carnicerías Reales.

In Royal Footsteps

The 16th-century slaughterhouse and market, now shorn of its original associations and preserved for its architectural value. The arcaded and cobbled patio of the old market, with its spiral stone staircase, exudes a special flair. The mullioned windows provide a wonderful view of the olive groves, and the setting is perfect for the occasional exhibitions staged here by local artists.

The Calle del Río runs past the Iglesia del Carmen to a magnificent fountain. The older Fuenta de la Salud (Fountain of Health) was created by Francisco del Castillo in the 16th century and consists of a mannerist-style façade with a stone latticework in the centre of which is a small niche with the Virgen de la Salud. The baroque Fuente del Rey (King's Fountain) built in the 19th century dominates the whole square. Water pours from the marble mouths of 139 gargoyles into the fountain's main basin and in the middle the chariot of Neptune and his wife Amphitrite surges through the waves. Both fountains are national monuments.

INSIDER TIP After you've ogled the lavish confection of white stucco in the Iglesia de la Asunción, enjoy **Asador La Muralla** (Calle Abad Palomino; tel: 957 70 18 56; www.asadorlamuralla.com).

---

212 A3

Parking
Car park in Plaza Palenque, at the west end of Carrera de las Monjas. Busy in the mornings.

Tourist Information
Plaza de la Constitución 3
www.turismodepriego.com

Iglesia de la Asunción
Plaza de Abad Palomino
Tue–Sat 11–1:30, Sun 10:30–noon

30 Baeza

Don't Miss	Magnificent architecture and a district court located in an old slaughterhouse – which may provoke a wry smile
Why	If you have to see Úbeda, you have to see Baeza
When	In the morning when everything is empty
Time	Until your journey through time is over
What Else	A walk along the old town wall as you look out over the endless rows of olives trees
In Short	A trip to the Renaissance

Surrounded by olive groves, wheat fields and vineyards, and perched high above the Río Guadalquivir valley, Baeza is an architectural pearl of the Renaissance with little modern encroachment on its historic buildings.

The best place to begin your exploration is in the Plaza del Pópulo with its exquisite Renaissance buildings. The Plaza is also known as Plaza de los Leones because of the ancient stone lions adorning its weatherworn fountain. From Plaza de Pópulo go through the imposing the twin archways Puerta de Jaén arch and the 16th-century Arco de Villalar and follow the road beyond for 250m (275yds) to reach the Paseo de las Murallas. This walkway leads along the edge of the escarpment with fine views across the surrounding countryside. Opposite the two archways, you will see the attractive facade of the old slaughterhouse, now the district court. The court used to convene in the Casa del Pópulo, now Baeza's tourist office. To the left, walk up the Escalerillas de la Audiencia to a narrow lane, Calle Romanones, that takes you to Plaza Santa Cruz and the Palacio de Jabalquinto, whose Gothic façade is studded with diamond-shaped bosses. The interior courtyard has a fountain and is surrounded by a double tier of arcades from which a fine baroque staircase leads to the upper floor.

Directly opposite the palace is the little Romanesque Iglesia de Santa Cruz with traces of Visigothic arches and of the mosque the church replaced. Through the Cuesta de San Felipe you come to the quiet Plaza de Santa María with its central fountain in the form of a triumphal arch. The square

is dominated by Baeza's Catedral de Santa María, which has a spacious Renaissance nave designed by Andrés de Vandelvira, the architect of many of Úbeda's buildings. The main altar has an exuberant altarpiece and there are a number of splendid *rejas* – wrought-iron grilles that screen side chapels. The cathedral was built on the site of a mosque.

Back on the Plaza del Pópulo, the Paseo de la Constitución is an inviting place to take a rest. The Paseo is lined by arcaded buildings and numerous bars and cafés. Stroll along the street that runs parallel to it in the north, Calle Benavides, for a look at the ornate 16th-century façade of the town hall.

Baeza's Old Town – here the Plaza de Santa Maria with the fountain designed by Ginés Martínez in front of the cathedral – is very well preserved

INSIDER TIP Join the locals at **La Góndola** (Paseo Portales Carbonería) and indulge in their delicious *patatas baezanas* (fried potatoes with mushrooms).

212 B4

Tourist Information
Plaza del Pópulo
953 77 99 82
http://turismo.baeza.net

Parking
There is convenient parking round the Paseo de la Constitución.

Palacio de Jabalquinto
Plaza Santa Cruz Mon–Fri 9–2

Iglesia de Santa Cruz
Plaza Santa Cruz Mon–Sun 11–1

Catedral
Plaza de Santa María Mon–Fri 10:30–2, 4–6, Sat 10:30–6, Sun 10:30–5
€4

㉛ Parque Natural de Cazorla y Segura

Don't Miss	Mountains reminiscent of Switzerland but in sunnier climes
Why	In order to work off a bit of energy outdoors
When	In spring when Spain's flowers are in bloom
Time	Until you want to get back to city life
In Short	The perfect place to explore your surroundings, on foot, horseback, in a kayak, on a bike or in a car

In the midst of a stunning natural backdrop, the La Yedra castle ruins tower over Cazorla

In the far northeast of Andalucía, the Sierra de Cazorla and the Sierra de Segura rise up out of the hill slopes of Jaén province. They are separated by the headwater of the Guadalquivir river. It is here that the watershed runs between the Mediterranean, into which the Río Segura flows, and the Atlantic, which is the destination of the Guadalquivir.

In the Parque Natural de Cazorla y Segura, rugged mountains rise to over 2,000m (6,562ft), with deep rocky gorges and thickly forested valleys, and tiny hilltop villages scattered throughout. The gateway to the park is Cazorla at the south-western edge of the Sierra de Cazorla. The attractive town straggles along the base of the mountain of Peña de los Halcones (Crag of the Falcons) beginning at its busy main square, Plaza de la Constitución. From here, the main street, Calle Dr Muñoz, leads to the far older Plaza de la Corredera, a lively square lined by cafés and shops. After you pass the town hall, you will come to the narrow Calle Gómez Calderón to the lookout point, Balcón del Pintor Zabaletato. It affords a view of the semi-derelict castle La Yedra, also known as *Las Cuatro Esquinas* – the "four corners". On the left of the castle is the ruin of the Santa María church.

Look out for the curiosity in Cazorla's Calle Negrillo: a house whose façade is adorned with dozens of bicycles

The Natural Park

The Sierras de Cazorla y Segura, together with lesser ranges, make up the largest natural park in Andalucía. The mountains of the park support forests of evergreen oaks and pines as well as native species such as elder, maple and juniper. There are over 1,200 species of plants, and the animals of the Sierras include red deer, fox, wild cat, Spanish ibex and wild boar. You may also see some of the birds of prey that congregate in the Sierras, including griffon vultures, golden eagles and peregrine falcons (sometimes visible from roadside vantage points). A network of good roads makes driving within the park area a pleasure. There are a few waymarked paths in the area around Cazorla and in the natural park. Local companies organise day walks, horse riding, mountain biking and four-wheel-drive trips into more remote areas.

You enter the park about 2km (1.25mi) east of Cazorla, just beyond the village of La Iruela with its tiny castle perched on a pinnacle of rock. A 34km (21mi) drive on A-319 northeast through the mountains will take you from Cazorla to the Centro de Interpretación Torre del Vinagre. The centre can be very busy in summer but it has excellent displays outlining the park's ecology. Nearby is a botanical garden with specimens of Sierra plant life.

INSIDER TIP Off to the park? Prepare a delicious picnic in **Cazorla.**

---

212 C4

Tourist Information Cazorla
Paseo del Santo Cristo 11
953 96 91 91
www.turismoencazorla.com

Parking
There is a car park in Plaza del Mercado, just down from the Plaza de la Constitución.

At Your Leisure

32 Medina Azahara

The ruins of the 10th-century palace-city of Medina Azahara lie about 10km (6.25mi) west from Córdoba.

The ruins of Medina Azahara still give a good impression of its former glory

The complex, recently elected a UNESCO World Heritage Site, was begun in 936 and in its heyday reflected some of the most sumptuous architecture and design of Moorish Al-Andalus. The main attraction is the superb Hall of Abd al-Rahman III, where the lavish marble carvings have been carefully restored. Medina Azahara is best reached by car. Every 20 minutes a bus shuttles visitors from the car park entrance of the excavation site 2km (1.25mi) away. There is a bus service from Córdoba, which it is best to reserve the day before at the tourist information office in Córdoba.

211 D4
10km (6.25mi) west of Córdoba
www. medinaazahara.org
Sun 10–5; Mid-Sep–March Tue–Sat 9–6; April–June Tue–Sat 9–9; June to mid-Sep Tue–Sat 9–3 Free with EU passport. Guided Tours: €18

Bus ab Córdoba
Departure: Avenida Alcázar
Tue–Fri at 11, Sat, Sun at 10, 11, and 4:30 in summer €8.50

33 Zuheros

The narrow streets of Zuheros are a delight to explore; their charm reflects the village's situation on a rocky hillside amid the Sierra Subbética hills near Priego de Córdoba. Built into the rocks above the houses are the remains of a Moorish castle. In Plaza de la Paz are the handsome Iglesia de la Virgen de los Remedios, next to it enthroned on a rock a fortress begun by the Moors in the 9th century. Zuheros is noted for its cheeses and olive oil. The Cueva de los Murciélagos (Cave of the Bats), with fascinating rock formations, lies about 4km (east of Zuheros.

211 E3

Tourist Information (Zuheros Museum)
Plaza de la Paz 1 957 69 45 45
www.zuheros.es/turismo

Cueva del Cerro de los Murciélagos
211 E3 957 69 45 45
Guided tours April–Sep Tue–Fri 12:30 and 5:30, Sat, Sun and public hols 11, 12:30, 2, 5, 6:30; Oct–March Tue–Fri 12:30 and 4:30, Sat, Sun and public hols 11, 12:30, 2, 4, 5:30 (phoning ahead advised) €7.50

34 Jaén

Jaén is worth visiting for its majestic cathedral, fine museums, restored Arab baths and its old quarter. The cathedral was started in 1248, from the 16th century it received its magnificent Renaissance makeover. The huge west façade is a dramatic display of elegant Corinthian columns and statuary, the whole framed by soaring twin towers. The cavernous interior has clusters of columns on a monumental scale, and the choir has exquisite carvings. The cathedral contains the Santo Rostro (Holy Face) claimed to be the cloth used by St Veronica to wipe Christ's brow on the way to his crucifixion. It is on public display every Friday.

Jaén's restored Arab baths, the Baños Árabes, lie beneath the 16th-century Palacio de Villadompardo (housing an arts and customs museum and a museum of native art). The splendid brickwork ceilings are pierced by star-shaped lights and supported by typically Moorish columns and horseshoe arches. A glass floor reveals Roman remains. The Museo de Jaén has Phoenician, Roman and Moorish artefacts and, in a building adjoining the main museum, a display of outstanding 5th-century BC stone sculptures. Moorish character survives in Jaén's labyrinthine quarters of La Magdalena and San Juan on the northeastern slopes of the scrub-covered hill of Santa Catalina, itself crowned by a ruined Moorish castle.

In the far northeast of Jaén province is Segura de la Sierra. Approached by a seemingly endless series of hairpin bends, this

Jaén's twin-towered cathedral is visible for miles

wonderful hilltop village has an old Moorish castle, restored Arab baths and a Renaissance church.

211 F4

Tourist Information: Calle de la Maestra
953 31 32 81 www.turjaen.org

Catedral
Plaza de Santa María
Mon–Fri 10–2, 4–8, Sat 10–2, 4–7, Sun 10–noon, 4–7 €5

Baños Árabes
Plaza de Santa Luisa de Marillac
953 24 80 68 Sat 9–10, Sun 9–3
Free with EU passport

Museo de Jaén
Paseo de la Estación 29
953 10 13 66 July, Aug Tue–Sun 9–3, Sep–March Tue–Sat 9–9, Sun 9–3
Free with EU passport

35 Baños de la Encina

Baños de la Encina has one of the finest hilltop castles in Spain. The 14 towers and massive keep of this Moorish fortress dominate the tiny village below. The Castillo de Bury Al-Hamma was built between 967 and 986 by the Córdoban Emirate as an outlying defence against belligerent clans in the nearby Sierra Morena and Sierra de Cazorla. The interior of the castle is now a gaunt empty space, but you can climb the great keep, the Tower of Homage, from which there are sweeping views. Guided tours only.

Skyline view of the village of Baños de la Encina

211 F4 Avenida José Luis Messía 2
953 61 33 38
www.bdelaencinaturismo.com
Guided tours (45 min.): Wed–Mon €3

36 Montoro

The town stands on a spur of land within a loop of the Río Guadalquivir that is spanned by a 15th-century bridge. The ochre and whitewashed houses blend in with the reddish colour of the hill on which Montoro is situated. Towering over the houses is the three-tiered, baroque tower of the Iglesia de San Bartolomé on Plaza de España. Opposite the church is the old ducal palace, now the town hall. North of the plaza, narrow alleyways lead into an older district, where you'll find the church of Santa María de la Mota, now a small museum of mineralogy and archaeology.

211 E4

Tourist Information:
Corredera 25 957 16 00 89
www.montoro.es/turismo

Santa María de la Mota
Plaza de Santa María Sat, Sun 10:30–2

Where to... Stay

Expect to pay per double room per night

€ up to €60

€€ €60–€90

€€€ €90–€140

€€€€ over €140

CÓRDOBA

Hotel Eurostars Conquistador €€€

The hotel is directly opposite the Mezquita, which is visible from the restaurant and some of the rooms. The air-conditioned rooms are relatively big. The restaurant serves international food as well as regional Andalucían dishes. On warm days, breakfast, lunch and dinner are in the pretty courtyard otherwise reserved for aperitifs.

215 E3

Magistral González Francés 3–5

957 48 11 02

www.eurostarsconquistador.com

Hotel y Hostal Maestre €–€€€

There is not much difference between the hotel and *hostal*, tucked down a quiet side street one block back from the river and even the prices vary very little. The rooms in the hotel are simple but comfortable. The hotel rooms look onto a gracious inner courtyard framed by arches, which means plenty of light; the Castilian-style furniture, gleaming marble and quality oil paintings add a touch of class. Rooms in the *hostal* are smaller, but the entrance patio is pure Córdoba with pots, plants, plates.

215 E3

Calle Romero Barros 4 & 6

957 47 24 10

www.hotelmaestre.com

Hotel Mezquita €€

The hotel is in a typical 16th-century Juderia house. It has retained an evocative historical ambience with paintings and antiques. There are original columns and stonework, plus a gracious central patio used for al fresco dining during the summer. The rooms have modern facilities and are furnished in a suitably regal fashion with satin drapes and ornate furniture. The location is ideal for sightseeing – right opposite the main entrance to the Mezquita.

215 D2

Plaza Santa Catalina 1

957 47 55 85

www.hotelmezquita.com

Los Omeyas €€–€€€

Located amid the tangle of back streets in Córdoba's former Jewish quarter, Los Omeyas has been refurbished to reflect the city's Andaluz heritage with arches, white marble and latticework. A central patio provides access to comfortable, tastefully decorated rooms with air conditioning. Try for one on the top floor for a view of the ancient tower of the great Mezquita, although tour groups tend to fill the place. Breakfast is a reasonable extra.

215 D3

Calle Encarnación 17

957 49 22 67

www.hotel-losomeyas.com

PRIEGO DE CÓRDOBA

Hostería de Rafi €

One of very few small *hosterías* in town, the Rafi is right in the centre, with shops and the best-known baroque churches all nearby. Rooms are fairly ordinary but the bathrooms are full-size and modern. A door from the lobby leads to the adjacent bar, which is usually packed with locals who've come to enjoy the good choice of tapas and light meals.

212 A3

Isabel La Católica 4

957 54 04 49

hosteriaderafi.es

JAÉN

Parador Castillo de Santa Catalina €€–€€€€

This is one of the most spectacular *paradores* in Spain, situated on the dramatic Cerro de Santa Catalina mountain amid the towers of a medieval Moorish castle. The rooms have luxurious canopied beds and balconies for marvelling at the view. The décor throughout is magnificent: a successful interplay of high-vaulted ceilings, baronial spaces and

Welcome to Parador de Úbeda!

Islamic decorative touches. The restaurant, serving typical Jaén dishes, is also recommended.
212 A3
El Castillo de Santa Catalina, Jaén
953 23 00 00
www.parador.es

BAEZA

Hotel Fuentenueva €€
This historic building, once a huge 16th-century palace, was divided into three separate living areas in 1812. During extensive renovation, the eleven rooms were extravagantly upgraded with marble floors, modern furnishings and bubbling fountains. From the Japanese roof garden with a pool, you can enjoy the wonderful view of Baeza's city centre.
212 B4
Calle Carmen 15
953 74 31 00
www.fuentenueva.com

ÚBEDA

María de Molina €–€€
The hotel is located on the historical central plaza in a 16th-century palace. Many of the original elements remain, such as the columned central patio, wall-hung tapestries and a magnificent stone fountain. Wicker furniture, ochre walls and plenty of palms and plants set the mood in the lobby and restaurant, while the rooms, solidly decorated with dark wood, have walk-in wardrobes and balconies overlooking Úbeda's grandest square.
212 B4
Plaza del Ayuntamiento s/n
953 79 53 56
www.mariademolina.es

Parador de Úbeda €€–€€€€
The Parador, housed in a 16th-century Renaissance palace, is located in the centre of the Old Town on the lovely Renaissance square Vázquez de Molina. Behind the main facade of the hotel, guests will discover a wonderful courtyard. Some of the rooms overlook the magnificent square in front of the hotel. Regional specialities can be enjoyed in the hotel restaurant. After the evening meal, the hotel bar is a convivial place for a drink.
212 B4
Plaza de Vázquez Molina
953 74 02 00
www.parador.es

Where to... Eat and Drink

Expect to pay for a three-course meal, incl. wine and service

€	up to €15
€€	€15–€40
€€€	over €40

CÓRDOBA

Almudaina €€€
One of the best addresses in Córdoba, situated in a 16th-century palace facing the Alcázar. Meals are served in six elegant dining rooms or the stunning glass-covered courtyard. Dishes include excellent regional dishes. The prices won't make you smile with pleasure, but everything else will.
214 C2
Campo Santos de los Mártires 1
957 47 43 42
www.restaurantealmudaina.com
Closed Sun dinner

El Caballo Rojo €€€
A typical Andalucían restaurant facing the Mezquita. You can enjoy some of the regional dishes in tapa size. Among the restaurant's highlights are the lavishly loaded dessert trolley, which you should not leave out.
214 C2
Calle del Cardenal Herrero 28 957 47 53 75 Daily 9–midnight
www.elcaballorojo.com

El Churrasco €€
Situated in the heart of the Judería, this excellent restaurant specialises in meaty dishes including its namesake *churrasco* (grilled meat in a spicy sauce), as well as fish. There's a charming interior patio and ten dining rooms with beams, exposed brick and evocative art work. If you feel like tapas, head for the adjacent bar.
214 C2 Calle Romero 16
957 29 08 19 www.elchurrasco.com
Closed Aug

El Rincón de Carmen €€–€€€
This 18th-century house in the heart of the Jewish quarter is perfect for a romantic dinner-for-two. The menu includes Andalucían dishes, such as *rabo de toro a la cordobesa* (oxtail), as well as Mediterranean fish dishes.
214 C2 Calle Romero 4 957 29 10 55
www.restauranterincondecarmen.es
Daily noon–4, 8–11:30

Taberna Plateros €–€€
This place dates from the 19th century. A large patio restaurant leads to more rooms and the traditional marbled bar. Photographs of late local bullfighter Manolete line the walls, and the patio is decorated with giddily patterned tiles and bricks. There is a great selection of tapas and the starters are a meal in themselves.
215 D3 San Francisco 6
957 47 00 42 www.tabernaplateros.com
Tue–Sat 8–4, 7:30–midnight

You can get some good tapas at Caballo Rojo

PRIEGO DE CÓRDOBA

Balcón del Adarve €€€
On the ground floor you can eat tapas and on the first floor good, more substantial meat and fish dishes are served. There is a wonderful view from the terrace over the surrounding countryside. Attentive service, good value for money.
212 A3 Paseo de Colombia 36
957 54 70 75 www.balcondeladarve.com
Daily from noon

BAEZA

Casa Juanito €€
The owners love to introduce ancient local recipes into their menu, so the dishes are tasty and unusual. Extra virgin olive oil is a standard ingredient, made from their own press. Other specialities include partridge salad, fillet of beef with tomatoes and peppers, and *alcachofas Luisa* (artichoke hearts with tomatoes and garlic).
212 B4 Av. Alcalde Puche Pardo 57
953 74 00 40 www.juanitobaeza.com
Tue–Sat 1:30–3, 8:30–11:30. Closed 24 and 31 Dec

CAZORLA

Mesón Don Chema €
Slightly off the beaten track, this restaurant is very popular nonetheless. Great tapas, nice staff.
212 B3 Escaleras del Mercado 2
953 71 05 29 Closed Tue

Taberna Quinito €
Tasty tapas are served here, which you can enjoy on the terrace when the weather is good.
212 B3 Plaza Santa María 7
953 72 15 07 Closed Tue

ÚBEDA

Restaurante El Marqués €€
A welcome addition to the centre of town, this hotel has an excellent restaurant, elegantly decorated in warm hues of ochre and cream with subtle lighting, modern furnishings and a sophisticated feel. It's a great place to sip an espresso, enjoy a light lunch or get serious with the three-course *menú del día* celebrating local cuisine with an imaginative nouvelle twist.
212 B4 María Molina Hotel,
Plaza del Ayuntamiento s/n 953 75 72 55
Daily noon–4, 8–midnight

Where to... Shop

Córdoba's long-established leather and filigree silver workshops produce exquisite goods. South of the city is the wine- and olive oil-producing area around Priego de Córdoba, while some of the best pottery in Andalucía is made by artisans in the town of Úbeda in Jaén province.

CÓRDOBA PROVINCE

For fashion and general shopping in Córdoba, head for the streets around Plaza de las Tendillas, especially Conde de Gondomar where you'll find chic dress shops, among them **Pampling Córdoba** (Calle Conde de Gondomar 5; tel: 857 80 07 66).

From there you eventually come onto Av. del Gran Capitán, which is also car free. Here, at the junction with Avenida Ronda de los Tejares you'll find Córdoba's **El Corte Inglés** department store.

The souvenir scrum round the Mezquita is fine for everyday gifts and postcards. For some of Córdoba's celebrated leather crafts, a better bet is such leading workshop as **Meryan** (Calleja de las Flores 2; tel: 957 47 59 02; www.meryancor.com), where besides Moorish-abstract decorated leatherware articles more in line with current fashion trends are also on offer.

In the **Zoco** craft market (Calle de los Judíos s/n; tel: 957 20 40 33; www.artesaniadecordoba.com), there are several shops selling ceramics, glass, clothes, leather, and filigree silverware.

There is also a highly entertaining **market** (Mon–Sat 8–2:30) in Plaza de la Corredera trading all kinds of local food and titbits on 27 stands, with a big and lively turnout on Saturday mornings.

As you head south towards Priego de Córdoba you enter olive oil and Montilla wine country. These sherry-like wines (though

The locally produced ceramics are brightly coloured and tastefully presented

with no added alcohol) come under the denomination of Moriles, after the main wine-producing town in the area. Priego de Córdoba is also a centre of olive oil production: around 80% of Spain's olive oil is produced in Andalucía.

JAÉN PROVINCE

Úbeda is noted for its fine ceramics which are distinguished by their beautiful dark green glaze.

Calle de Valencia is the town's "potters' quarter", where there are several top workshops such as Pablo Tito with adjoining Museo de Alfarería Paco Tito (Calle Valencia 22; tel: 953 75 14 96; www.pablotito.es) and nearby Cerámica Alameda (Cno. El Cementerio; tel: 953 75 18 03; www.ceramicaalameda.net).

In the extension of Calle Valencia, Alfarería Góngora (Cuesta de la Merced 32; tel: 953 75 46 05) is also good for high-quality ceramics and craftwork. In Calle Real, Úbeda's old main street, there are one or two shops that still sell goods made from esparto grass, a long-established craft in the area.

In the Sierra de Cazorla browse round the stalls in Cazorla's daily market in Plaza de Andalucía and then look at the typical village shops in Calle Dr Muñoz, with their local goods and food products.

For Sierra crafts and gifts, the natural park's information centre, the Centro de Interpretación at Torre del Vinagre (tel: 953 71 30 17), has plenty to choose from.

Where to... Go Out

You will find lots of event information for Córdoba at www.andalocio.es. The daily Spanish-language newspaper is *Córdoba*. Ask at the tourist office for a free copy of the listings guides.

NIGHTLIFE

You'll find lively dance and music bars on Calle Cruz Conde just north of Plaza de las Tendillas.

FLAMENCO

One of the best venues for "classical" flamenco in Córdoba city is the Tablao Flamenco Cardenal (Calle Buen Pastor 2; tel: 691 21 79 22; www. tablaocardenal.es), just a five-minute walk from the Mezquita. The Tablao is located in the Casa Palacio del Conde de Torres Cabrera, a former 18th-century manor house with beautiful inner courtyards. (flamenco sessions Mo–Thu at 8:15pm, Fri, Sat at 9pm).

Another good flamenco venue is La Bulería (Calle Pedro López 3; tel: 957 48 38 39).

Among the few authentic flamenco temples still left in Spain is El Tablao de Bodegas Campos (Calle Lineros 32; tel: 636 74 74 71). Sessions start at 8:30, followed by dinner. Reservations are advised.

THEATRE

Córdoba has a fine theatre in its Gran Teatro (Avenida del Gran Capitán 3; tel: 957 48 02 37; www.teatrocordoba.org) staging excellent music, dance and drama presentations. You can get a monthly programme of events from the theatre or tourist office.

LEISURE AND SPORTS

Córdoba's Hammam Al Ándalus (Calle Corregidor Luís de la Cerda; tel: 957 48 47 46; www.hammamalandalus.com) are traditional Moorish-style steam baths with hot and cold water and massages. There is also a *tetería* (tearoom) where you can relax afterwards.

For outdoors enthusiasts, there is plenty of adventure in the mountainous Parque Natural de Cazorla y Segura (p. 132).

You can of course just set off on your own, but on the website www.turismoencazorla.com (in Spanish) you will find numerous organised activities under "Ocio and Multiaventura" including wheel-drive tours into the remoter areas, as well as horse treks and mountain biking, rafting, kayaking and canoeing, mountain climbing, paragliding and guided walks.

Cazorla (Calle Ximinez 17; tel: 953 71 00 73; www.tierraventuracazorla.com) offers a similar programme.

Sultry summer night in Seville: It is warm and the quiet murmuring of the people at the tables fills the streets

Sevilla and Huelva

Vibrant Sevilla (Seville), towns steeped in history and breathtakingly beautiful nature feature high in this part of Andalucía.

Pages 142–177

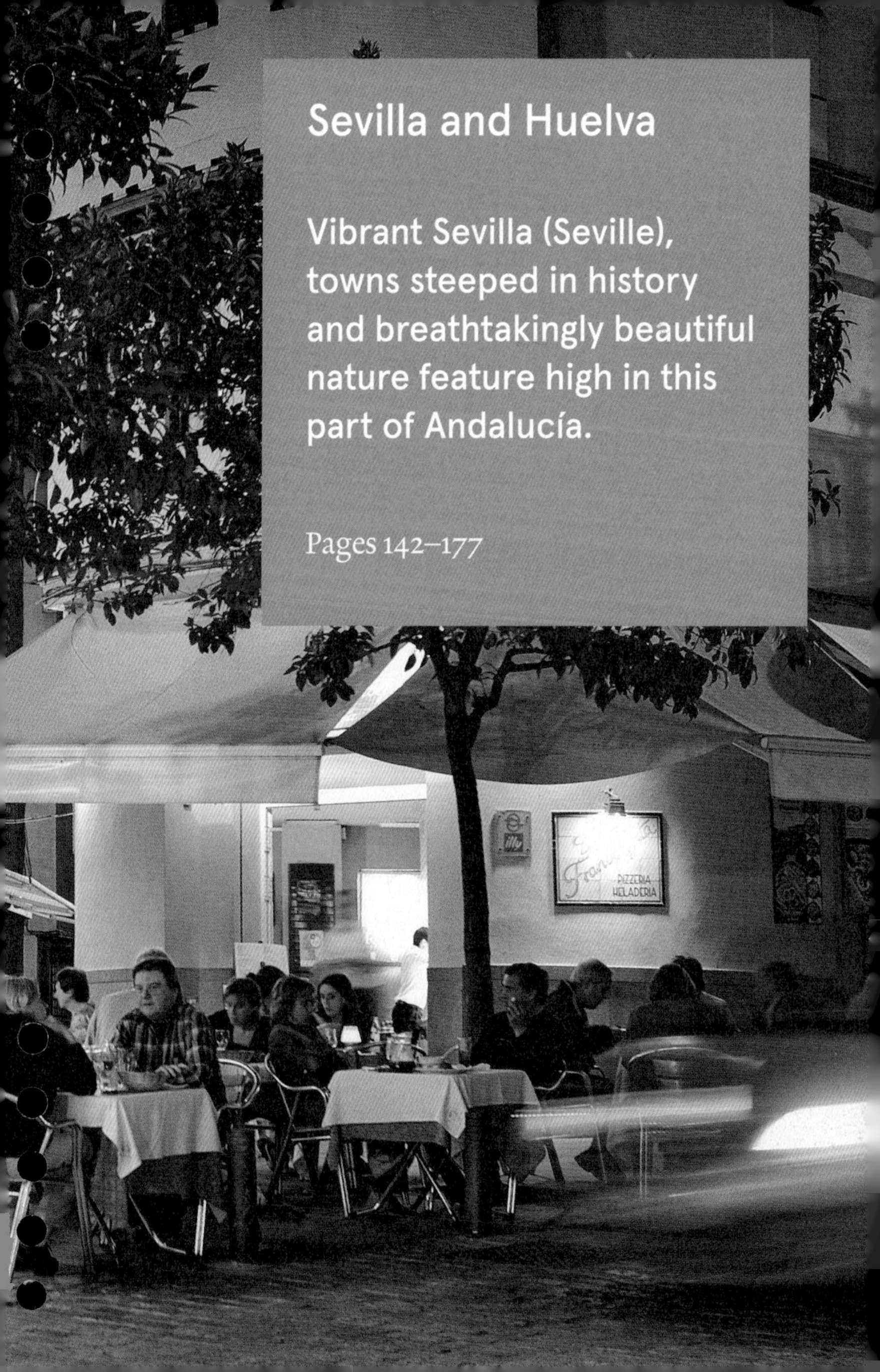

Getting Your Bearings

The city of Seville is the essence of all things Andalucían, a city of enduring excitement and spontaneity, of orange trees and flamenco; a city where the jingle of horse-drawn carriages is still heard in quiet streets and flower-filled parks and where modernistic buildings blend happily with Moorish palaces, majestic churches and medieval streets. It is where you find the best tapas bars in Spain and where a hint of pleasurable expectancy is always in the air.

Seville is one of the hottest places on mainland Europe. Thus, it is no wonder that the town does not wake up until a lot of other are going to bed – nights in Seville have a lot to offer. Out in the larger province beyond the city are lesser-known but fascinating places to visit such as the old Roman city of Itálica, the walled town of Carmona, with its Moorish streets and Roman necropolis, and historic Écija.

On the coast is Huelva. The capital of the province of the same name is an industrialised port that has no great sights, but an excursion to the northern part of the province. is well worthwhile. Here, in the natural park Sierra de Aracena, you will find the friendly hill town of Aracena, famous for its limestone caverns, the Gruta de las Maravillas. All around Aracena there are sprawling cork oak forests (*dehesas*) in which tiny villages have nested, seemingly forgotten by time. Huelva's southernmost coastline, the Costa de la Luz, has one of the longest and most remote beaches in Andalucía. In the east lies the huge delta of the Río Guadalquivir and the Parque Nacional de Doñana, a vast area of wetlands, sand dunes and scrubland that is a wildlife site of world importance.

TOP 10

3 ★★ Sevilla

6 ★★ Carmona

9 ★★ Parque Nacional de Doñana

Don't Miss

37 Aracena & Gruta de las Maravillas

At Your Leisure

38 Écija

39 Itálica

40 Minas de Río Tinto

41 Costa de la Luz (Huelva)

42 El Rocío

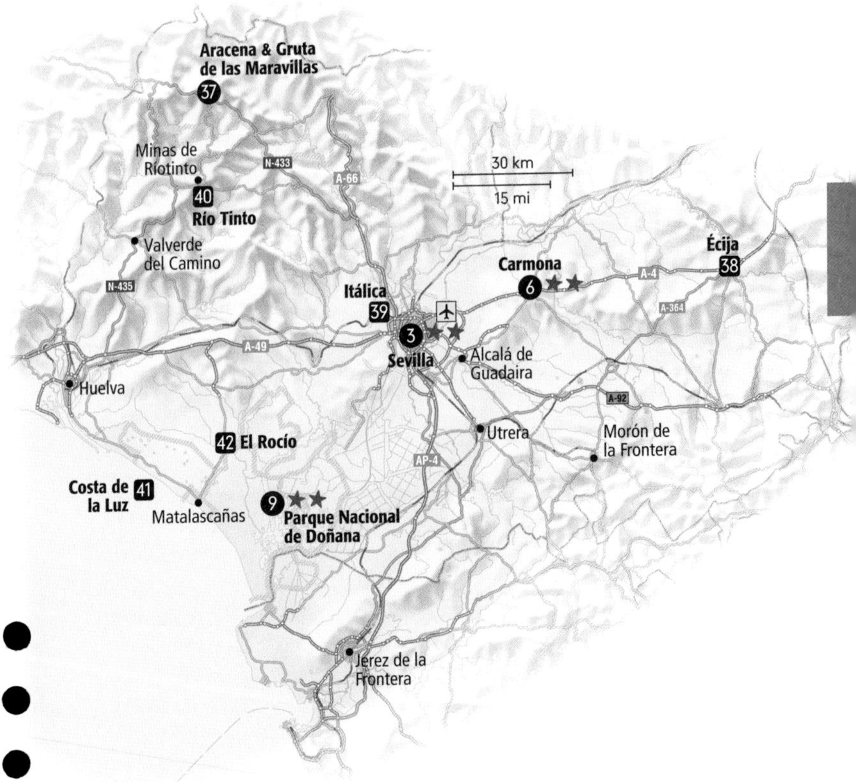

My Day With Pilgrims, Romans and Flamenco

What many don't know: Sevilla (Seville), a byword for vibrancy and joie de vivre, is also one of the starting points of the famous Camino de Santiago routes. Today you follow part of the pilgrim's path on the Vía de la Plata make a leap in time to the Romans in Itálica and end the day with excellent flamenco.

8am: First Traces

Only experts will recognise the markings of the Camino de Santiago trail in ❸ ★★Sevilla: Set off towards the southwest corner of Seville Cathedral on the Avenida de la Constitución in front of Puerta de San Miguel. On the other side of the road, on the round arched portal, you will see a blue tile with yellow scallops – it is the first way mark of the Vía de la Plata Camino de Santiago route. Were you to follow it, you would, after about 1,000km (620mi), eventually arrive in the Galician Santiago de Compostela.

First, go to the main portal. 32 figures of saints flank the spectacular Puerta de la Asunción, one of them is Saint James, recognizable thanks to his pilgrim's hat and cape with scallop. Can you find him?

Now you follow the Camino de Santiago route, albeit not 1,000km (620mi), but at least 1km: At the end of the west façade turn off left into

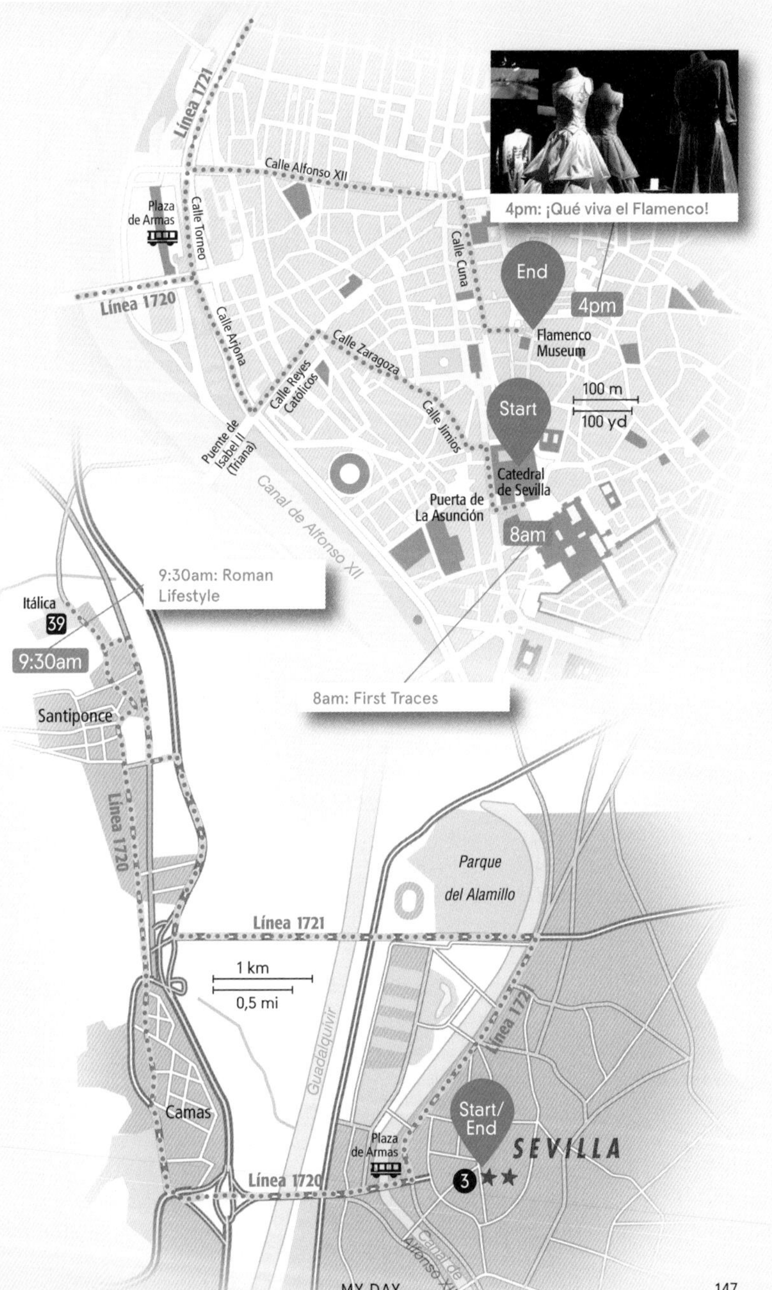

4pm: ¡Qué viva el Flamenco!
Línea 1721
Calle Alfonso XII
Plaza de Armas
Calle Torneo
Calle Cuna
End
4pm
Línea 1720
Calle Arjona
Calle Zaragoza
Flamenco Museum
Calle Reyes Católicos
100 m
100 yd
Start
Calle Jimios
Puente de Isabel II (Triana)
Catedral de Sevilla
Puerta de La Asunción
Canal de Alfonso XII
8am
9:30am: Roman Lifestyle
Itálica
39
9:30am
8am: First Traces
Santiponce
Línea 1720
Parque del Alamillo
Línea 1721
1 km
0,5 mi
Guadalquivir
Línea 1721
Camas
Start/ End
Plaza de Armas
SEVILLA
Línea 1720
3
Canal de Alfonso XII

Standing side by side: admire the religious figures on the main portal of Seville Cathedral (above left); in the Flamenco Museum people show a different kind of fervour (right page below)

the Calle García de Vinuesa and then immediately right into the Calle Jimios. Calle Zaragoza leads into Calle Reyes Católicos, on which you turn off left on to wander over Puente de Triana. The Camino de Santiago route leads over the Guadalquivir to the Roman town of Itálica; however you take the Calle Arjona off to the right leading to the bus station Plaza de Armas, about 500m further on, and take the bus.

9:30am: Roman Lifestyle

After the hustle and bustle of Seville, 39 Itálica offers some welcome tranquillity. The greenery around the amphitheatre offers welcome shade, while the uncovered mosaics of some of the villas testify to the good taste of the Romans. It is easy to imagine that this was not exactly one of the poorer residential areas.

The Roman road once extended to Gijón on the Atlantic. The Arabs called it the *Balata*, fortified road; this became the Vía de la Plata (Silver Way), on which Christians went on pilgrimage to the tomb of St John.

It was not only the pilgrims who used the route, however: At the end of the ninth century, the Muslim commander Almansor raided Santiago de Compostela and had Christians carry the bells from the cathedral on Vía de la Plata to Córdoba where they were turned into lamps. When the Christians reconquered Córdoba in 1236 the Moors were made to carry them back to Santiago in exactly the same way.

The Romans enjoyed a good lifestyle in Itálica, as these ground mosaics show (right above). Seville's inhabitants and visitors indulge in similar joie de vivre when they sit by the river (above)

2pm: Back to the Fray!

After visiting Itálica, it is time to return to Seville on the bus. Stroll for a while along the river or slip back via for instance Calle Alfonso XII into the urban hustle and bustle. Treat yourself to a bite to eat somewhere, either on the river bank or in one of the side streets!

4pm: ¡Qué viva el Flamenco!

Seville is the heartland of the Flamenco – a visit here is not complete unless you have been to see one of the shows. Insiders regard the performances in Museo del Baile Flamenco (p. 163) with the dancer Cristina Hoyos as being particularly authentic. Ideally, you should put yourself in the mood by doing a tour of the partly interactive exhibition of the museum. The chances are that you will find yourself doing one or two flamenco pirouettes yourself on your evening walk.

ℹ

Estación Plaza de Armas
218 A3 to Itálica: Express line 1721 Mo–Fr 9 am (journey time about 20 min.) to Seville no. 1720 on the full and half hours (journey about 30 min.) approx. €1

❸★★ Sevilla

Don't Miss	Andalucía's vibrant capital
Why	Because no other city so skilfully combines the grandeur of the past and the vitality of the present
When	Certainly not in the height of summer! It is much too hot!
Time	Stay until you have soaked up the flair of the city; then you can draw on it later.
How	Bullfight, flamenco, feria – this city sparkles!

Sevilla (Seville), bestriding the broad Río Guadalquivir, exudes charm and joie de vivre. The everyday life of the *Sevillanos* is played out with equal verve in the bars, fine restaurants and during Spain's most exuberant festival, the *Feria de Abril*.

An inscription on the Puerta de Jerez reads: "Hercules built me; Julius Caesar surrounded me with walls and high towers; the Holy King conquered me". It remains questionable whether Hercules really founded Seville. What is fact though, is that when the Romans arrived in around 206BC and drove out the Carthaginians, there was a settlement there called Hispalis, which was an important harbour for Caesar. In 712, the Moors ended the rule of the Visigoths. As Ichbilîja, it flourished under the Almohad Caliphate in the 12th century.

In the 16th century, Seville became Spain's most important port of departure to America. In the 17th century, this golden age ended owing to the silting of the Guadalquivir. In 1929, the Iberoamericana Exhibition took place here.

In the heart of the city three buildings created an ensemble now listed as a UNESCO World Heritage Site: the Alcázar, the palace of the Muslim and Christian rulers, the cathedral containing the tomb of Christopher Columbus, and the Archivo General de Indias with its important colonial records.

ⓘ

210 C3

Tourist Information
218 south of B1
Avenida de las Delicias 9
☎ 954 2 34 65 www.visitasevilla.es

Parking
There is out-of-centre parking near Santa Justa railway station, at Calle Luis de Morales. Some of the Seville Metro underground stations in the suburbs offer inexpensive parking facilities.

Sundowner by the Guadalquivir

One of the most beautiful places to experience the sunset in Seville is by the Guadalquivir. Between the Puente de San Telmo and Puente de los Remedios bridges, you will find some charming riverside bars, such as the Terraza Martini Sevilla. From a prime position overlooking the water as it slowly flows past, you can sip on an aperitif and enjoy the *hora violeta*, the blue hour, that twilight time when the sky assumes a velvety blue hue.

Terraza Martini Sevilla, Paseo de las Delicias 3

La Catedral & La Giralda

Seville's Cathedral of Santa María de la Sede is the largest Gothic church in the world, a treasure house of monumental architecture and great sculptures, paintings and decorative craftwork.

After Seville was wrested from the Moors by Fernando III in 1248, the mosque was consecrated as the cathedral of the Kingdom of Seville. From 1401, building began of the new cathedral over the meanwhile very dilapidated mosque, a project which would drag on for over 500 years. Now the largest Gothic cathedral in the world, it is 116m (380ft) long, 76m (249ft) wide and the main nave is 37m (121ft) high.

The Giralda

The exterior focus of the cathedral is the Giralda tower built by the Moorish Almohad rulers of Seville between 1184 and 1198: The *Sevillanos* revere the 97.5m (320ft) high tower as the emblem of the town. The original minaret was remodelled into a belfry with 25 bells in the 16th century by the Spanish. It was crowned by a statue representing Faith, in the form of a weathervane, a *giraldillo*, from which the tower's name derives. The filigree structure is a perfect symbiosis of Moorish architecture and elements of the Renaissance. Instead of steps, the tower has 35 ramps – thus enabling the sultan to ride his horse right up to the lookout platform, from which he could enjoy the view over the entire city.

The entrance to the Giralda is in the northeast corner of the cathedral, immediately as you enter the building through the Puerta de la Concepción. From the top, you are presented, as in the days of the sultan, with a fantastic view of Seville and of parts of the roof construction in the Orange Tree Courtyard of the cathedral.

The Cathedral

The Gothic cathedral is entered through the Puerta del Perdón (Gate of Absolution) on the north side. Beyond it lies the Patio de los Naranjos (Patio of the Orange Trees), where worshippers carried out ritual ablutions before entering the

The Giralda, the bell tower, once a minaret, towers above the piers and pinnacles of the cathedral

mosque. Towering above the patio is the intricate façade of the Puerta de la Concepción, the doorway through which you enter the cathedral proper. Take some time to appreciate the size of the building's cavernous interior. Located in the centre of the huge central nave, built during the period from 1401 to 1507, are the Capilla Mayor, the main chapel, with the Coro (Choir). The gilded and painted *retablo* (altarpiece) of the Capilla Mayor is one of the cathedral's treasures. The vast screen is composed of 45 carved panels depicting scenes from the life of Christ and featuring over 1,000 biblical figures. The focus of this awesome Gothic masterpiece is a silver-plated cedar statue of the Virgen de la Sede (the Virgin of the Chair). The choir has 117 stalls, each one intricately carved.

During the 16th century the Capilla Real (Royal Chapel), which has an imposing *retablo* in stone, was set up behind the Capilla Mayor. Also dating back to the 16th century is the Sacristía Mayor on the south side of the cathedral, a beautiful domed chamber in Renaissance style by Diego de Riaño and

Catedral de Santa María de la Sede

According to traditional accounts, the members of the cathedral chapter said, "Let us build a church so beautiful and so grand that those who see it finished will think we are mad." Their wish was fulfilled. At a length of 116m (380ft), 76m (249ft) wide and a height of 37m (121ft), it is the largest Gothic church in the world.

❶ Giralda: The tower was originally the minaret for the main mosque.
❷ Gallery: The viewing gallery is at a height of 70m (229ft).
❸ Fountain: The octagonal-shaped fountain is the remains of the Muslim *midhâ*, the basin used for ritual cleansing.
❹ Library: The library of the cathedral chapter possesses i.a. handwritten papers by Columbus and the Bible of Alfonso X.
❺ Sagrario: This baroque building contains a *retablo* (altarpiece) with Pedro Roldán's *Descent from the Cross*.
❻ Nave: "Notre Dame de Paris could walk without bending her head down the central nave." (Théophile Gautier).
❼ Choir: The choir stool is Gothic. The Capilla de la Concepción Chica on the south wall contains the *La Cieguecita*, a wooden sculpture of the Virgin Mary.
❽ Capilla Mayor: The *retablo* is the dominant piece here: at almost 30m (100ft) in height and 20m (65ft) in width, it is the largest altarpiece in the world.
❾ Capilla Real: Fernando III's body rests in the silver shrine. To the left lies his son Alfonso X, and to the right his wife Beatriz de Suabia.
❿ Sacristía Mayor: It contains the key of Seville (1248), a reliquary of Alfonso X, a reliquary of the Cross found by Saint Helena, the "Tenebrario" by Bartolomé Morel

and Pedro de Campana's painting *Descent from the Cross*.

⓫ Capilla de San Antonio: Here you will find *The Baptism of Christ* and *The Vision of St Anthony by* Murillo.

⓬ Capilla de Santiago: contains a picture of St James at the Battle of Cavijo by Juan de Roelas and a painting by Valdés Leal (*San Lorenzo*).

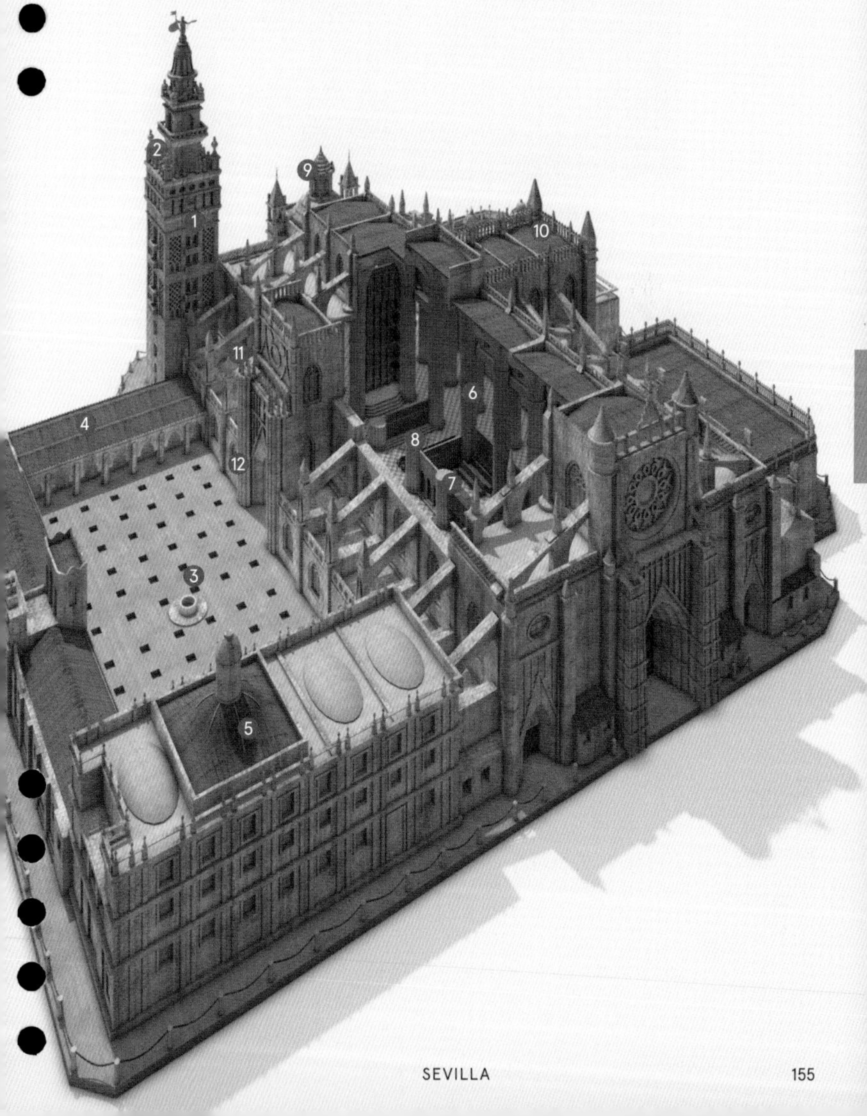

Columbus' tomb in the cathedral: four heralds (symbolising the four kingdoms León, Castilla, Navarra and Aragón) carry the stone sarcophagus

Diego de Siloé. Apart from the Sacristía Mayor, of particular interest in the Sacristía de los Cálices, built in 1529, are the many paintings, which include Goya's *Las santas Justa y Rufina* and Valdés Leal's *San Lázaro con Santa Marta y María Magdalena*.

Adjoining the Sacristía de los Cálices is a striking monument to Christopher Columbus depicting the great sailor's coffin. For a long time, it was a controversial point as to whether the seafarer's remains were actually inside. After Columbus' death in 1506, he was buried in Seville, but in 1596 transported to Santo Domingo on Haiti and from there to Havana, Cuba, where Arturo Mélida sculpted a tomb which was installed in the cathedral (1892). When Cuba "was lost" in the Spanish-American war of 1898, Columbus was returned to Seville. A DNA test carried out in 2006 that compared samples from the tomb with DNA from family members finally confirmed that the remains in the coffin really were those of Christopher Columbus.

INSIDER TIP Stop for a drink at the **Cervecería Giralda** (Calle Mateos Gago 1; tel: 954 22 82 50; www.cerveceriagiralda.com; noon–midnight) and enjoy a magnificent view of the cathedral at the same time.

Catedral Santa María de la Sede and Giralda
218 B2 Plaza Virgen de los Reyes 954 21 49 71
Mon 11–3:30, Tue–Sat 11–5, Sun 2:30–6
C1, C2, C3, C4 €9 (free Mon 4:30–6)

Reales Alcázares

The Alcázar located immediately opposite the cathedral was originally the fortress-palace of the Moorish rulers who worked on it from the 10th century onwards. The layout of the palaces reflects classic Islamic architecture, with central courtyards from which individual halls and chambers lead off to all sides. Great use is made of painted stucco and of tiles known as *azulejos* (p. 17), which form a dazzling kaleidoscope of geometric patterns. Not the least of the Alcázar's delights are the beautifully kept gardens.

Seville's original Reales Alcázares was built from 913 on the ruins of Roman and Visigothic fortifications. The interior of the building dates almost wholly from the later Christian era. After the conquest of Seville by Fernando III, the Christian kings moved in here. Pedro I, commonly called Pedro the Cruel (reigned from 1350 to 1369) decided to build his mistress María de Padilla a regal residence. He had Moorish architects and craftsmen brought in from Granada and Toledo, who built the palace section named after him and with it one of the most beautiful examples of Moorish architecture in Spain. The Catholic kings altered quite a few of the rooms; under Carlos V a new extension was added.

Visiting the Reales Alcázares

Beyond the entrance vestibule is the Patio del León (Court of the Lion) and, beyond that, the larger Patio de la Montería (Hunting Court). To the right of the latter is the Cuarto del Almirante (Admiralty Hall), established by Isabel I de Castilla as a suite of rooms in which to plan voyages to the Americas. The finest room is the Sala de Audiencias (Audience Hall) with an *artesonado* ceiling, a fine model of Columbus's vessel the *Santa María*, and a 16th-century *in situ* altarpiece, *The Virgin of the Navigators*, portraying Columbus, Amerigo Vespucci and other voyagers.

You next enter the true Palace of Pedro I. In the central courtyard, the Patio de las Doncellas (Court of the Maidens), a space rich with multi-lobed arches and beautiful lattices of stone, a frieze of *azulejos* clads the lower walls and a central

From the Plaza del Triunfo, you enter through the high walls surrounding the stunning Alcázar into the Patio del León, a courtyard full of orange trees and flowers. The Alcázar gardens bring together Islamic and Renaissance styles in a marvelous manner.

fountain sends a slim column of water into the air. The patio is encircled by richly decorated rooms leading one into the other through narrow doorways. The two-storey Salón de los Embajadores (Room of the Ambassadors), next to it, is the oldest and most beautiful room in Alcázar. It is crowned with a magnificent stalactite dome (1420) made of cedarwood.

A stairway in the corner of the Patio de las Doncellas leads to the gloomy 17th-century Salones de Carlos V. From near the Estanque del Mercurio, a passageway leads you past a cafeteria into a covered coach hall, the Apeadero, and then to the exit.

---

218 C2 Patio de Banderas 954 50 23 24
Daily April–Sep 9:30–7; Oct–March 9:30–5
Café C1, C2, C3, C4
From €11.50 (children under 16 free); to avoid queues, it is worth buying the ticket online, audio guide possible.

Barrio de Santa Cruz

Alongside the cathedral and Reales Alcázares are the narrow streets and plazas of Barrio de Santa Cruz, a welcome antidote to the traffic-jammed main streets of the city. Santa Cruz was the *aljama*, or Jewish quarter, of medieval Seville. Much of the original *barrio* was destroyed after a vicious pogrom in 1492, but a lot was also preserved. As you wander through the streets, you will catch tantalising glimpses of lovely central patios through wrought-iron grilles.

The El Rinconcillo (Quiet Corner) tavern-restaurant is in a building that dates back to 1670

A peaceful little enclave that many visitors seem to miss is Plaza de Santa Cruz; the wrought-iron cross at its centre symbolises the original Iglesia de Santa Cruz, destroyed by Napoleonic troops. Another pretty square is Plaza de Doña Elvira with its central fountain and dappled shade. On the *barrio's* eastern boundary are the pleasantly shady Jardines de Murillo (Murillo Gardens), and everywhere you turn there are bars and cafés. You can experience fantastic flamenco in the Museo del Baile Flamenco. Renowned flamenco dancer Cristina Hoyos (Seville 1946) opened the museum here in 2006. What makes it particularly special is that besides the exhibits regarding the history and culture of dance, visitors can also see high-calibre flamenco every day.

Museo de Bellas Artes

One of Spain's major art galleries, the Museo de Bellas Artes (Fine Arts Museum) is located in the former Convento de la Merced Calzada, right on the west border of the Old Town. With its hushed galleries and peaceful central patio, this lovely building is a pleasure in itself. The collection focuses on the works of the Sevillan Baroque (Zurbarán, Murillo) and 19th-century Andalucían painting.

The permanent collection is displayed in 14 of the convent's rooms. The highlight of any visit must be Room V, the one-time chapel of the convent. Here works by two of Seville's most important painters, Francisco de Zurbarán and Bartolomé Esteban Murillo, are on show, as are works by Goya, Velázquez, El Greco, Murillo's contemporary Juan de Valdés de Leal and sculptors such as Pedro Millán. Even the chapel is worth seeing, and the dome of the chapel is aglow with restored paintings. In a small chamber round to the right is Murillo's ravishing *Virgin and Child*, known as *La Virgen de la Servilleta* because it is said to be painted on a dinner napkin.

Rooms XII and XIV show 19th- and 20th-century art. In Room XII look for Gonzalo Bilbao's sentimental but persuasive evocation of the world of *Carmen* and the Seville Tobacco Factory, *Las Cigarreras. Noche de Verano en Sevilla*, by the Impressionist painter born in the Andalucían capital can also be seen here.

Casa de Pilatos (Pilate's House)

This palace which now belongs to the Dukes of Medinaceli combines Moorish, Gothic and Renaissance elements in such a winning way that the result is almost on a par with the Alcázar. Construction started in 1492 and was completed around 1520. Since the master of the works had travelled to Palestine the year before, it was generally assumed that the building was a copy of the house of Pontius Pilate in Jerusalem. The house is laid out around a spectacular patio, which is entered through an entrance modelled on a triumphal arch and made of Carrara marble; completed in 1532, it is by the Genoese artist d'Aprile. Work since the mid-20th century has restored the house to its original splendour. A conducted tour takes you through a succession of chambers and salons exquisitely decorated and furnished.

Plaza de España & Parque de María Luisa

From the mid-19th century, what is now the Parque de María Luisa was the private garden of the Palacio de San Telmo; in 1893 Infanta María Luisa de Borbón gave it to the town. From 1911, based on the designs of French landscape architect Jean-Claude Nicolas Forestier, it was turned it into

a public park and became the venue for the Ibero-American Exposition of 1929. Today the 340,000m² (407.000yd²) park is an oasis of tree-filled gardens, resplendent with colourful ceramics, ornamental bridges and follies, and in summer bright with geraniums and bougainvillaea. The main stage of the *Iberoamericana* Exhibition was Plaza de España northeast of Parque de María Luisa. It is a huge crescent of arcaded redbrick building with curving staircases. At ground level, a series of brightly coloured tile mosaics display the coats of arms of Spain's main provinces. In front of the crescent is a canal-style lake, criss-crossed by ornamental bridges, where people drift sedately in little rowing boats. In the south is the pretty Plaza de América, flanked by the Museo Arqueológico (Archaeological Museum) whose collections range from prehistory to the Moors, and the Museo de Artes y Costumbres Populares (Museum of Folk Art), which displays artefacts and costumes from the 18th and 19th centuries. Both were built as part of the 1929 Exhibition.

The central courtyard of Casa de Pilatos is a two-storey arcaded structure; the round arches are adorned with Moorish motifs. In the middle of the courtyard is a fountain with dolphin designs and a Janus head

Impressive: The crescent-shaped Plaza de España

Plaza Nueva & Calle Sierpes

To the north of the cathedral is the bustling Avenida de la Constitución leading to Plaza de San Francisco. Off to the left past the 16th-century Ayuntamiento (city hall) with its Renaissance façade, you will come to the Plaza Nueva. Plaza Nueva has little architectural appeal but buzzes with life in the evenings. The *Sevillanos* meet here during the day to chat in the shade of the large plane trees, and in the evening a livelier crowd takes over. This is where political meetings and other major events take place. From here, stroll north along Calle Sierpes, Seville's great shopping street, crammed with shops of every kind, its side streets alive with tapas bars. Between 2006 and 2011 German architect Jürgen Mayer built a spectacular eyecatcher, popularly known as Las Setas de la Encarnacíon (Incarnation's Mushrooms; officially Metropol Parasol) in a square just a short walk from the Sierpes: the wonderfully curved wooden roof offers a fantastic lookout point, while numerous events take place in the space below.

Torre del Oro, Plaza de Toros de la Maestranza, Triana

The languid flow of the Guadalquivir River exudes a sense of calm and space. On the east side is the Torre del Oro, a 12th-century Moorish tower that now houses a small maritime museum. It earned its "Golden Tower" name because of the shining golden tiles that used to adorn its facade. From the jetty below the tower, the Cruceros Torre de Oro boats set off every 30 minutes for a one-hour tour. Further north along the Paseo de Cristóbal Colón is Seville's huge baroque bullring, La Maestranza, claimed as the finest bullring in the world. A little further, you can cross the Guadalquivir on the Puente de Isabel II to reach the district of Triana, once Seville's main gypsy quarter, home of flamenco and of ceramic production.

Isla de la Cartuja

Further north, Isla de La Cartuja, an island in the Guadalquivir River, was the venue of Seville's Expo '92. The Carthusian monastery which gave the island its name, now houses the Andalucían Contemporary Art Centre (Centro Andaluz de Arte Contemporáneo). On the eastern side of the island is the large amusement park, Isla Mágica.

Museo del Baile Flamenco
218 C3 Calle Manuel Rojas Marcos 3 954 34 03 11
www.museoflamenco.com
Museum: 10–7. 2–3 daily shows
€10

Museo de Bellas Artes
218 A3
Plaza del Museo 955 54 29 31
Mid-June to mid-Sep Tue–Sun 9–3:30; mid-Sep to mid-June Tue–Sat 9–7:30, Sun 9–3:30 C1, C2, C3, C4
€1.50 (free with EU passport)

Casa de Pilatos
218 C3
Plaza de Pilatos 1 954 22 52 98
May–Sep 9–7, Oct–April 9–6
C1, C2, C3, C4 (for Plaza San Agustín)
€8–€10

Plaza de España & Parque de María Luisa
218 C1
Avenida de Isabel la Católica
Bus C1, C2, C3, C4 Free

Museo Arqueológico
218 south of C1 Plaza de América
955 12 06 32 July, Aug Tue–Sun 9–3; Sep–June Tue–Sat 9–9, Sun and holidays 9–3 Free with EU passport

Museo de Artes y Costumbres Populares
218 south of C1
Plaza de América 954 71 23 98
July, Aug Tue–Sun 9–3; Sep–June Tue–Sat 9–9, Sun and holidays 9–3
Free

Setas de Sevilla
218 C3 Plaza de la Encarnación 14
Viewing platform 10–10
setasdesevilla.com

Cruceros Torre del Oro
218 B1 Muelle del Marqués del Contadero (below Torre del Oro)
954 56 16 92 crucerosensevilla.com
May–Sep 11–10; Oct–April 11–7
€17 € (children under 12 free)

Centro Andaluz de Arte Contemporáneo (CAAC)
218 west of A4
Cartuja de Santa María de Las Cuevas
955 03 70 70 www.caac.es
Tue–Sat 11–9, Sun 10–3:30 €3

Isla Mágica
218 north of A5
Avenida de los Descubrimientos s/n
902 16 17 16 www.islamagica.es
May–Sep daily 11–7 or midnight
€32

❻ ★★ Carmona

Don't Miss	Typical little Andalucían town full of history
Why	You will be hard put to find such a charming Old Town anywhere else
When	Anytime
Time	A day
What Else	A tapas break, surrounded by arcades, on the Plaza de Abastos
In Short	Exactly the right choice for those looking for a leisurely tour

Carmona sits enthroned on a bare hill ridge in the middle of the Vega de Corbones, one of the most fertile stretches of land in Andalucía. The historic centre ranks it among the most exquisite little towns in Andalucía, only surpassed by Baeza and Úbeda. Carmona also possesses a first-class cultural landmark in the form of an extensive Roman burial ground.

There are about 1,000 tombs in Carmona's Necrópolis Romana dating from about 2BC to AD4, about 250 of which have been uncovered. There are conducted tours of the site, but you can easily find your own way around. The site museum has displays of mosaics, gravestones and funerary pottery.

Visiting the Old Town

The main town of Carmona is entered by an impressive Roman gateway, the Puerta de Sevilla. You can reach the upper walls and battlements of the gateway through the tourist office. Across busy Plaza Blas Infante from the Puerta de Sevilla, outside the walls, is the 15th-century Iglesia de San Pedro, its tower built in the form of Seville's Giralda. On Carmona's palm-fringed central square, Plaza de San Fernando, is a splendid Renaissance building Carmona's *ayuntamiento* (town hall). A Roman mosaic of the head of Medusa is displayed in its patio. The weekly market is held on the Plaza de Abastos. Towering over Plazuela del Marqués de las Torres is the Gothic Iglesia de Santa María la Mayor; look for a column with a Visigothic calendar

inscribed in the stone. At the eastern end of the town is the refurbished Roman gateway, the Puerta de Córdoba.

Carmona's pretty Old Town exudes plenty of Andalucían flair

INSIDER TIP Enjoy a drink, even as a non-resident, at Carmona's exclusive **Parador** (p. 173) hotel in the renovated Alcázar del Rey Pedro. In the 13th century, Pedro the Cruel had the former Moorish fort turned into his favourite palace. If you're feeling flush, stop off for lunch or dinner.

---

210 C3

Tourist Information
Alcázar de la Puerta de Sevilla
954 19 09 55
www.turismo.carmona.org

Parking
There is limited parking inside the Puerta de Sevilla and random parking around Plaza de San Fernando.

Necrópolis Romana
Avenida de Jorge Bonsor 9
600 14 36 32
April–June Tue–Sat 9–9, Sun 9–3; July to mid-Sep Tue–Sun 9–3; mid-Sep–March Tue–Sat 9–6, Sun 9–3
Free

Iglesia de San Pedro
Calle San Pedro
Enquire about opening times at the Tourist Information Office €1

Ayuntamiento (with mosaic)
Calle El Salvador 2
954 14 00 11 www.carmona.org
Mon–Fri 8–3 Free

Iglesia de Santa María la Mayor
Calle Martín López de Córdoba
Mon–Sat 10–2 and Mon–Fri 5–7
€3 (incl. museum)

❾ ★★ Parque Nacional de Doñana

Don't Miss	Wetland with unique landscape
Why	The Spanish Carmargue enthuses not only birdwatchers
When	In October, when the migrating birds arrive, or in May when everything is green and flowering
Time	Until you have spotted an Iberian lynx…
What Else	Visit El Rocío, the neighbouring town with Western flair
In Short	Fantastic photos of fabulous countryside

The wilderness of the Doñana National Park forms one of Spain's largest conservation areas and is one of the most important wetland sites in the world. It serves as a haven for native birds, such as the endangered Spanish Imperial Eagle, migratory birds and an exciting range of mammals.

The park covers an area of more than 540km² (510mi²) around the delta of the Río Guadalquivir, which borders it on the east. To the south, it stretches to the estuary of the river opposite Sanlúcar de Barrameda and in the west from Matalascañas on the Atlantic to El Rocío. This region has always been sparsely populated – the climate of the marshes (*marismas*) being too hostile for comfort, with malaria rampant there until the mid-20th century.

A lot of deer live in the Parque Nacional Coto de Doñana

From Hunting Ground to Conservation Area

After the expulsion of the Arabs, Alfonso X Christianised the area in the 13th century and had religious houses built. From the 15th century, the Dukes of Medina Sidonia were using the area as a hunting ground. In 1595, the 7th Duke of this family, Alonso Pérez de Guzmán, erected a palace for his wife Doña Ana there, now a research centre. Over a period of time, the name *Coto de Doña Ana* became *Coto de Doñana.*

At the end of the 19th century, English hunter and natural scientist Abel Chapman drew attention to the abundance of

Numerous migrant birds spend the winter here, or take a break on their way to Africa and socialise with the species resident here

bird life, after which keen English egg collectors wreaked havoc on the ecological system. In 1900, the dukes sold the area to the sherry baron William Garvey. Conservationists started to lobby for the creation of a national park, which ultimately resulted in the establishment of the "Parque Nacional Coto de Doñana" in 1969 originally covering an area of 370km² (143mi²); in 1978 it was extended. Since 1994, the park has been a UNESCO biosphere reserve. Around 300,000 birds migrate from northern Europe to the Doñana *marismas* in October each year, then head north again in March. Winter is thus the best time for dedicated birdwatchers to visit.

During the El Rocío pilgrimage at Whitsun, it is not possible to visit the park

Several visitor centres manage entrance to the Donaña. The Centro de Recepción del Acebuche is the main information centre, offering exhibitions, souvenirs and a café. Tours can be arranged here in all-terrain vehicles.

Dogs are not allowed (with the exception of guide dogs)

INSIDER TIP **Coto de Doñana** is a great picnic area, so stop off at a delicatessen and pick up some fresh bread, Manchego cheese, *jamón serrano* and a couple of bottles of Rioja.

210 B2

Centro de Recepción del Acebuche
Off A483, 5km/3 mi north of Matalascañas,
959 43 04 32 www.donanavisitas.es
Daily 8–3 and 4–8 in summer, until 7 in winter
Guided tours: €30. Tour with all-terrain vehicle (about 80km/50mi, 3–4 hours); reservation necessary.

Doñana Reservas – Visitas Guiadas
Av. de la Canaliega s/n, El Rocío
959 44 24 74
www.donanareservas.com
Guided tours (3.5–4 hours): from €30

Centro Recepción Las Rocinas
off A483, on southern outskirts of El Rocío 959 43 95 69
Daily 8–3 and 4–8 in summer, until 7 in winter

㊲ Aracena & Gruta de las Maravillas

Don't Miss	A market town and an impressive dripstone cave
Why	You can see the most beautiful "backsides" here!
When	Ideally when it is hot – then the cave feels pleasantly cool
Time	As long as you like
What Else	After visiting the cave, it is time to go on up to the castle, so that you can enjoy the view.
In Short	Thoroughly enjoyable: sensuous indulgence

Aracena lies in the north of the Huelva province, at the heart of the Sierra de Aracena, an area of smooth-browed hills covered with cork-oak forests (*dehesas*).

The Gruta de las Maravillas is said to have been discovered by a 19th-century shepherd seeking lost sheep

The main tourist attraction here is the 1.2km (0.75mi) long cave system Gruta de las Maravillas (Grotto of Marvels); a 45-min. tour leads through galleries and passageways that bristle with fantastic stalactites and stalagmites and a series of small lakes. Lighting and piped music add to the theatrical effect. The guide's commentary is in Spanish, but many of the features speak for themselves. Highlights include the Sala de los Culos (Room of the Backsides), where certain deposits carbonate resemble well-rounded parts of the human anatomy. In the caves, the temperature is a constant 16–19°C (61–66°F) range, and humidity is almost 100% – so wear something warm!

Lively Market Town

Back on the surface, it's pleasant to stroll around Aracena's cobbled streets and its busy main square, Plaza Marqués de Aracena. Located in the old town hall in pretty Plaza Alta is the information centre for the surrounding natural park Sierra de Aracena

On the hilltop above the town, beyond a 16th-century brick gateway, are the ruins of a Moorish castle along with the adjoining Iglesia de Nuestra Señora del Mayor Dolor, an impressive medieval church (13th–15th century) with a richly adorned *mudéjar*-tower; beside it is the ruin of the Arab castle.

At www.audioguiasaracena.es, you can download audio guides in MP3 format (in Spanish and English) on the local sights

Aracena is the centre of *Jamón Ibério* – the finest but also most expensive ham in the world. Numerous shops sell this traditionally cured delicacy, which you can also try in one of the bars down towards the end of town. The area's main *jamon*-producing village is Jabugo, located 20km (12.5mi) to the west. Basically, a distinction is made between the *Jamón Serrano* that comes from the white domestic pig and *Jamón Ibério*. The latter is only made from the typically black pasture pigs, Cerdo Ibérico, an old endemic race on the Iberian Peninsula. If you are interested in learning about the history of the Iberian ham, then you should plan a visit to the Museo del Jamón. Seven exhibition rooms in the museum are dedicated to this local speciality.

INSIDER TIP What could possibly be better here than a *Jamón Ibérico* **picnic**? All you need to do is find the perfect place for it.

210 B4

Tourist Information
Calle Pozo de la Nieve,
Plaza San Pedro (also ticket office for the Gruta de las Maravillas)
663 93 78 76
www.aracena.es

Parking
There is a car park in Plaza San Pedro at the entrance to the town from the N433. Pay the fee to the attendant.

Gruta de las Maravillas
Off Plaza San Pedro
959 12 82 06/12 83 55
Daily 10:30–1:30, 3–6. Guided tours Mon–Fri every hour, Sat, Sun every half hour. Tickets from tourist centre opposite entrance to caves.
Tours limited to 35 people at a time; waits of an hour or two at busy periods.
€9. Combined ticket (caves, castillo, Museo del Jamón): €12

Museo del Jamón
Calle Gran Vía s/n 663 93 78 70
Mon–Fri 11:15–1:15, 4:15–6:15, Sat, Sun 11:15–1:30, 4:15–6:30. Guided tours 11:30, 12:30, 1:45, 4:30, 5:30, 6:45
€3.50, free audio guide

At Your Leisure

38 Écija

Écija's 13 churches, their baroque towers steepled and domed and gleaming with coloured tiles, have earned the town its nickname "Town of Towers". There is a fine central square, Plaza de España, dotted with palm trees. Écija's remarkable secular buildings include Palacio de Peñaflor, the long elegant curve of its balconied façade painted with colourful frescos, and the interior rich with plasterwork and marble. Palacio de Benamejí houses the small Museo Histórico Municipal, providing excellent background to the town's history, and tourist information.

Écija is dubbed Ciudad de las Torres, the "City of Towers".

211 D3

Tourist Information
Elvira 1 955 90 29 33
www.turismoecija.com

Palacio de Peñaflor
Calle Castellar
Mon 10–1:30, 4:30–6:30, Sat 10–2, 5:30–8, Sun 11–2 €2

Museo Histórico Municipal
Palacio de Benamejí, Plaza de la Constitución 1 June–Sep Tue–Fri 10–2:30, Sat 10–2:30, 8–10, Sun and public hols 10–3, Oct–May Tue–Fri 10–1:30, 4:30–6:30, Sat 10–2, 5:30–8, Sun and public hols 10–3 €3

39 Itálica

The remains of one of the most important cities of the Roman Empire lie 9km (5.5 mi) north of Seville. Itálica was established in 206BC as a military camp after the Romans defeated the Carthaginians. Its military and economic importance soon increased, and it was the birthplace of the emperors Hadrian and Trajan. Only a small section of the once 52ha (128 acre) town has been excavated, but it is still well worth a visit. On view is the amphitheatre that once held 3,000 people, foundations of villas and mosaics, including a magnificent Neptune motif.

210 C3
Avenida de Extramadura 2, Santiponce 955 12 38 47
April–June Tue–Sat 9–9, Sun 8–3; July to mid-Sep Tue–Sun 9–3; mid-Sep to March Tue–Sat 9–6, Sun 9–3
Free with EU passport

Impressive: the evocative ruins of Itálica, the first Roman town in Spain

40 Minas de Riotinto

For almost 5,000 years, iron ore, copper and silver, were mined near the Río Tinto. What remains is a landscape that is so bizarre that even NASA was interested in it because of its similarity to the conditions on Mars. Vivid colours – rust red, emerald green and ochre – stain the slopes and slag heaps. In the late 19th century the mines were sold to British and German banks, who began to excavate on a massive scale. Since 2015, Atalaya Mining from Cyprus has been mining smaller quantities of copper here. The village of Minas de Riotinto is unattractive, but its Museo Minero (Mining Museum) tells a dramatic story through its excellent displays on geology, archaeology and social history. As part of a guided tour, you can go into a tunnel, equipped with helmet and miner's lamp, and walk along a 200m (656ft) long subterranean tunnel. Equally fascinating is the 12km (7.5mi) round trip with the 100-year-old mine train through the eerily beautiful mining landscape.

210 B4

Museo Minero
Parque Minero de Riotinto, Plaza Ernest Lluch ☎ 959 59 00 25
parquemineroderiotinto.es
mid-July to Sep 20 10:30–3, 4–8; Sep 21 to mid-July until 7 Museum: €5. Mining tours: €5–€14. Train trips: €11. Combined ticket: €19

41 Costa de la Luz (Huelva)

Travel a few kilometres southeast of the estuary of the Río Tinto and Río Odiel, with its factories and refineries, and you reach a largely uninhabited coastline and a beach of golden sand that runs for 30km (18.5mi) between the resorts of Mazagón and Matalascañas. The beach, backed by

Real pulling power is needed to move the decorated wagons along during the pilgrimage in El Rocío

pine-covered sand dunes, is accessible from only a few places on the coast road, behind which lies the Parque Nacional de Doñana (p. 166). The most convenient beach access points are at Mazagón and Matalascañas. Both resorts get very busy in summer; Mazagón may be too close to the estuary mouth for some, and at Matalascañas the beach is backed by hotel complexes. 7km (4.5mi) south-east of Mazagón is the Parador de Mazagón where there is public parking above a popular section of beach. Before going to the Parador, it is worth making a little excursion off to the right to see the *Pino centenario*, an impressive 300-year-old pine. About 9km (5.5mi) further down the road there is a roadside car park (Cuesta Maneli) from where you can take a stroll along a boardwalk, through pine and juniper-covered dunes, to the remote Playa Cuesta de Maneli.

210 A3

42 El Rocío

To the first-time visitor, El Rocío, a village on the western edge of Doñana National Park, resembles a Wild West town. Broad and mostly deserted sandy roads traverse the sleepy village with its whitewashed colonial-style houses.

El Rocío is the centre of the Romería del Rocío (p. 205). Each Whitsun, up to half a million *romeros* (pilgrims) from Spain and abroad descend on the town of El Rocío and its about 800 remaining residents to pay boisterous homage to *Nuestra Señora del Rocío* (Our Lady of the Dew), aka *La Blanca Paloma* (The White Dove), whose revered image is kept in El Rocío's enormous white-painted church. Most of the buildings in El Rocío are owned by *hermandades,* brotherhoods of devotees, who often stage minor celebrations.

210 B3

Where to... Stay

Expect to pay per double room per night

€	up to €60
€€	€60–€90
€€€	€90–€140
€€€€	over €140

ARACENA

Finca Valbono €€€

In a nature reserve surrounded by rolling hills, and with a choice of self-contained cabins or hotel rooms, Finca Valbono is the perfect place for a family to stay. You can choose between 21 holiday cottages with self-catering facilities or one of only six hotel rooms. There is a pool, hiking and bridle paths. The restaurant specialises in meat dishes with a few down-to-earth choices for children.

210 B4
Carretera de Carboneras, Km 1
959 12 77 11
www.fincavalbono.com

Los Castaños €€

This elegant hotel is just a few minutes' walk from the caves, and has plenty of shops, restaurants and bars on the door-step. The rooms are modern and spacious with balconies. The best view over Sierra de Aracena is from the dining room.

210 B4 Avenida Huelva 5
959 12 63 00
www.loscastanoshotel.com

CARMONA

Parador de Carmona €€€–€€€€

A stunning clifftop location, with sweeping views across the flat plain of the River Corbones. The public rooms surround a central Moorish-style patio, and the bedrooms are large and luxuriously furnished; all look out either onto the inner courtyard or the valley. If you can't afford a room, have a drink at the bar or check out the excellent restaurant (p. 174).

210 C3 Alcázar s/n
954 14 10 10
www.parador.es

SEVILLA & SURROUNDING AREA

Casual Sevilla Don Juan Tenorio €€

This hotel has an unbeatable location. It is on a small square surrounded by trees in the heart of Barrio de Santa Cruz. All 21 rooms take their theme from the theatre play *Don Juan Tenorio*, which playwright José Zorrilla set here in the 16th century. The rooms are on two storeys, were recently renovated, simply furnished and squeaky clean.

218 C2 Plaza de los Venerables 5
955 54 44 16
www.casualhoteles.com

Hotel Alfonso XIII €€€€

Seriously luxurious at prices to match, this five-storey rococo building was built during the 1929 Expo in the *mudéjar*/Andalucían revival style. Even if you can't afford to stay a night, sip a sherry overlooking the plant-filled central patio, surrounded by antique furniture, hand-painted tiles, crystal chandeliers and acres of marble and mahogany. The rooms are predictably sumptuous and the service professional and efficient.

218 C1
San Fernando 2 954 91 70 00
www.hotel-alfonsoxiii-sevilla.com

Hotel Londres €

This simple but comfortable place is located near the Museo de Bellas Artes and the main shopping district. There are plenty of bars, cafés and restaurants within the vicinity and the cathedral is a mere 10-minute walk away. The rooms here are simple but comfortable and there are some with balconies. Look for the plaque to Manuel Machado (fellow poet and brother of the more famous Antonio) which is across from the door of the hotel.

218 A3 San Pedro Mártir 1, El Arenal 954 21 28 96
www.londreshotel.com

La Cartuja de Cazalla €€

Around 90km (55mi) to the northeast of Seville, the hotel doubles as a Centre for Contemporary Culture. The magnificent stone building is a restored 15th-century

Carthusian monastery set in beautiful grounds. Just right if you are seeking some out-of-town peace. The hotel also rents out a large artists' studio for painting, sculpting and pottery workshops.
218 A3 Carretera Cazalla-Constantina A455, Km 2.5, Cazalla de la Sierra, Seville
684 30 27 18
www.cartujadecazalla.com
Closed 24–26 Dec

Where to... Eat and Drink

Expect to pay for a three-course meal, incl. wine and service

€	up to €15
€€	€15–€40
€€€	over €40

ARACENA

Restaurante Casas €€
There's not much wall space left at this typical Sierra Morena restaurant specialising in the region's famous ham and pork. A mixture of mirrors, plates, religious pictures, and various pots and pans are the backdrop to the cosy beamed dining room. The food represents honest, home-style cooking at its best.
210 B4 Calle del Pozo de la Nieve
959 12 80 44
www.restaurantecasas.es
Daily noon–5

CARMONA

Molino de la Romera €€–€€€
This 15th-century mill has retained much of its original character with ancient cobbled floors, arches and patio. The bar does a brisk evening trade in drinks and tapas for a predominantly student crowd, while the restaurant has a typical Andalucían menu with *gazpacho*, salads and soups, *tortilla*, fried fish, grilled meat and various seafood dishes. For something more formal, there is also a fabulous *mesón* (period-décor restaurant), open at weekends only, located in an evocative, church-like space with its own bar and fireplace.
210 C3 Sor Ángela de la Cruz 8
954 14 20 00
www.molinodelaromera.com
Tue–Sat 1–4, 8–11:30, Sun 1–4. Closed 24 and 31 Dec

Restaurante Parador de Carmona €€€
A former Moorish fortress provides a superb setting, and the dining room with its vaulted ceiling, chandeliers and clifftop views makes this restaurant a winner for special occasions. The menu is select, with an emphasis on game, particularly partridge and venison; the house wine is excellent.
210 C3 Calle Alcázar s/n
954 14 10 10 www.parador.es
1:30–4, 8:30–11. Closed July and 24 Dec

Dine in aristocratic fashion at Parador de Carmona

SEVILLA

Casa Robles €€
Not far from the cathedral, this traditional restaurant specialises in seafood with more than a dozen types of shellfish served daily. Juan Robles conjures up the dishes in the kitchen of his family business, founded with his father in 1954. In the meantime, his daughter Laura Robles is in charge of affairs and is making a name for herself with her desserts that can be placed somewhere between traditional and avant garde.
218 B2 Calle Álvarez Quintero 58
954 21 31 50 www.casa-robles.com
1–4:30, 8–1. Closed 24 Dec for dinner

El Corral del Agua €€
In one of the prettiest situations in the heart of the Barrio de Santa Cruz, this restaurant

is housed in a former 18th-century palace and has a lovely patio filled with brilliant red geraniums. The food here is traditional and reliably good with dishes including filet of Iberian pork with grape sauce or an oxtail house speciality.
218 C2 Callejón del Agua 6
954 22 48 41 www.corraldelagua.es
Closed Sun and Nov 15 to Feb 12

Habanita €€
Habanita, one of Seville's few vegetarian restaurants, is tucked down a side street in the buzzing Alfalfa *barrio*, within easy walking distance north of the city centre. The reasonable prices here attract students and travellers alike and the menu is vast, with an emphasis on Cuban and Mediterranean dishes. There are some real one-offs like yucca with garlic, plus black beans, tamales and strict vegan fare. They also have some lactose-free meals.
218 C3 Calle Golfo 3
606 71 64 56 (mobile) www.habanita.es
Mon–Sat noon–4:30, 8:30 to late

Patio San Eloy €
In this famous bar there's enough tilework for a mini *alcázar*, with *azulejo* steps providing additional seating. Popular with students, shoppers and business people alike, the tapas menu includes a vast range of multi-tiered sandwiches with interesting fillings plus the usual *tortilla* (omelette), *jamón* and olives, best washed down with an ice-cold *fino* direct from the barrel.
218 B3 San Eloy 9e
954 50 10 70 www.patiosaneloy.com
Daily 11:30–11:30

Pizzería San Marco €€
Not your usual fast-food Italian, this one is housed in an authentic Arab Bath, giving it a great atmosphere – rather like sitting inside your own private mosque. The menu has a good range of typical pizza and pasta dishes, and the place is usually packed. Enjoy a glass of house Rioja while you wait at the Bar.
218 C2 Calle Mesón del Moro 6
954 21 43 90 www.sanmarco.es
Tue–Sun 1:30–4:30, 8:30–12:30

Restaurant La Cueva €€
This restaurant is a picture-postcard sort of place, with a charming choice of terraces and patios for dining al fresco. Ochre walls, cobbles and columns complete the look, while the indoor dining room is hung with all the matador paraphernalia – including the bull (his stuffed head, that is). The prices are reasonable, also for the three-course *menú del día*, and the dishes are solidly Andalucían, with a selection of good fish choices and an above-average paella.
218 C2
Rodrigo Caro 18 954 56 29 80
www.restaurantelacueva.eu
Tue–Sat 12:30–3:30, 7:30–11:30

Where to... Shop

The city of Seville encourages chic fashion, but there are top-quality gift and jewellery shops too, as well as shops specialising in ceramics and traditional crafts. Huelva cannot match Seville for general shopping, but you can buy some of the finest jamón serrano and other food products that you'll ever taste.

CARMONA

For excellent pottery look in Taller de Cerámica at María Jurado Pérez (Urb. El Socorro 229 F www.mariajurado.es).

For typical rural goods, visit Carmona's morning market just off Calle Domínguez de Aposanto.

HUELVA PROVINCE

The shopping paradise of Huelva can be found in the multi-storey Centro Comercial Aqualón. You can enjoy a lovely view of the river from the top floor (Glorieta Norte; www.ccaqualon.com). The choice includes a wide range of shops, cinemas, restaurants and bars.

Aracena's La Trastienda de Jabugo (Calle San Pedro 36; tel: 959 12 71 58; latrastiendadejabugo.es) sells all manner of cured and cooked meats, but the widest (though priciest) choice is in the village of Jabugo (p. 188).

Enticing selections of *jamón*, *chorizo* (spicy sausage) and *salchichón* (salami) are all on sale at top outlets such as La Cañada de Jabugo (Carretera San Juan del Puerto-Cáceres 2; tel: 959 12 12 07).

Down on Huelva's Costa de la Luz there are few out-of-the-ordinary shopping options, but the main information centre of the Parque Nacional de Doñana, the Centro de Recepción del Acebuche (p. 167), has a useful gift shop that sells craftwork from the area.

SEVILLA

Seville's main shopping area lies between the bustling Plaza Nueva and adjacent Plaza de San Francisco. Central to it all is the pedestrianised Calle Sierpes, which has a vast range of shops selling clothes, shoes, leather goods, children's wear and ceramics.

For the ultimate in style, Max Mara (Plaza Nueva 3; tel: 954 21 48 25) has up-to-the-minute fashions, as does top Spanish style house Zara (Plaza del Duque de la Victoria; tel: 954 21 48 75).

Purificacion García is known for its minimalistic designs (Plaza Nueva 8; tel: 954 50 11 29). Numerous stores sell brands such as Mango, Blanco, Massimo Dutti, Pull & Bear.

For something quintessentially Spanish, Sierpes has a number of splendid shops selling flamenco scarves and veils, shawls and shoes, including María Rosa (Calle Cuna 13; tel: 954 22 24 87).

Away from Sierpes, try Artesanía Textil (García de Vinuesa; tel: 954 56 28 40; http:/ artesania-textil.com), just west of the cathedral, where you can buy place mats, wall hangings and tablecloths in the finest Andalucían styles.

And check out Sombrería Maquedano (Sierpes 40; tel: 954 56 47 71) for stylish hats and impeccable service.

For jewellery of the highest quality, try Joyería Abrines (Calle Asunción 1; tel: 954 27 42 44; www.abrines.es) and Joyería Casa Ruiz (O'Donnell 14; tel: 954 22 21 37 and Calle Sierpes 68; tel: 954 22 77 80).

Near the north end of Sierpes is a branch of the department store El Corte Inglés (Plaza del Duque de la Victoria).

For something less mainstream, have a look round the jewellery and clothes market, staged Wed–Sat in Plaza del Duque de la Victoria itself.

La Campaña (tel: 954 22 35 70), at the north end of Calle Sierpes, has a superb selection of cakes and pastries. Other good shopping areas include the narrow Calle Hernando

The Calle Sierpes in Seville is a shopping paradise

Colón that leads from Alemanes, opposite the main entrance to the cathedral, to Plaza de San Francisco, and is packed with gift, clothes and souvenir shops.

In Barrio de Santa Cruz (p. 159), in with the souvenir shops are some classy shops. One such is Aqua Ispal (Rodrigo Caro 16; www.aquaispal.es), a very stylish perfumery and accessories shop near the Reales Alcázares (p. 157).

For ceramics try Martian Ceramics (Calle Sierpes 74; tel: 954 21 34 13), El Postigo (Arfe; tel: 954 56 00 13), Cerámica Nazaret (Feria 15), or across the river in the Triana district, Azulejos Santa Isabel (Alfarería 12; tel: 954 33 36 18).

Where to... Go Out

Seville's monthly listings magazine *El Giraldillo* (www.elegirhoy.com) can be bought at kiosks, or is sometimes available free at tourist offices.

NIGHTLIFE

There are plenty of music bars in Seville's Plaza de la Alfalfa area, a few streets east of Calle Sierpes. On the west bank of the Río Guadalquivir is Calle del Betis where there are a number of lively music bars fronting the Triana district.

FLAMENCO

Seville is big on flamenco and there are any number of "spontaneous" venues.

There are also some fairly phoney shows; to be recommended is El Arenal (Calle Rodo 7; tel: 954 21 64 92; http://tablaoelarenal.com), a long-established venue with twice-nightly *tablaos* (p. 26) and optional dinner.

At the heart of the Barrio de Santa Cruz (p. 159) are Los Gallos (Plaza de Santa Cruz 11; tel: 954 21 69 81; www.tablaolosgallos.com) and El Tamboril (Plaza de Santa Cruz).

The popular La Carbonería (Calle Céspedes 18; tel: 954 22 99 45) often has flamenco on Thursday and Monday nights, and at other times, but rarely before 10pm.

THEATRE

Seville's Teatro de la Maestranza (Paseo de Cristóbal Colón 22; tel: 954 22 33 44; www.teatrodelamaestranza.es), near the bullring, stages outstanding productions of opera, classical music and jazz.

Teatro Lope de Vega (Avenida María Luisa; tel: 954 47 28 28; http://teatrolopedevega.org) also puts on a programme of theatre, music and dance.

BULLFIGHTING

At Seville's magnificent 18th-century bullring, La Maestranza (Paseo de Cristóbal Colón; tel: 954 22 45 77; www.realmaestranza.com), top *corridas* are always packed out, and to get a ticket, even for the sunny side, you need to book well ahead. The season runs from Easter Sunday to October, with big names fighting during June and July and novices taking up the rest of the calendar. Fights are on Sunday evenings and on every evening during the *Feria de Abril* (p. 205). It is always best to try to buy tickets directly from the box office at the ring or online.

OUTDOOR ACTIVITIES

The Aracena area of the Sierra de Aracena has numerous opportunities for walking and it's worth checking at Aracena's tourist office (www.turismosierra dearacena.com) for information on guided walks and cycle trips. They can usually provide maps of the trails.

On Huelva's Costa de la Luz (p. 171) there are opportunities within Coto de Doñana National Park (p. 166) for more intensive birdwatching trips. You can also take part in a car tour of the park (contact the Centro de Recepción del Acebuche or Doñana Reservas, El Rocío; tel: 959 44 24 74, www.donanareservas.com).

Equestrian fans can even birdwatch from horseback on day-long rides through the Doñana marshland (contact Doñana Ecuestre, El Rocío; tel: 674 21 95 68, www.donanaacaballo.com). Don't forget the insect repellent!

Wild and romantic: The gorges and rugged crags of Sierra de Grazalema make it an exciting place to go hiking

Walks & Tours

Villages in spectacular land-scapes, and the enchanting legacy of the Moors – you'll learn a lot about Andalucía on these excursions.

Pages 178–189

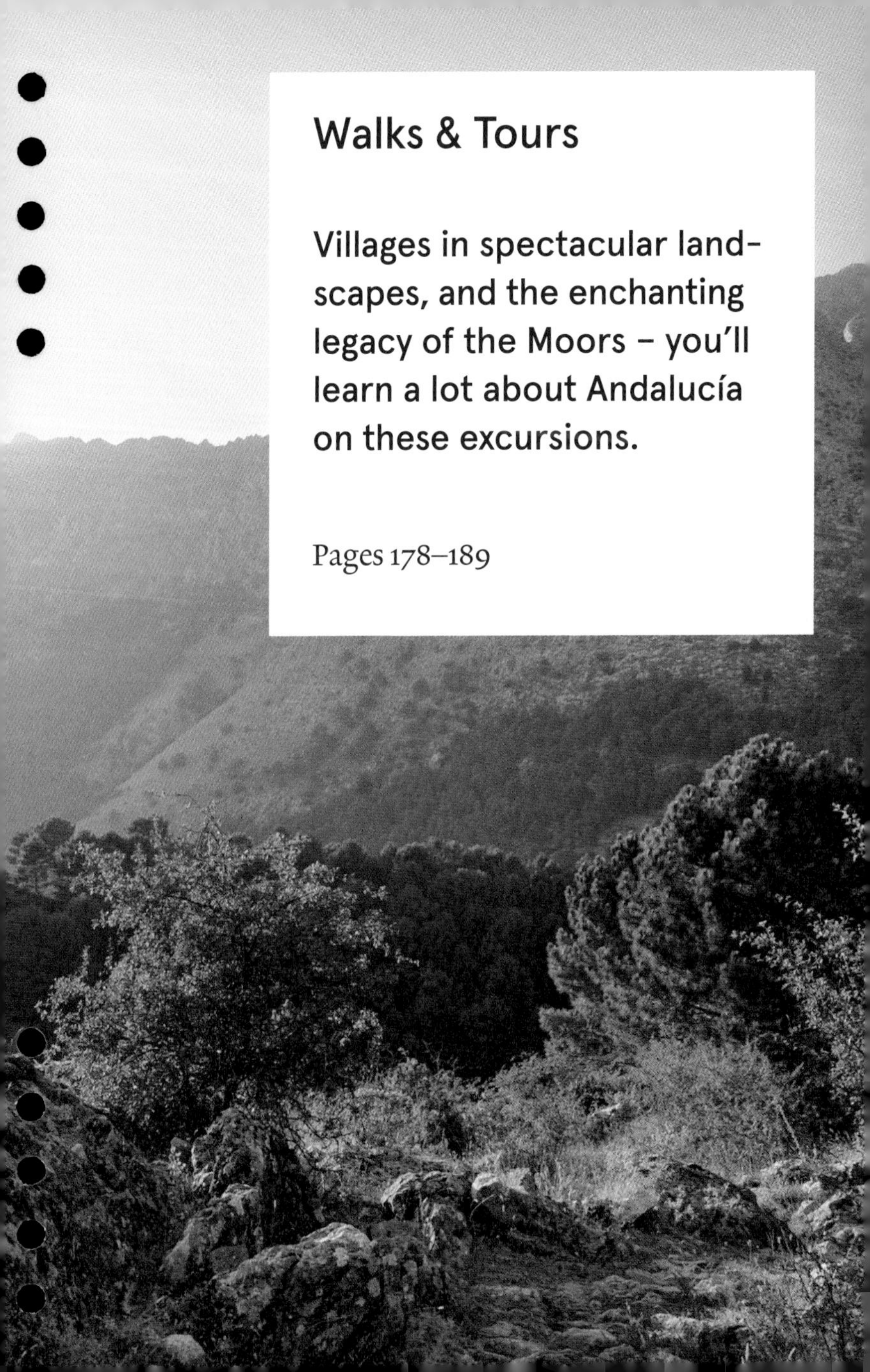

Granada's Albaicín

What	Walk in an old Moorish quarter
When	Late morning: The morning sun is not too hot and there is a lot going on – or otherwise in the evening
Distance	3km (2mi)
Time	2–3 hours
Start/End	Plaza Nueva ➔ 216 C2

Granada's picturesque old Moorish quarter, the Albaicín, is explored on this circular walk that offers stunning views of the Alhambra and the Sierra Nevada on the way.

1–2

From Plaza Nueva walk through Plaza Santa Ana past a church, the Iglesia de Santa Ana y San Gil, and along Carrera del Darro. Down on your right the minuscule Río Darro filters its way. As you walk along the street you pass first the Moorish bridge, the Puente de Cabrera, and then the Puente de Espinosa. On the opposite bank are the ruins of an 11th-century gateway, the Puerta de los Tableros, and of a bridge, the Puente del Cadí. Look left for the alleyway called Bañuelo with, just left of the entrance, the 11th-century Arab baths, El Bañuelo.

2–2

Continue along Carrera del Darro, passing the Convento de Santa Catalina de Zafra where you can buy delicious almond cakes from the nuns, and the Museo Arqueológico (p. 88) on your left. Keep on past the wide terrace of Paseo del Padre Manjón, known also as Paseo de los Tristes because priests once publicly prayed here; today it is crammed with café tables served from the long line of bars along the street front. The Alhambra towers above.

3–4

Just past the Café Bar La Fuente, turn left up narrow Calle Horno del Oro. Go up steps at the top of the alley, then turn right up some more steps. Cross a lane and continue up Calle Valenzuela. At its top go up more steps to the left. At the next

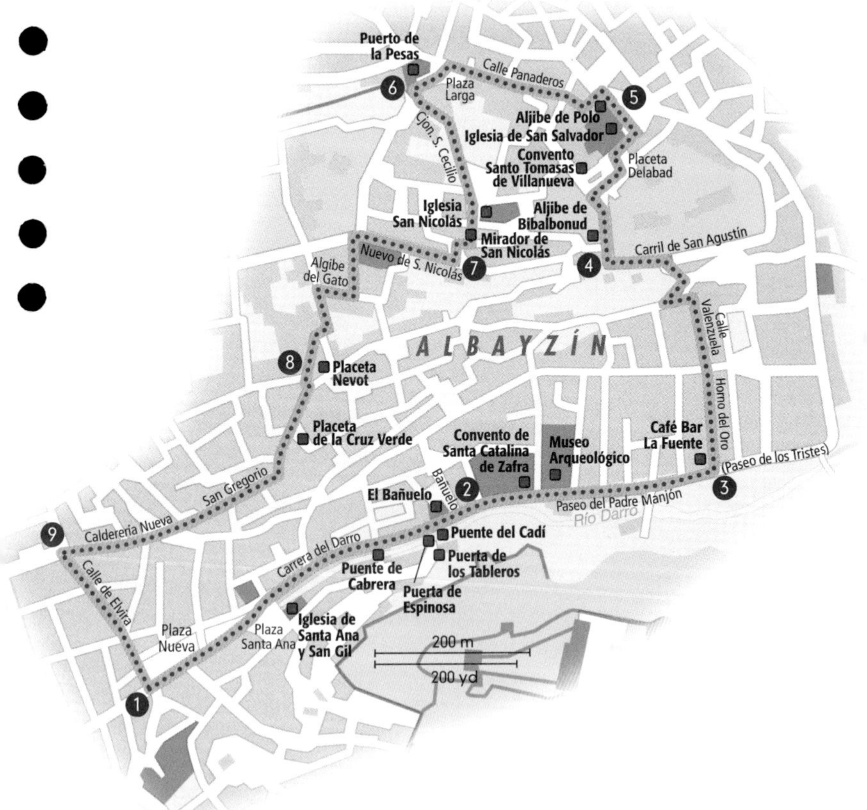

opportunity turn off sharply right and then immediately afterwards sharply left through Carril de San Agustín and at the top left again. There are fine views of the Alhambra to your left.

4–5

Follow the lane round to the right. Pass the Convento Santo Tomás de Villanueva (Tomasas) into Carril de las Tomasas. Pass the Aljibe de Bibalbonud, a brick-built Moorish well, and go alongside the wall of the church of San Salvador. The church was built on the site of the former mosque.

5–6

Leave the church and turn left, and then left again into Calle Panaderos. Pass another old well, the Aljibe de Polo, and

continue past small local shops and characterful bars to reach Plaza Larga. Cross the plaza to its opposite corner and go under the Puerta de la Pesas, an arched gateway in the old walls of the Alcazaba Vieja.

It doesn't matter what time of day it is: The view from Albaicín on Granada is fantastic

6–7

Beyond the arch, climb some steps into Placeta de las Minas, turn left along Callejón San Cecilio and follow the lane round right to reach Plaza del Cementerio de San Nicolás and th Iglesia San Nicolás. To the right of the church is a Moorish cistern. Immediately in front of the church is the Mirador de San Nicolás, Granada's most famous viewpoint.

7–8

Go down the steps right-hand side of the Mirador, keep downhill, then go right along Camino Nuevo de San Nicolás. Follow this towards the right and turn left onto narrow Cuesta María de la Miel, then at a T-junction turn right along Algibe del Gato. In a few metres, go down left and then round right and into Placeta Nevot. On the right-hand side of the square is an Arabic-style building with a fine arched doorway.

8–9

Keep going downhill and on through Placeta de la Cruz Verde (from where you'll get a fleeting glimpse of the Alhambra). Continue down San Gregorio, then along Calderería Nueva passing Granada's "Arab quarter". At the T-junction with Calle de Elvira, turn left to return to Plaza Nueva.

INSIDER TIP Take a breather on the Plaza del Cementerio de San Nicolás in **Café-Bar-Restaurante Kiki** (Plaza Cementerio de San Nicolás 9; tel: 958 27 67 15; Thu–Tue noon–5).

Convento de Santa Catalina de Zafra
Mass: Mon–Sat 1, Sun 9

Iglesia de San Salvador
Mon–Sat 11:30–1, 5–6:30

Sierra de Grazalema

What	Car tour to the *Pueblos Blancos* through magnificent countryside
When	At any time, although the nicest time is when the griffon vultures are nesting, because the drive can be wonderfully combined with a walk through the Garganta Verde.
Distance	80km (50mi)
Time	4–5 hours
Start/End	Grazalema → 211 D2

The *Pueblos Blancos*, the "white towns" of Málaga and Cádiz provinces, are in reality small mountain villages of white-washed houses set amid the spectacular mountains of the Parque Natural Sierra de Grazalema. This tour takes you to some of the finest.

1–2

Leave Grazalema, sheltering beneath the rocky peak of Peñón Grande, by the Ronda road. The road winds uphill beneath huge overhanging cliffs. At a junction, keep ahead along the A374, signed Ubrique. Follow the road beneath the impressive rocky crags of the Sierra del Caillo and pass Villaluenga del Rosario, the highest village in Cádiz province.

2–3

Continue through the valley known as La Manga (The Sleeve) where rocky slopes rise to either side and stone walls wriggle along the base of the cliffs. Soon, the road bends sharply to the right just after a picnic spot and viewpoint. In about 1km (0.5mi) turn off right at a junction, signed Benaocaz, and enter the village. The village, an 8th-century Moorish settlement, is a typical *pueblo blanco*. Encircling the main square, Plaza de las Libertades, are pillars with small ceramic tiles picturing local landmarks.

3–4

Continue to follow the local bypass (A-374) towards Ubrique. After about 7km (4mi), you will see Ubrique down to the left

below the knife-edged crag of the Cruz de Tajo. From here, take the A373 towards El Bosque.

4–5

Watch for signposts for El Bosque and for a junction on the right, signed Benamahoma and Grazalema. Bear right here, then keep right at the next junction on to the A372, signed Benamahoma, Ronda and Grazalema. The road now climbs towards the Sierra del Pinar, passing above Benamahoma, another attractive *Pueblo Blanco*. It celebrates its Moorish heritage with a colourful festival that includes mock battles between "Moors and Christians" on the first Sunday of August. Continue along the A372 with views of limestone crags on your right. In 8km (5mi) turn left, signed Zahara de la Sierra.

5–6

You now enter a beautiful area of mountains swathed in cork oak and holm oak and large numbers of pinsapo pines, a conifer that has had a tenuous continuity since the last European Ice Age but which now flourishes in the Parque Natural Sierra de Grazalema. The road climbs steadily through a spectacular series of S-bends to reach the Puerto de Palomas (Pass of the Doves) at 1,357m (4,452ft), from where it descends through more S-bends. About 5km (3mi) below the pass, there is a car park on the left from where a path leads to the spectacular Garganta Verde ravine. This breathtaking path, on which if you are lucky you will also spot some griffon vultures, can only be used if you have the necessary permit, available from the visitor centre. Dogs are not allowed in this area. Continue towards Zahara de la Sierra and you will soon pass an olive oil production centre, El Vínculo – Molino de Aceite Alojamiento Rural, which is open for visits during normal working hours (p. 69).

6–7

There are parking spaces just before you reach the narrow entrance to Zahara de la Sierra and it is advisable to park here. Zahara is one of the loveliest of the *Pueblos Blancos*. The village clings to a rocky hill crowned by a 12th-century castle. Its narrow main street leads to a central plaza overlooked by the baroque church of Santa María de Mesa and with a *mirador* giving fine views of the reservoir, the Embalse de Zahara, below. The castle is reached from the square by a rocky path; the views from its battlements are well worth the effort.

The easiest way to reach the road above the reservoir is to leave the car park at the village entrance and drive back towards the El Vínculo olive oil production centre but turn off left just before at the junction towards Algodonales. Then follow the signposts twice to the right towards Arroyo Molinos and drive onto the A2300 alongside the reservoir.

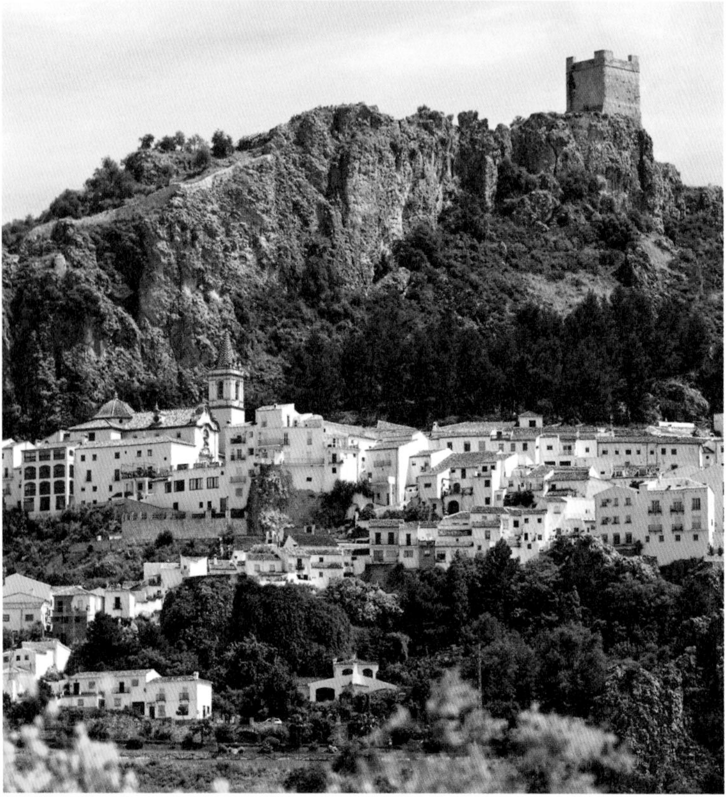

The Moorish castle dominates the village of Zahara de la Sierra

At the end of the lake a sign indicates "Grazalema 10km" bringing you back onto the road you started out on.

INSIDER TIP At Benaocaz, the **Restaurante Nazarí** (Calle Lavadero 12; tel: tel: 653 27 53 20), is the place for quality local dishes in an atmospheric setting. At Zahara de la Sierra, the restaurant **El Rincón de la Ermita** (Calle San Juan 14; tel: 956 12 32 16) offers a good selection of Spanish dishes.

Visitor Centre, El Bosque
Federico García Lorca, 1, El Bosque ☎ 956 70 97 33
cvelbosque@reservatuvisita.es

It is best to send a mail or phone to obtain access permits to Garganta Verde.

Sierra de Aracena

What	A drive through a whole different world
When	Preferably in summer
Distance	60km (37mi)
Time	2–3 hours (longer if stops are made at villages and points of interest along the way)
Start/End	Aracena → 210 B4

The Sierra de Aracena is a world of wooded hills traversed by roads that wind lazily between delightful villages where cobbled streets spill down to a central plaza, its fountain brimming with crystal-clear water even in high summer.

1–2

Leave Aracena by Plaza San Pedro, just beyond the car park, and take the road leading south west, signed Alájar. Drive down an avenue lined with plane trees. Keep ahead at the next junction, signed Alájar, and immediately enter the beautiful hill country of the Sierra de la Virgen. You need old-fashioned driving skills here: the HU8105, twists and turns through woods of chestnut, ash and oak. Soon you catch glimpses of the tiny village of Linares de la Sierra, in the valley below.

The village is worth a short diversion. Park on the road above Linares and stroll downhill to the main square; every household has an individual mosaic of pebbles, like a stone doormat, outside its door.

2–3

Continue along the HU8105 to reach a turn-off on the left that descends to the larger village of Alájar. Above is the rocky outcrop of Peña de Arias Montano, with caverns said to have served as human shelters from prehistoric times (before the village, follow the road sign to the right!). Located below is the Ermita de Nuestra Señora de los Ángeles. This was the retreat of 16th-century cleric and scholar Benito Arias Montano. He was confessor to Philip II, who visited the hermitage and meditated in a nearby cave (below the modern car park). A large rock beside the cave has been known ever since as the King's Chair.

3–4

Back on the HU8105, carry on to a junction with the Huelva road, the N435. Opposite is the Hostal el Cruce, which has a good tapas bar. Continue through wooded country towards on HU8105 to Almonaster. A detour just before the village takes you up to the right along a side road with a gravel surface through a series of hairpin bends to reach 912m (2,992ft) high Mirador del Cerro San Cristóbal. There are two viewpoints on the summit: one overlooks Almonaster from below a thicket of radio transmitters; the other is reached along a track that leads off from near the road end and offers tremendous views to the west across the Sierra Pelada and to the northeast, the Picos de Aroche.

Back on HU-8105 you will immediately reach Almonaster on the right. Here you will find a beautiful 10th-century mosque, built partly into a rock face. It has little horseshoe arches in brick, supported by what are probably Roman and Visigothic columns, recalling, in miniature, the arches of Córdoba's Mezquita. From the adjoining minaret tower you can look down into the bullring. To view the inside of the mosque, ask for the key at the town hall in the village square.

4–5

Continue from Almonaster on the HU8105 for about 5km (3mi). At the junction with the main N433, the Portugal–Seville road, turn right to Aracena and Sevilla. In about 7km (4.5mi) turn off for Jabugo.

Everything is green and flowering: Spring in the Sierra de Aracena

5–6

The otherwise quiet little village of Jabugo is the centre of the *jamón* (ham) curing industry. On reaching the first buildings, turn right, signed Centro Urbano, into a quiet, cobbled street where you have a fair chance of parking. Walk up

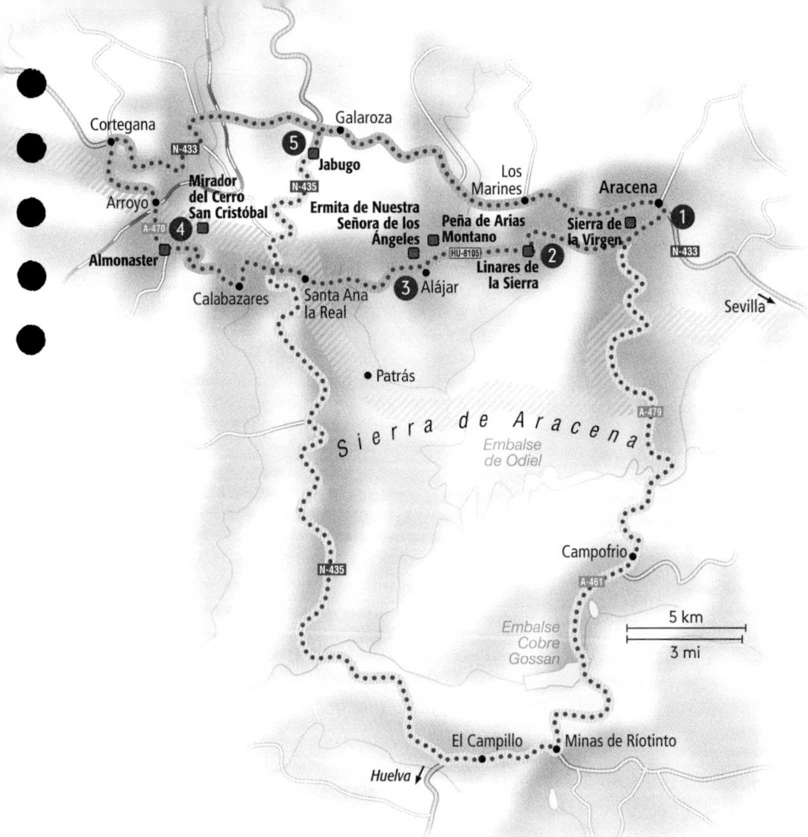

the street and keep left at a junction, then go immediately left and up Calle Silencio, a road lined with shops selling *jamón* and other meats.

From Jabugo return to the N433 and turn right to reach Aracena. The drive can be extended to take in a visit to dramatic landscapes of the Río Tinto mining area. This adds 60km (37mi) to the main drive. To do this leave Jabugo by its southern exit and take the N435 and the A461 to Minas de Ríotinto and after the visit continue to Aracena (A461 and A479).

INSIDER TIP The bars and cafés in Jabugo offer snacks and meals featuring local *jamón*. But, be warned: the often high prices may spoil your appetite.

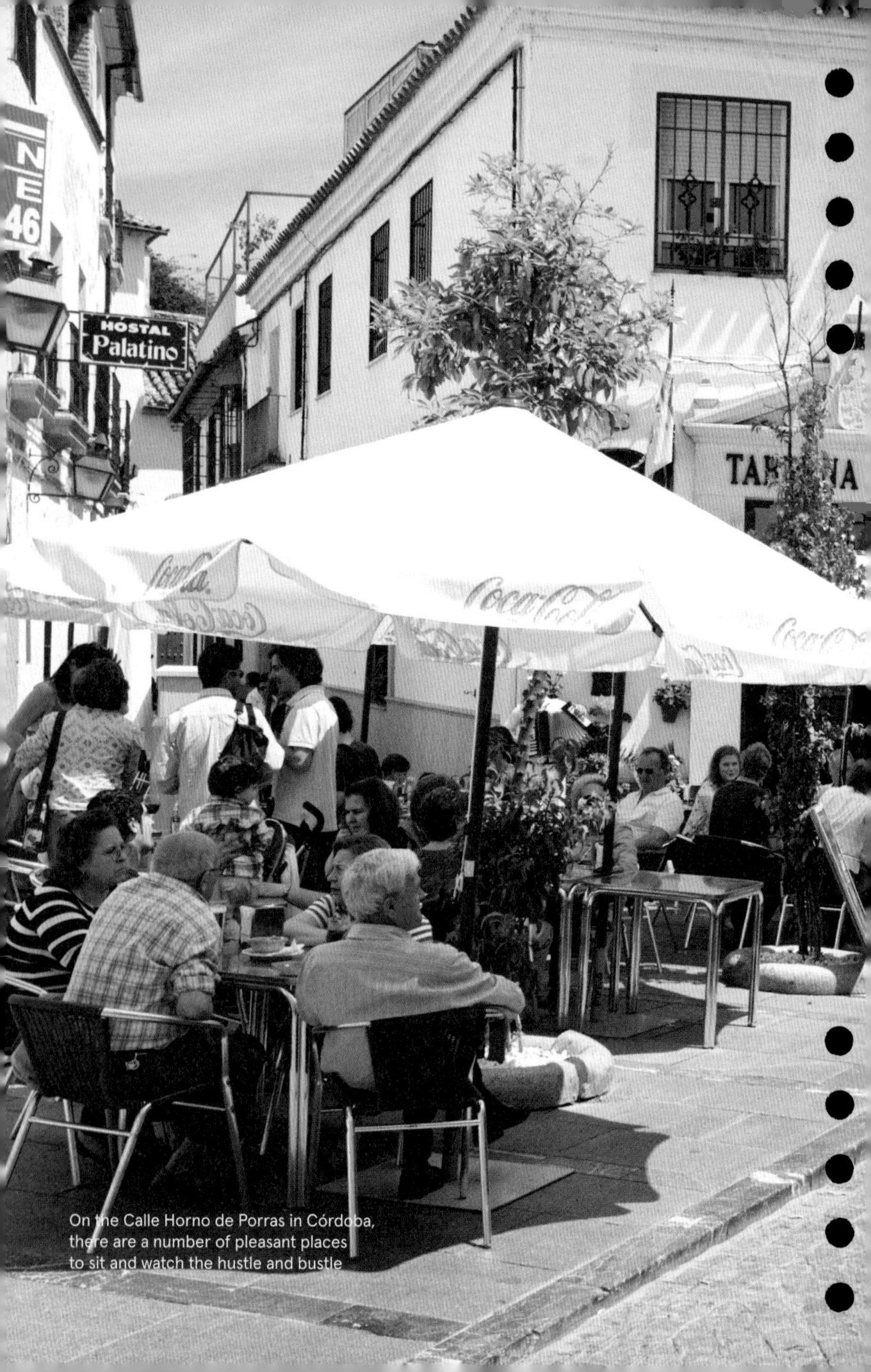

On the Calle Horno de Porras in Córdoba, there are a number of pleasant places to sit and watch the hustle and bustle

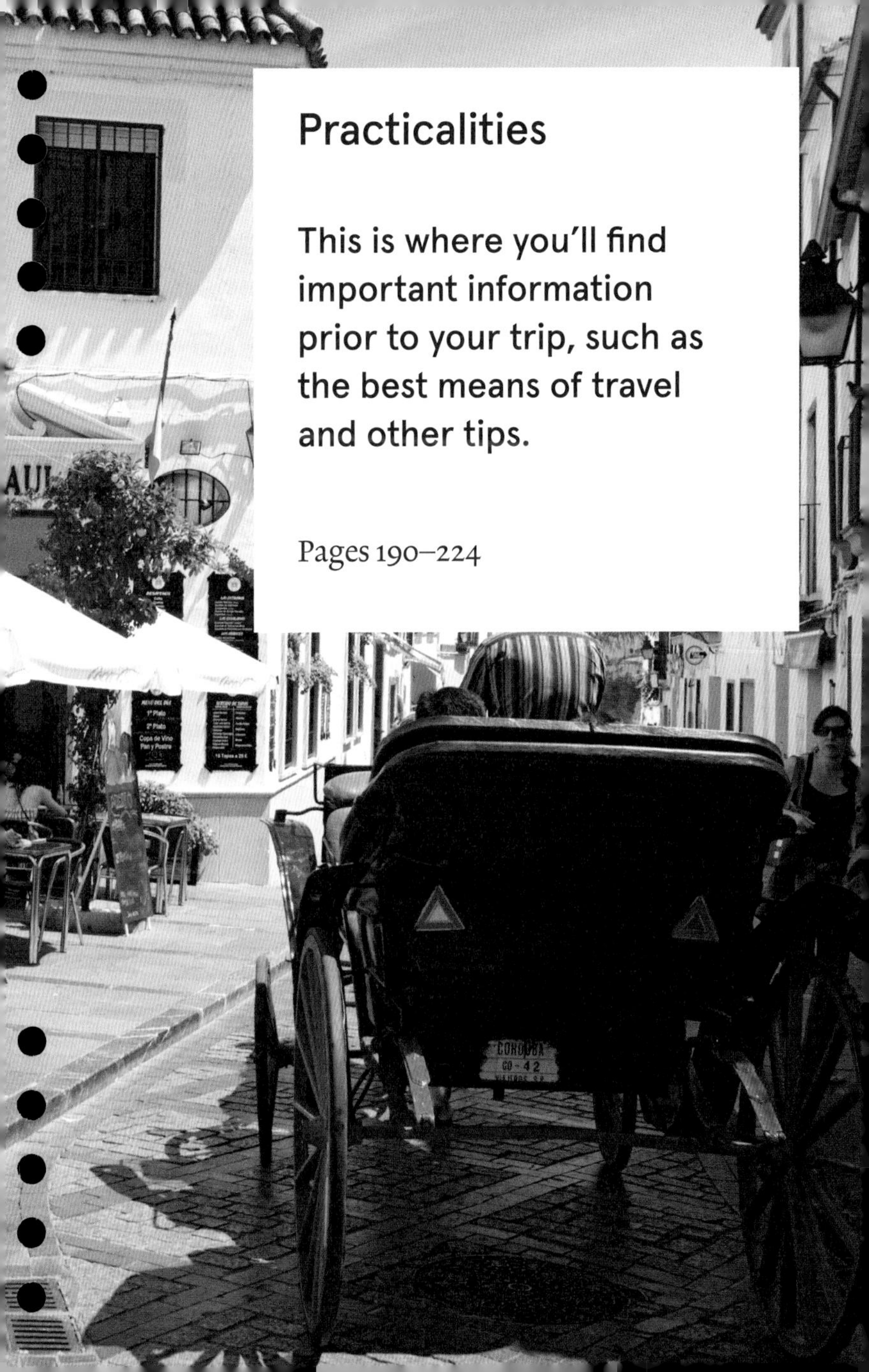

Practicalities

This is where you'll find important information prior to your trip, such as the best means of travel and other tips.

Pages 190–224

BEFORE YOU GO

Advance Information

Spanish Tourist Offices
In the UK
1st Floor, 100 George Street, W1U 8NU London
tel: +44 020 73 17 20 11
www.spain.info/en_GB

In Ireland
Callaghan House, 13-16 Dame Street
D02 HX67 Dublin
tel: +353 016 350 200
www.spain.info/en

In Canada
2 Bloor Street West, Suite 3402
M4W 3E2 Toronto-Ontario
tel: 001-416-961-4079
www.spain.info/en

In the U.S.
60 East 42nd Street, Suite 5300 (53rd Floor)
New York, NY 10165-0039
tel: 001-212-265-8822
www.spain.info/en_US/

Consulates and Embassies
British Consulate Málaga
Calle Mauricío Moro Pareto 2,
Edificio Eurocom
29006 Málaga, Spain
tel: 0034 952 352 300

Office of the Governor, Gibraltar
The Convent, Main Street, GX111AA, Gibraltar
tel: 00350 200 45440
www.gov.uk/world

Consulate of Ireland, Málaga
Galerias Santa Monica,
Avenida Los Boliches, 15
29640 Fuengirola, Málaga, Spain
tel: 0034 952 475 108
www.dfa.ie/irish-embassy/spain

U. S. Consulate
Calle de Serrano, 75
28006 Madrid, Spain
tel: 0034 915 872 200
https://es.usembassy.gov

Canadian Embassy
Torre Espacio, Paseo de la Castellana, 259D
28046 Madrid, Spain
tel: 0034 913 828 400
www.canadainternational.gc.ca/spain-espagne/

Embassy of Australia
Torre Espacio, Paseo de la Castellana, 259D
28046 Madrid, Spain
tel: 0034 913 536 600
https://spain.embassy.gov.au

Concessions
Holders of an International **Student** Identity Card (ISIC) can get some concessions on entrance fees.
Children and Senior Citizens over 65 pay less or even sometimes nothing at all for admission tickets. Children under four can travel free-of-charge on Spanish trains and, from the age of four till eleven, children only pay 60% of the normal fare. Seniors over 60 and students can also purchase discounted tickets.
Many museums and tourist sights offer **free admission** on certain days in the week; find out which days they are when you are there! In many cases, admission is free for EU citizens but a symbolic price of €1.50 for everyone else.

Currency & Foreign Exchange
Spain has adopted the **euro**. Notes are in denominations of 5, 10, 20, 50, 100, 200, 500; coins come in 1, 2, 5, 10, 20 and 50 cents and 1 and 2 euros.
Credit cards, exchange: Most hotels and businesses will accept the major credit cards (VISA, MasterCard and Diners Club), and this cashless payment is also quite common for smaller sums. It is rare for there to be a minimum, amount. Generally, all that is needed is the PIN number; very occasionally some form of identification (a passport or ID card) is requested.
Travellers cheques can be cashed in banks or at main post offices for a fee, but you have to show a passport.
There are **ATMs** in many small villages, although there can very occasionally be

a problem when using foreign cards to withdraw cash or pay for something. It is thus always advisable to have some cash with you if you are going on an excursion to areas that are a bit more remote.

Customs

The import of wildlife souvenirs from rare and endangered species may be either illegal or require a special permit. Before purchase you should check customs regulations.

The movement of goods for private purposes is largely duty free within the European Union (EU). Maximums do apply, however: e.g. 800 cigarettes, 10 litres (330oz) of spirits. Souvenirs up to a combined value of €430 (travelling by plane) or €300 (travelling by car, bus or rail) are also duty free.

Electricity

The power supply is 220–240 volts. Sockets take standard continental-style plugs with two round pins. Visitors from the UK require an adaptor (often available at the airport). Visitors from the USA will require a voltage transformer.

Health

Insurance: Citizens of EU countries receive reduced-cost emergency health care with relevant documentation (**EHIC**, European Health Insurance Card). Private doctors and clinics do not accept the EHIC; you will have to pay for any treatment yourself, unless you have additional insurance to cover such occurrences.

Where to go in case of illness?: In such cases, contact a state health centre (*Centro de Salud*). These can be found in most larger towns; they often have a 24-hour emergency service. In smaller places there are, if anything, only *consultorios*, little doctors' practices which are only occupied for a few days and hours in the week. Most bigger towns have one or more hospitals.

Travelling With A Disability: Facilities in Andalucía for travellers with disabilities are improving as more hotels install ramps, special lifts and toilets, etc. For information and advice contact RADAR (tel: 020 7250 3222, www.radar.org.uk).

Dental treatment normally has to be paid for in full as dentists operate privately. A list of *dentistas* can be found in the yellow pages of the telephone directory. Dental treatment should be covered by private medical insurance.

Pharmacies: If you are suffering from a slight indisposition, you can – before deciding to find a doctor – try a local pharmacy (*farmacia*, distinguished by a large green cross) first. In general, the pharmacists are very competent and helpful and can provide you with the medication you need. Many medicines that are prescription drugs in other countries are freely available from the pharmacy in Spain.

Safe Water: Tap water is generally safe to drink. Mineral water (*agua mineral*) is cheap and widely available. It is sold *sin gas* (still) and *con gas* (carbonated).

Sun and safety: The sunniest (and hottest) months are July and August, when daytime temperatures are often into the 40s, and around Seville at times even over 40°C (104°F). Try to avoid the midday sun, use a high-factor sun cream during most months, and get used to the sun gradually.

National Holidays

People celebrate a lot in Andalucía. Each year, the towns and villages all pay homage to their patron saint with a big *fiesta*, and there are other smaller celebrations and national public holidays:

1 Jan	*Año Nuevo* – New Year's Day
6 Jan	*Epifanía del Señor*, better known as *Día de los Reyes* – Epiphany
28 Feb	Andalucían Day (regional)
Mar/Apr	*Semana Santa* – Easter
1 May	*Fiesta del Trabajo* – Labour Day
15 Aug	*Asunción de la Virgen* – Assumption of the Virgin
12 Oct	*Fiesta Nacional de España* – Hispanic Day
1 Nov	*Todos los Santos* – All Saints' Day
6 Dec	*Día de la Constitución Española* – Constitution Day
8 Dec	*Inmaculada Concepción* – Feast of the Immaculate Conception
25 Dec	*Navidad* – Christmas Day

Personal Safety

Spain is one of the safest holiday destinations in Europe; that also applies to Andalucía. However, here especially in the big tourist centres, tricksters and pickpockets ply their trades; at the blink of an eyelid, they make your bag, camera or unattended luggage disappear or break into a car.

You should report every incident to the police. The first contact points are the three types of police that there are in Spain: the ***Policía Local*** (the local police, blue and neon green uniforms, mainly based in the town halls), the ***Policía Nacional*** (blue uniforms; these police stations are generally only to be found in bigger towns, tel: 091) or the ***Guardia Civil*** (green uniforms; also responsible for traffic violations, tel: 062 or 112).

The national police and *Guardia Civil* also have an "**ALERTCOPS**" app for your smartphone. This app, which is free of charge, can be installed in Spanish or English. In emergencies (theft, assaults, sexual violence), you can make direct contact with the police. Information is available at: https://alertcops.ses.mir.es.

You can avoid a lot of the trouble by taking simple **precautions**: Do not leave any valuables on the beach, by the pool or in a parked car. Put your valuables in the hotel safe, including your cheque and credit cards when you don't need them. Make sure you know and have the numbers you need to get your mobile phone or credit cards blocked, should this be necessary. Don't carry your camera or handbag over your shoulder but preferably across your chest like a satchel. Don't be too trusting of people you don't know, and avoid lonely and dodgy areas at night.

Staying in Touch

Post

Smaller post offices *(correos)* are generally open 8:30–2:30 (Sat 9:30–1). The main post offices in the provincial capitals are open from 8:30–8:30. At www.correos.es (also in English), you can locate the nearest post office, including details about the opening times. It is expensive to send packages abroad from Spain; it costs around €33 for anything over 2kg, and for anything up to 2kg there is the new *Paquete Internacional light* for around €20. Stamps (*sellos*) can also be bought at tobacconists (*estancos*).

Telephones

All telephone numbers throughout Spain now consist of nine digits, and no matter where you call from, you must always dial all nine digits. Fixed connections begin with the number 9 or 8, mobile phones with 6, in future also 7. Free service numbers start with 800 or 900, and when they incur costs for the person calling with 901 or 902.

Many **public telephones** (*teléfono*) take **phone cards** (*credifone*), which are available from post offices and some shops for €6 or €12.

International Dialling Codes

dial 00 followed by:

UK:	44
Ireland:	353
USA/Canada:	1
Australia	61
Spain	34

Mobile/cell phones (móvil):

The network coverage and G4 reception is good almost everywhere. It is only in very remote and/or mountainous areas that the reception is restricted or even non-existent.

Internet Access

Most restaurants, bars and hotels offer WLAN access (*zona WiFi*), as do many museums or other sights. The service is generally free of charge, but you occasionally have to ask for the password (*clave, contraseña*). Some public places also have *zonas WiFi*.

Emergency Numbers

For all kinds of emergency, the emergency number is ☎ 112
In tourist areas, the operator can also take the call in English.

Time

Spain is one hour ahead of Greenwich Mean Time (GMT +1), but from late March until the last Sunday in September, summer time (GMT+2) operates.

Travel Documents

Travellers need a passport. National driving licences and motor vehicle registration certificates are recognised. Dogs and cats travelling from the EU need an EU Pet Passport as well as a microchip with their identification number. At least 30 days need to have passed since the rabies vaccination, and not more than a year.

If your pet is travelling from outside the EU, for example USA, Canada, or Australia, the same rules apply as above, and a licensed vet must also complete a non-commercial EU health certificate for Spain within ten days of your travel date.

When travelling with your own car, you need a valid driving licence, the vehicle's registration certificate and proof of your third party liability insurance.

When to Go

Andalucía is essentially an all-year-round destination, whereby the best time to go there is during the period between autumn and spring. The summer has various disadvantages: in July and August in particular, it can be extremely hot. The areas around Seville and Córdoba have some of the highest temperatures on the Iberian Peninsula, in Montoro (Córdoba province) a temperature of 47,3°C (117°F) was measured in July 2018. In Seville, the café terraces had to be cooled down with a fine water spray. What is more, August is the month the Spanish traditionally go on holiday: hotels restaurants and sights are crammed packed and the risk of accidents on the road increases. At Easter, it is usually sunny but not yet hot. However, about half of Spain uses the ***Semana Santa*** for a short holiday. For this reason, many areas are fully booked a long time in advance.

The summer months (from about June to September) and the Easter week are the **high season** (*temporada alta*), and this is reflected in the higher prices.

The best time to visit is in May and early June when there is plenty of sunshine, and the average daytime temperature is 23 to 25°C (73–77°F). Visitor levels are not too high and there is a choice of accommodation. Prices in the **mid and low season** (*temoprada media* bzw. *baja*) are generally lower. September and October can be delightful, with the sunny weather lingering well into autumn. **Winter** temperatures on the coast and in low-lying regions are pleasant, but in the mountains expect chilly to very cold weather. Winter can also bring heavy rain and high winds

GETTING THERE

Arriving by Air

From the UK There are inexpensive flights to Málaga-Costa del Sol Airport with easyJet from i.a. Bristol, Stansted, Liverpool and Glasgow; Ryanair from Bournemouth, Glasgow and Southend-on-Sea and with Jet2 from Leeds, Newcastle, Blackpool and Manchester. EasyJet also flies to Gibraltar from Gatwick and Manchester. Scheduled flights to Málaga, Seville and Gibraltar are available with BA from Heathrow and Gatwick, and to Málaga and Seville with Iberia from Heathrow. Iberia flies from Heathrow to Madrid for connections to Almería, Granada and Jerez de la Frontera. Charter flights from the UK to Málaga, Almería, Seville and Jerez de la Frontera often have spare seats. Information regarding all Spanish airports is available at www.aena.es or at: 902 404 704.

From Dublin and Belfast Aer Lingus has direct flights from Dublin and Belfast to Málaga, while easyJet has cheap flights from Belfast to Málaga.

From Australia, New Zealand, America and Canada There are no direct flights, but national carriers from all four countries fly to Madrid and Barcelona where connections can be made.

Airports

Information regarding all Spanish airports is available at www.aena.es or by calling tel: 902 40 47 04.

Málaga-Costa del Sol International Airport

The airport, 12km (7.5mi) south of Málaga city, is the main point of entry for most visitors.

An **electric train service** (Línea C-1) between Málaga city and Fuengirola connects with the airport (terminal T3), Torremolinos and Benalmádena. The way to the station is signposted. Tickets are obtained from a machine by the end of the footbridge. You will pay more if you buy your ticket on the train. Trains to Málaga city run from 7am, then on the half hour until midnight; journey time: 12 minutes.
Bus service: Línea A Exprés runs between the airport and Málaga city every 30 minutes, 7am–midnight. Journey time is about 15 minutes (€3). The end destination in the town centre is Plaza del General Torrijos.
A **taxi** to Málaga city costs about €18–€30; to Marbella up to €60. Licensed taxis (white) line up outside the airport exit.
When leaving the airport **by car**, follow signs "San Julián/N 340 Málaga". At the next roundabout the blue signpost directs you to the MA-21 motorway towards Málaga. Depending on the traffic, you will reach the town centre, harbour in around 30 minutes.

Seville Airport
The airport lies about 12km (7.5 mi) northeast of Seville city centre.
Bus Línea EA (Especial Aeropuerto) to city centre runs from about 5:20am to 1:15am every hour (€4).
Taxi to the city centre costs €20–€31.
In a **car,** follow the blue signposts to Sevilla (A4); it is a good 20 minutes to the centre.

Granada Airport
Aeropuerto Federico García Lorca lies about 20km (12.5mi) west of Granada city.
After flight arrivals **city bus No 0245** goes from the airport to the city centre from 5:45am to 10:30, every 1–2 hours (€2.90).
A **taxi** to the city centre (bus station, Av. de Juan Pablo II) costs €21–€24.

Almería Airport
Almería Airport (tel: 902 40 47 04) lies about 10km (6mi) east of Almería city.
Bus No 30 runs between the airport and the city centre (Rambla de Belén) approximately every 70 min., from 7:10am to 10:10pm.
A **taxi** to the Puerta de Purchena costs €20–€25.

Arriving by Rail
Travelling by train from the UK to Andalucía is time-consuming and can take anything from up to 30 hours. You need to first travel to Paris, then change trains, changing once more at the Spanish border for connections to Madrid. There are further connections from Madrid to Córdoba, Seville and other main Andalucían cities.

Estación de María Zambrano, Málaga
The main railway station (Málaga RENFE) lies west of the harbour near the city centre.
Electric train (Línea C-1) connects to Alameda Centro.
Several **buses** go to Alameda Principal

Estación de San Justa, Sevilla
From the main station, **Metro** Line 1, to the Avenida Carlos V; it is a five-minute walk from the "Puerta de Jerez" stop to the cathedral.
Taxis to the cathedral area cost about €8, plus €2 for luggage.
The **tourism information desk** can book hotels.

Granada Railway Station
The station, on Avenida de Andaluces, is about 1.5km (1mi) from the city centre.
Several **bus lines** run between the station and Gran Vía de Colón and Los Reyes Católicos at the city centre.
Taxis cost about €6 to Los Reyes Católicos.

Almería Railway Station & Bus Station
The railway station and bus station share the arrival/departure concourse on Plaza de la Estación (Estación Intermodal Almería).
It is a short **walk** of about 700m to the seaward end of Avenida Federico García Lorca (Rambla de Belén).

Córdoba Railway Station
The station is about 1.7km (1mi) northwest of the Mezqita.
Bus No 3 connects to Plaza de las Tendillas and continues to the riverside in front of the Mezquita.
Taxis cost about €6 to the Mezquita area.

Arriving by Bus

Travel **by bus** from the UK to Andalucía is also time-consuming; at least 24 hours to Madrid, over 30 hours to Málaga. The cost can be more expensive than the cheaper flights.

Málaga Bus Station

The bus station (estabus.malaga.eu; tel: 952 35 00 61) is adjacent to the railway station at Paseo de los Tilos.

For connections to the city centre, see Railway Station above.

Sevilla Bus Station

Seville has two bus stations. International arrivals and arrivals from other Spanish cities outside Andalucía come in at Plaza de Armas by the Guadalquivir (www.autobuses plazadearmas.es; tel: 955 03 86 65).

Buses from Andalucía's other main cities arrive at Prado de San Sebastián (tel: 955 47 92 90) north of the Plaza de España.

Granada Bus Station

Carretera de Jaén (tel: 902 42 22 42), about 3km (2 miles) from the city centre on Av. de Juan Pablo II.

City buses SN1 and SN2 run to the centre.

Taxis cost about €7–€8 to the city centre

Córdoba Bus Station

The bus station (www.estacion autobus-escordoba.es; tel: 957 40 40 40) is next to the railway station in Av. Vía Augusta.

Bus No 3 takes arrivals from the bus station (tel: 957 40 43 83) to the city centre.

Taxis cost about €5

Arriving by Car

You can drive to Spain via Calais, Rouen, Tours, Bordeaux, San Sebastián, Burgos, Salamanca and Cáceres. Motorway toll charges (one way) through France and Spain amount to about €140. Given the distance between the UK and Spain (e.g. London–Seville approx. 2,200km/1,350mi), it is advisable to plan two to three days for the journey.

A route planner with travel cost evaluation (petrol and toll) can be found at www.via michelin.es.

GETTING AROUND

Train

There are train connections to all major towns in Andalucía. High-speed train services run to Córdoba, Seville and Málaga. RENFE (Red Nacional de Ferrocaril de España) is the national rail network. Services between main cities are generally fast, comfortable and efficient. Services to smaller towns and throughout rural areas are much slower, but are often scenic. Stations and halts in rural areas can be several kilometres from the main settlement that they serve; public transport is usually not available and you may need to phone for a taxi.

For general enquiries about **RENFE** services throughout Andalucía; tel: 902 32 03 20.

The RENFE website is in Spanish and English; www.renfe.es. The site also provides information about apps for your smartphone.

Cercanías are city and suburban link trains, though services may extend to nearby provincial towns. They are fast and fairly cheap.

Media Distancia are intercity links. They are fast and comfortable. High-speed trains, known as ***AVE*** (Tren Alta Velocidad) is the national high-speed service into Andalucía from Madrid to Córdoba and Seville.

It is advisable to **reserve a seat** on mainline trains. You can buy **tickets** and reserve seats at city-centre travel agents that display the RENFE sign. Most city railway stations have a queuing system at ticket desks: you must first take a numbered slip from a machine signed *"Venta anticipada"*, then watch for your number to appear on indicators above the desks.

Bus

Andalucía has an excellent regional bus service run by a number of companies. Buses, in general, are reliable and comfortable and fares are usually about 25% less than for similar journeys by train. In rural areas bus travel is often faster than train or is the only option.

Depending on the route and season, buy **tickets** as early as possible (preferably the day before). There can be long queues, especially in the mornings, at the weekends and during school holidays.

Most bus stations sell the tickets from one desk, but at **Málaga bus station** the Alsina Graells company ticket office handles the main services inland and the Automóviles Portillo company handles Costa del Sol, Cádiz and coastal routes to the east. Services are greatly reduced on Sundays and public holidays.
Luggage goes in the hold, but there is room under the seat in front of you for a normal-sized case or bag.

Driving
Avoid, where possible, driving right into the cities. Private vehicles are not allowed into many of the Old Town districts (*centro histórico*), and where this is not the case, the narrow streets and confusing one-way systems mean driving is not a lot of fun. You are not allowed to park on yellow lines; you will have to pay a parking fee for the blue designated spaces. Pay the parking attendant or feed the machine, as applicable. Driving in Andalucía is fairly stress-free away from cities and towns.
Keep as far to the right as possible on single-carriageway roads – Spanish drivers love to cut things a little close when overtaking. Congestion on the **N340** main road along the Costa del Sol can be daunting.
Drive on the **right-hand side** of the road. **Seat belts** must be worn in front seats and in rear seats where fitted. The **blood alcohol limit** is 0.5%.When **turning left** outside localities, you will find that the more major roads have their own lanes, which first go off to the right and then cross the main street (*raqueta*). There are a lot of roundabouts. As in England, the vehicles already in the roundabout have right of way. You must carry a **warning triangle**, a **set of replacement bulbs** and a **reflective jacket**.
The **speed limit** on the *autopistas* (toll motorways) and *autovías* (free motorways) is 120kph (75mph). On dual carriageways and roads with periodic overtaking lanes it is 100kph (62mph) and on rural roads 90kph (56mph). The maximum speed on urban roads is 50kph (31mph) and 30kph (16mph) in residential areas. It is advisable to adhere to these regulations. During the holiday period, the police carry out a lot of speed checks, and the fines are painfully high (in excess of 20km/h: €100, then, depending on the gravity of the offense €300–€600); for payment within 20 calendar days, you receive a 50% discount.
Fuel is available as *gasolina sin plomo* (unleaded) with 95 and 98 octane and *gasóleo A* (diesel), sometimes also as biodiesel. Most garages take credit cards. Carrying canisters full of petrol or diesel in the car is forbidden.
There are two types of motorway in Spain: the toll-free **Autovías** (e.g. A7) and the **Autopistas** (e.g. AP7), which are subject to tolls. You can pay the toll in cash or with a credit card.

Hiring a Car
You have to be at least 21 to hire a car and in possession of a credit card. Some rental companies demand that young drivers have at least two years' experience before they can hire one of their cars.
Book ahead at peak times. From the UK, try **Budget** (tel: 08701 56 56 56; www.budget.co.uk) or **Europcar** (tel: 08706 07 50 00; www.europcar.com).
On-the-spot hiring can be done at airports and at most city railway stations. A good hire company is **Rentacarspain** (www.rentacar-spain.com) with offices in Málaga and Seville, for example).
Always **check** bodywork, tyres, undercarriage and inside trimmings of your hire car and indicate any damage to the hirer before driving off. Check in particular the hazard light system and if there are high-visibility safety vests for everyone travelling in the car.
In the event of a **breakdown**, follow the instructions on your car-rental agreement. Make certain that there are portable warning symbols with your hire car and use these to warn other traffic no matter where you break down. If using your own car use the procedures outlined in your insurance or motoring association membership.
You will be expected to return the car with the same amount of **petrol** as when you left.

Taxi
Taxis in Andalucía have metres. Fares are generally cheaper than in northern Europe, but expect a change to an increased rate as soon as you leave city limits, or late at night, at weekends and during holidays. A surcharge is also likely for luggage carried.

Bike Rental
The mild winter temperatures make cycling a good option in Andalucía. However, there have been an increasing number of serious accidents involving cars in the last few years. Bicycle helmets are obligatory.
You can find additional information about bike rental and guided tours at: http://www.bike2malaga.com/en; www.eurobike.en and http://www.sierranevada.cc.

ACCOMMODATION

This guide recommends a cross-section of places to stay, ranging from *paradores* (the state-owned chain of top-quality hotels) to small family-run *hostales* (modest hotels). In the more popular tourist destinations, it is advisable to book ahead.

Prices are for a double room per night.

€	up to €60
€€	€60–€90
€€€	€90–€140
€€€€	over €140

Finding a Room
If you have not reserved a room, the local tourist office will have a list of accommodation; most are prepared to call ahead to check if there is a room available. Or you locate a room using the relevant platforms, such as www.booking.com or www.airbnb.com. Note, most hotels are only required to retain a reserved room until 6pm unless you have given your credit-card details in advance. If you have a pet or small child with you, inform the hotel when booking. Only a small number of hotels allow you to take pets along with you; check when you are booking.

Checking In and Out
You will be asked to produce your passport when you check in; this will be used to complete a registration form. Check-out time is normally noon in hotels, although at some *hostales* and *pensiones* it is 11am; always find out in advance, to avoid paying an extra day. If you are staying in cheaper accommodation and plan to leave early, advise the front desk. Hotels will normally store your luggage until the end of the day and call a taxi for you.

Types of Accommodation
Paradores
Paradores are an expensive but special option. They tend to be converted castles, palaces and monasteries and most successfully retain the historical character of the building, while incorporating modern bathrooms, air conditioning and all the luxurious trimmings that you'd expect from a first-class hotel. They are often furnished with magnificent antiques and original works of art. There are some 16 *paradores* in Andalucía. Advance booking is recommended (www.parador.es)

Hotels
Spanish hotels are officially classified with one to five stars (*estrellas*) by the Ministry of Tourism, depending on the amenities.
A **five-star** hotel is truly luxurious with a price to match. You can expect facilities such as a WiFi, tennis court, swimming pool and gym, as well as nightly entertainment.
A **four-star** hotel is slightly less deluxe, but still first-class.
A **three-star** hotel is considerably lower in price but the rooms are perfectly adequate and will include TV and air conditioning.
A **one- or two-star** hotel is more basic and relatively inexpensive. When booking such accommodation, enquire about the exact location and facilities provided, as standards can vary.
Many hotels offer family rooms with – for a surcharge – extra beds.

Hostales
Hostales often provide better accommodation and value for money than cheap hotels.

Not to be confused with a youth hostel, a Spanish *hostal* is essentially a small hotel, in a category of one to two stars. With few exceptions they provide straightforward accommodation at a reasonable price, with the option of en-suite bathroom. There are some charming small *hostales* in Andalucía, particularly in the major cities where they are invariably situated in the historic quarter of town. Unlike a hotel, they don't normally have a bar or restaurant.

Pensiones

There is not a great deal of difference between an *hostal* and a *pensión*, except that the latter is more like a boarding house and will often have a shared bathroom. You can expect your room to be clean but spartan and you will have to supply your own soap and shampoo, although towels and blankets should be provided. There is usually a dining room.

Budget Accommodation

Camas or ***habitaciones*** are the closest Spanish equivalent to a B&B, usually advertised in the windows of private houses and the upper floors of bars and *ventas* (p. 202), perhaps with the phrase *"camas y comidas"* (bed and meals). A *fonda* is a small inn offering basic no-frills accommodation.

Most **youth hostels** (*albergues juveniles*) are usually situated out of town and can be packed with schoolchildren during holiday periods – and are best avoided.

Camping

Andalucía has some excellent campsites. These are routinely inspected and approved by the Spanish tourist authority, and classified under **four categories**: L (luxury), then first, second and third class, according to their amenities. However, even the most basic campsite must have 24-hour surveillance, be within a fenced area, provide unlimited drinking water, have first-aid and fire-prevention facilities, and toilets and showers. There is sometimes an extra charge for hot water. Camping is forbidden on beaches and may result in a fine.

Seasonal Rates

Minimum and maximum rates are established according to the season, as well as the facilities provided. In popular summer resorts, such as those of the Costa del Sol, Easter (*semana santa*) and July/August are the high season (*temporada alta*) when room rates can increase by 25%. In winter resorts, as in the Sierra Nevada, high season is, logically, winter. Outside the main season (*temporada media, temporada baja*), many hotels offer discounts, and some will have reduced prices at weekends. *Paradores* can be particularly good value then.

During national holidays and local *fiestas* such as Seville's *Feria de Abril*, accommodation costs more and is harder to find.

FOOD AND DRINK

Andalucía has the climate, coast and terrain to produce a wonderful range of raw ingredients: swordfish (*pez espada*), mussels (*mejillones*), cockles (*berberechos* and *almejas*) and fresh anchovies (*boquerones*) for seafood lovers; baby goat (*choto*) and rabbit (*conejo*), both popular in this part of Spain, for meat eaters; and beautiful fruit and vegetables according to season – purple figs, glossy red peppers, curly green chard or brilliant orange pumpkin.

Price per person for a three-course meal, including wine and service.

€	up to €15
€€	€15–€40
€€€	over €40

Meal Timetable

Breakfast (*desayuno*) is usually between 8–10, and is fairly simple: It generally consists of coffee with toasted white bread or baguette (*tostada*), which locals prefer topped with olive oil or crushed tomato with olive oil (*tomate y aceite*). Spiral-shaped *churros* and hot chocolate are another popular choice, or *magdalenas* (little biscuits). However, most Spaniards drink coffee in the morning, either strong and black (*café solo*), with hot milk (*café con*

leche), or black with a dash of milk (*café cortado*). If you find the coffee too strong, you may prefer the more diluted *americano* or decaffeinated, *descafeinado*.
Lunch (*almuerzo*) is between 1:30 and 4:30 – and you will not find many restaurants that serve lunch earlier or later. There are usually three or four courses, starting with soup and/or salad. The Andalucían classic is *gazpacho*. The main is a choice between fish or seafood, or meat and vegetables. Often the choice of desserts is limited to caramel custard (*flan*), ice cream or fresh fruit. Most average restaurants offer an economical menu of the day (*menú del día*).
A **tapa** is usually served to accompany your beer, sherry or a cold glass of white wine during the day.
Dinner (*cena*) is eaten between 8:30 and 11, and during the summer it may well extend to midnight or even later. This meal varies from being light to heavy, depending on personal preferences. Few restaurants offer their cut-price menu in the evening.

Andalucían Cuisine

The best-known Andalucían dish is ***gazpacho***, served cold in summer and made from blended tomatoes, cucumbers, peppers, garlic, bread, vinegar and olive oil.
A thicker version, known as *salmorejo* in Córdoba and *porra antequerana* around Málaga, is also popular. *Ajo blanco* is a chilled soup made with almonds, garlic and grapes.
Tortilla española (or *tortilla de patata*), the Spanish omelette with onions and potatoes are popular as a tapa or a small snack between meals. A plain omelette is a *tortilla francesa*.
With around 800km (500mi) of coastline, a lot of **fish** (*pescado*) and **seafood** (*mariscos*) are served. ***Chiringuitos***, located on beaches, are the best places to find economically priced fish such as fresh charcoal-grilled anchovies (*boquerones*). Some beach cafés are less expensive than restaurants, others seem to add the sea view to the price of the food. When the *chiringuitos* are particularly popular, you will not get a table without a reservation. *Paella* originally came from Valencia and has since become an essential part of a Spanish holiday. The traditional form is made of rice and chicken and rabbit, white and green beans; it is also made with fish and seafood and in many other variations.
Popular **meat dishes** (*carne*) include loin of pork (*lomo de cerdo*), chops (*chuletas*), spicy sausage (*chorizo*) and roast suckling pig (*cochinillo*). Some of the best Spanish mountain ham (*jamón serrano*) originates from the Alpujarras region. The *jamón ibérico*, regarded as a delicacy, comes from the area around Jabugo in Huelva.
Salads (*ensalada*) tend to be a combination of lettuce (*lechuga*), tomatoes (*tomate*) and onion (*cebolla*). Many vegetable dishes (*verdura*) are seasona, such as oyster mushrooms (*setas*) fried with garlic and parsley, and fresh asparagus prepared with scrambled eggs (*revuelto*).
Desserts (*postres*): As well as ice cream (*helado*) and caramel custard with cream (*flan* or *crema catalan*), you may find rice pudding (*arroz con leche*), vanilla whip (*natillas*) and fresh fruit on the menu.

Where to Eat

Andalucía has an eatery for every kind of hunger.
Ventas, rural restaurants that traditionally catered to farm workers and travellers, still serve hearty home-style cooking, though nowadays the clientele is a mix of construction workers, business people and, on weekends, families.
Chiringuitos are beachside restaurants serving fresh seafood.
There's plenty of choice when it comes to **cafés** and **bars**, including *tascas* that specialise in tapas, and *bodegas* where you can sample wine or sherry straight from the barrel.
Restaurants, ranging from sophisticated places serving international cuisine to ethnic and fast-food joints, are found in the Costa resorts and main cities. Spanish restaurants tend to specialise in seafood, game and meat dishes.
Teterías are Moroccan-style tea shops serving a wide choice of herb teas (*infusiones*), accompanied by traditional Arab pastries.

Tipping

There is a lot of discussion about tipping in Spain. It is not that common and lower than elsewhere. A Spanish tip is an average of 5%, but there is rarely any arithmetic involved. It's more a matter of just leaving spare change. Most foreigners tip as they would in their own countries. Give what you think is appropriate for the service offered.

What to Drink

Beer (*cerveza*) is extremely popular – many Spaniards prefer it to wine. Spanish beer is fairly strong (around 5%). A freshly tapped beer is a *caña*, which generally comes in an ice-cold glass. For something lighter, try a normal shandy (*clara*) or a tasty, more lemony alternative *clara con limón*. A *cervecería* is a bar that specialises in beer and usually has several brands on tap, plus a wide range of bottled and imported beers.

Rioja is perhaps the most famous of Spanish **wines**, but there are 40 other wine denominations in Spain. Red wine is *tinto*, white wine *blanco*. You may want to try a house wine (*vino de la casa*) or, for a refreshing alternative, a *tinto de verano*: red wine with lemonade (*gaseosa*).

Sangría is a delicious red wine punch that combines wine, cognac, other liqueurs and *gaseosa* with slices of citrus fruit.

The sweet Málaga wine (D. O. Málaga, Sierras de Málaga and Pasas de Málaga) is made from muscat grapes grown in the Axarquia region.

Sherry (*fino, manzanilla, amontillado, oloroso*) is naturally a popular aperitif here.

Cocktails and spirits are much cheaper in Spain than in most other countries and the measures are generous. Many Andalucíans will have a brandy (*coñac*) or *anís* with their morning coffee.

The usual choice of fizzy soft drinks is available. Other **non-alcoholic drinks** include fruit juice (*zumo*) and *Bitter Kas*, the latter similar in flavour to Campari.

For something different, try ice-cold ***horchata***, a nutty milk-like beverage made from tiger nuts (*chufas*).

SHOPPING

In Andalucía's glitzy coastal resorts and major cities, top-name fashion salons exist side by side with shops selling traditional flamenco wear. In every region, you'll find *alfarerías* (pottery workshops) and *talleres* (craft studios) producing colourful ceramics and fabrics, leatherwork and silverware (craft traditions that have their origins in the region's Moorish past). You'll also find tempting delicatessens, wine shops and pâtisseries in every city, and colourful local markets, where you can buy a range of regional specialities.

Fashion

All main cities – Málaga, Granada, Seville, Córdoba and Cádiz – and the chic Costa del Sol resorts of Marbella and Puerto Banús, have a huge number of clothes and shoe shops. You can buy anything from top-of-the-range Armani or Gucci to affordable and bargain clothes and accessories.

Jewellery

There are many jewellery shops in the Costa del Sol resorts, although with some outlets you would be wise to know something about what you are buying. Long-established jewellers are also found in the main shopping areas of cities and larger towns.

Souvenirs

You can buy souvenirs that range from tacky T-shirts to traditional pottery in just about every city and large town in Andalucía. Most shops that are wholly dedicated to mass-produced souvenirs are concentrated around major attractions, such as Córdoba's Mezquita and Seville's Barrio Santa Cruz area.

The more authentic outlets that sell fine pottery and other traditional Andalucían craftwork can still be found. The main streets and seafront *paseos* of the major Costa del Sol resorts are lined with gift shops, and at peak season an additional layer of pavement stalls hawk cheap souvenirs.

Antiques and Art

For interesting pieces with a genuine Spanish pedigree – a cut above the usual "souvenir" – search the antiques and fine-arts shops scattered throughout the centres of main cities like Granada and Seville.

Crafts

Andalucían **ceramics** reach international standards, not least in such regional centres as Úbeda (p. 124) and Níjar (p. 102). Andalucía is particularly noted for vivid and colourful tile work in a tradition that goes back to the Moorish era. In Córdoba you will find outstanding **leatherwork** and **filigree silverware**, while Granada is a centre for **marquetry**. The mountain areas of Andalucía, especially the Alpujarras (p. 93) and the Sierra de Grazalema (p. 61), are good places to find traditional fabrics and clothing such as ponchos, as well as small rugs and bedcovers, known as *jarapas*.

Culinary

The hill regions of the Alpujarras in Granada province and the Sierra Morena in Seville province are famous for their ***jamón serrano*** and ***jamón ibérico*** (cured ham) respectively; villages such as Trevélez (p. 95) in the Alpujarras, and Aracena (p. 168) and Jabugo (Huelva province) in the Sierra Morena, have shops devoted to *jamón* and other meats.

You can find own-label brands of **sherry** in the big-name *bodegas* of Jerez de la Frontera (p. 48), El Puerto de Santa María (p. 63) and Sanlúcar de Barrameda (p. 62), while in specialist shops in main towns and wine-producing areas, you will find every kind of sherry, wine and liqueur on sale.

Department Stores

Spain's shopping success story is the **El Corte Inglés** chain of mega-stores, which has branches in Seville, Granada, Córdoba, Málaga and the Costa del Sol. Some, like Málaga's, are crammed with departments that specialise in just about anything you could want.

Markets

Town and village markets are excellent sources of fresh food. Colourful, noisy, good-natured and, above all, bursting with life, they can be an entertainment in themselves. In general, every town holds a market once a week (*mercadillo*).

Best Markets

For fish: Sanlúcar de Barrameda (p. 62), Almería (p. 96)
For mixed fish, meat, fruit and vegetables: Cádiz (p. 58), Málaga (p. 55)
For clothing and general goods: Fuengirola (p. 53), Córdoba (p. 116)

Village Shops

Village hardware and general goods shops can sell anything from local pottery to straw hats, spices and condiments, colourful shawls and neckties. You'll pay a fraction of the price for such items that you would pay in town, while they have a far more authentic pedigree than a typical resort souvenir.

Opening Hours

Most **shops** in Andalucía open 9–2 and 4:30–8:30 Monday to Saturday, although there is individual flexibility at either end. Large **department stores** and **malls** open Mon–Sat from about 10am to as late as 10pm. In the tourist areas, such as the Costa del Sol, lots of **supermarkets** are also open on Sunday mornings, and even all day in larger towns.

Banks normally open Mon–Fri 8:30am to 1/2pm

The opening times of **museums** and **tourist sights** change from summer to winter, and there is sometimes even an interim period (spring and autumn) with different times. Generally, the opening times are longer in summer, but due to the fact that it gets so hot in summer there are some places in Andalucía that the opening times are actually shorter in the summer. It is not unusual for the opening times to change from year to year; the information in this guide corresponds with the relevant times stated when this book went to print.

Payment

In main cities and larger towns, credit cards are accepted in most shops and stores. This is essentially true for countryside towns as well, but it is always better to ask in advance if you are not quite sure!

Etiquette

Andalucíans enjoy browsing in shops and you will have no problems about doing so as a visitor. To avoid any misunderstandings, shoppers should ask the assistant's permission before handling goods. However, in chic fashion salons you will be assumed to be serious about buying and here you may receive one-to-one attention as soon as you enter. In the wall-to-wall shopping of the resorts, shopkeepers and stallholders are sometimes overly attentive.

ENTERTAINMENT

There is no lack of organised evening entertainment in Andalucía's towns and villages, from nightclubbing to flamenco watching. Most cities have cinemas and the Costa del Sol has a number of casinos. For the outdoor enthusiast there are plenty of activities, and children are more than catered for on the Costa del Sol where there is a whole range of fun parks (p. 163).

Nightlife

The main **clubbing circuit** is on the Costa del Sol. Most clubs **open** their doors at 10 or 11pm, but you'll have the place to yourself until at least 1am, and things often don't really get going until 3 or 4am.
There are **cinemas** in all the major cities and in most large towns. Most foreign-language films are dubbed in Spanish rather than subtitled. Cinemas in Málaga, Fuengirola and Marbella show original version films.
There are plenty of opportunities to see **flamenco** (p. 24).

Special Events

Festivals are an essential and exuberant part of Andalucían life. The calendar of events is fullest from Easter through to June (p. 205).
The main **bullfight** season runs from Easter to October, but there are novice fights into November on the Costa del Sol. Hotels often organise bus pickups. For major rings, tickets are often booked well ahead by locals. Prices can be as high as €140 but start at about €15. Even Costa del Sol *novilladas* may cost you from €30 to €60, although they should be much less. For more information see p. 22.

Outdoor Activities

The windier Atlantic coast, especially at Tarifa (p. 63), between Gibraltar and Cádiz, is one of the world's best **windsurfing** and **kitesurfing** venues, while the opportunities for **scuba diving**, **waterskiing** and **paragliding** are increasing.
Boat trips are an enjoyable option and in the Gibraltar and Tarifa area, there are special **dolphin-watching** boat trips available.
Specialist "golf villages" proliferate on the Costa del Sol. On the Costa golf courses in general you may find that you need to book well in advance for a round, and provide a handicap certificate. Fees vary, but can be hefty on some of the more upmarket courses where you may even have difficulty in making a casual booking (p. 71 for details). A good source of information about golf in Andalucía is the **Real Federacíon Andaluza de Golf** (Sierra de Grazalema 33-5-1B, Málaga; tel: 952 22 55 90, http://rfga.org).
Andalucía's magnificent mountains offer endless opportunities for adventure holidaying, whether it's basic **walking** along the numerous tracks and paths in Las Alpujarras (p. 93), the Sierra de Grazalema (p. 61) and the Sierras de Cazorla y Segura (p. 132) or **horse riding** and **cycling** on organised trips with expert guides. Ask at tourist offices.
For information on angling, contact **Spanish Fishing Federation** (tel: 915 32 83 53; www.fepyc.es).
You can also go for the wilder edges of **adventure sport** and try rock climbing, abseiling, canoeing, paragliding and hang-gliding.

CALENDAR OF EVENTS

In Andalucía, you will find festivals, *fiestas* and *ferias*. The *fiesta* originated as a rural holiday and the *feria* as a country fair, and even in big cities their outdoor nature survives, with horses and bulls still figuring largely in the proceedings. And then there are, of course, the religious festivals.

Andalucíans have long been noted for their love of festival and fun. "Every day seems to be a holiday," commented the 19th-century writer Richard Ford, in a rather sniffily English way, on his first visit. The English politician and writer Benjamin Disraeli was more enthusiastic. "It is all the sun," he exclaimed when he visited Andalucía in 1830 after an illness and felt rejuvenated.

February
Carnaval Spectacular carnivals in Cádiz and Málaga and, to a lesser extent, Córdoba, Carmona, Nerja and many other towns and villages, are held in the days preceding the beginning of Lent.

March/April
Semana Santa Religious processions are staged in all the main cities and in many country towns and villages throughout Holy Week, which precedes Easter.

April
Feria de Abril Seville's April festival, held about two weeks after Easter, is a week-long celebration. It is the biggest and most colourful festival in Spain.

May
Feria del Caballo Colourful horse fair, with marvellous displays of equestrianism (Jerez de la Frontera, early May).
Moros y Cristianos (Moors and Christians) Carnival Mock battles (Pampaneira, Las Alpujarras, 3 May).
Fiesta de los Patios Many of Córdoba's beautiful private patios open to the public (early May).
Romería del Rocío The biggest religious pilgrimage and festival in Spain (El Rocío, seventh week after Easter, p. 166).
Feria de Primavera Puerta de Santa María wine festival (last week in May).
Feria de la Manzanilla Sanlúcar de Barrameda wine festival (last week in May).
Corpus Christi Processions and celebrations in many places (late May/early June).

June
Feria de San Bernabé Marbella's very lavish festival (second week in June).
Fiestas Patronales de San Antonio Festival with mock battles between "Moors" and "Christians" (Trevélez, Las Alpujarras, 13–14 June).
Moros y Cristianos Festival in Mojácar (10 June).
International Guitar Festival Córdoba (two weeks June/July).

July
International Festival of Music and Dance at the Alhambra (Granada, late June/early July).
Virgen de la Mar Almería's lively summer festival (last week in July).

August
Feria de Málaga Málaga's summer festival (mid-Aug).
Sanlúcar de Barrameda Horse Races along the beach at Sanlúcar (last two weeks in Aug).
Feria de Grazalema Village festival includes bull-running (last week in Aug).
Fiestas Patronales San Augustín Mojácar festival (last week in Aug).

September
Fiesta de la Vendimia Major wine festival at Jerez de la Frontera (first/second week in Sep).
Romería del Cristo de la Yedra Baeza's main festival (7 Sep).
Feria y Fiesta de Pedro Romero Ronda festival featuring bullfighters in 18th-century costume, plus flamenco (first two weeks in Sep).

October
Fiesta de San Miguel Festival at Úbeda and in many other towns and villages (1 Oct).
Feria de San Lucas Jaén's main festival (mid-Oct).

USEFUL WORDS AND PHRASES

In Andalucía, people speak standard Spanish (*castellano*) but with a strong local dialect, which principally entails them omitting consonants. In very rural areas, this can mean that even people with a good command of Spanish will not understand a word. In tourist areas, you will generally find that people speak English, but the Spaniards are happy when you at least try to use a few words of Spanish.

Greetings and Common Words

Do you speak English?	**¿Habla inglés?**
I don't understand	**No entiendo**
I don't speak Spanish	**No hablo español**
Yes/no	**Sí/no**
OK	**Vale/ de acuerdo**
Please	**Por favor**
Thank you (very much)	**(Muchas) gracias**
You're welcome	**De nada**
Hello/goodbye	**Hola/adiós**
Good morning	**Buenos días**
Good afternoon/ evening	**Buenas tardes**
Good night	**Buenas noches**
How are you?	**¿Qué tal?**
Excuse me	**Perdón**
How much is this?	**¿Cuánto vale?**
I'd like...	**Quisiera/ me gustaría**

Emergency!

Help!	**¡Socorro!/¡Ayuda!**
Could you help me please?	**¿Podría ayudarme por favor?**
Could you call a doctor please?	**¿Podría llamar a un médico por favor?**

Directions and Travelling

Aeroplane	**Avión**
Airport	**Aeropuerto**
Car	**Coche**
Boat	**Barco**
Bus	**Autobús/guagua**
Bus stop	**Parada de autobús**
Station	**Estación**
Ticket (single/ return)	**Billete (de ida/ de ida y vuelta)**
I'm lost	**Me he perdido**
Where is...?	**¿Dónde está...?**
How do I get to...? the beach the telephone the toilets	**¿Cómo llego a...? la playa el teléfono los servicios**
Left	**Izquierda**
Right	**Derecha**
Straight on	**Todo recto**

Accommodation

Do you have a single/double room available?	**¿Tiene una habitación individual/doble?**
With/without bath/toilet/ shower	**Con/sin baño/lavabo/ ducha**
Does that include breakfast?	**¿Incluye el desayuno?**
Could I see the room?	**¿Puedo ver la habitación?**
I'll take this room	**Cojo esta habitación**
One night	**Una noche**
Key	**Llave**
Lift	**Ascensor**
Sea views	**Vistas al mar**

Days

Today	**Hoy**
Tomorrow	**Mañana**
Yesterday	**Ayer**
Later	**Más tarde**
This week	**Esta semana**
Monday	**Lunes**
Tuesday	**Martes**
Wednesday	**Miércoles**
Thursday	**Jueves**
Friday	**Viernes**
Saturday	**Sábado**
Sunday	**Domingo**

Numbers

0	**cero**
1	**una/uno**
2	**dos**
3	**tres**
4	**cuatro**
5	**cinco**
6	**seis**
7	**siete**
8	**ocho**
9	**nueve**
10	**diez**
11	**once**
12	**doce**
13	**trece**
14	**catorce**
15	**quince**
16	**dieciséis**
17	**diecisiete**
18	**dieciocho**
19	**diecinueve**
20	**veinte**
21	**veintiuno**
22	**veintidós**
30	**treinta**
40	**cuarenta**
50	**cincuenta**
60	**sesenta**
70	**setenta**
80	**ochenta**
90	**noventa**
100	**cien**
101	**ciento uno**
110	**ciento y diez**
120	**ciento y veinte**
200	**doscientos**
300	**trescientos**
400	**cuatrocientos**
500	**quinientos**
600	**seiscientos**
700	**setecientos**
800	**ochocientos**
900	**novecientos**
1,000	**mil**
¼	**un cuarto**
⅓	**un tercio**
½	**medio**
¾	**tres cuartos**
1st	**primero**
2nd	**Segundo**
3rd	**tercero**
4th	**cuarto**

Restaurant

I'd like to book a table	**Quisiera reservar una mesa**
A table for two please	**Una mesa para dos, por favor**
Could we see the menu, please?	**¿Nos trae la carta, por favor?**
What's this?	**¿Qué es esto?**
A bottle/ glass of...	**Una botella/ copa de...**
Could I have the bill please?	**¿La cuenta, por favor?**
Service charge included	**Servicio incluido**
Waiter/waitress	**Camarero/a**
Breakfast	**Desayuno**
Lunch	**Almuerzo**
Dinner	**Cena**
Menu	**La carta**

Menu Reader

a la plancha	grilled
aceite	oil
aceituna	olive
agua	water
ajo	garlic
almendra	almond
anchoas	anchovies
arroz	rice
atún	tuna
bacalao	cod
berenjena	aubergines
bistec	steak
bocadillo	sandwich
café	coffee
calamares	squid
cangrejo	crab
carne	meat
cebolla	onion
cerdo	pork
cerezas	cherries
cerveza	beer
champiñones	mushrooms
chocolate	chocolate
chorizo	spicy sausage
chuleta	chop
conejo	rabbit
cordero	lamb
crema	cream
crudo	raw

cubierto(s)	cover (cutlery)
cuchara	spoon
cuchillo	knife
embutidos	sausages
ensalada	salad
entrante	starter
espárragos	asparagus
filete	fillet
flan	crème caramel
frambuesa	raspberry
fresa	strawberry
frito	fried
fruta	fruit
galleta	biscuit
gambas	prawns
gazpacho andaluz	gazpacho (cold soup)
guisantes	peas
habas	broad beans
helado	ice cream
hígado	liver
huevos fritos/ revueltos	fried/ scrambled eggs
jamón serrano	ham (cured)
jamón York	ham (cooked)
judías	beans
judías verdes	french beans
jugo	fruit juice
langosta	lobster
leche	milk
lechuga	lettuce
legumbres	pulses
lengua	tongue
lenguado	sole
limón	lemon
lomo de cerdo	pork tenderloin
mantequilla	butter
manzana	apple
mariscos	seafood
mejillones	mussels
melocotón	peach
melón	melon
merluza	hake
mero	sea bass
miel	honey
naranja	orange
ostra	oyster
pan	bread
papas arrugadas	Canarian-style boiled potatoes
patata	potato
patatas fritas	fries
pato	duck
pepinillo	gherkin
pepino	cucumber
pera	pear
perejil	parsley
pescado	fish
pez espada	swordfish
picante	hot/spicy
pimientos	red/green peppers
piña	pineapple
plátano	banana
plato principal	main course
pollo	chicken
postre	dessert
primer plato	first course
pulpo	octopus
queso	cheese
rape	monkfish
relleno	filled/stuffed
riñones	kidneys
salchicha	sausage
salchichón	salami
salmón	salmon
salmonete	red mullet
salsa	sauce
seco	dry
solomillo de ternera	fillet of beef
sopa	soup
té	tea
tenedor	fork
ternera	beef
tocino	bacon
tortilla española	Spanish omelette
tortilla francesa	plain omelette
trucha	trout
uva	grape
verduras	green vegetables
vino blanco	white wine
vino rosado	rosé wine
vino tinto	red wine
zanahorias	carrots
zumo	juice

Road Atlas

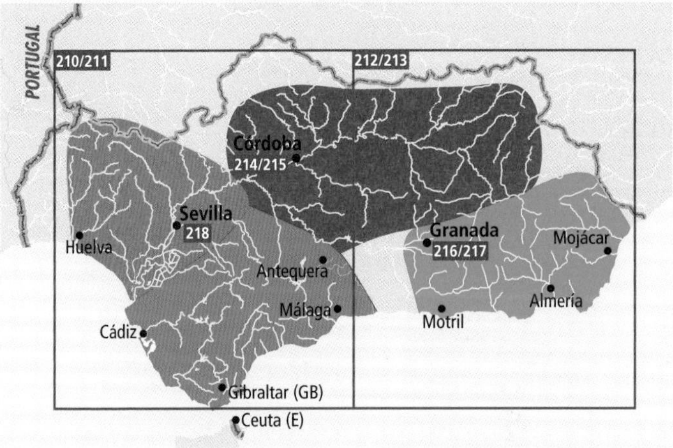

Key to Road Atlas

- A-7 Motorway
- A-381 Dual carriage-way
- A-369 Trunk road
- A-2226 Main road
- Secondary road
- Road under construction
- Dirt road
- Lane
- Footpath
- Ferry
- National boundary
- Regional boundary
- National park
- International airport
- Regional airport

- Castle, Fortress; Ruin
- Monastery; Church, chapel
- Point of interest
- Archaeological site
- Radio or TV tower; Windmill
- Cave; Lighthouse
- Peak; Pass
- Skiing area
- Windsurfing; Marina
- (Swimming) beach
- 2 ★★ TOP 10
- 11 Don't Miss
- 15 At Your Leisure

1 : 1 700 000

0 — 10 — 20 km

0 — 5 — 10 mi

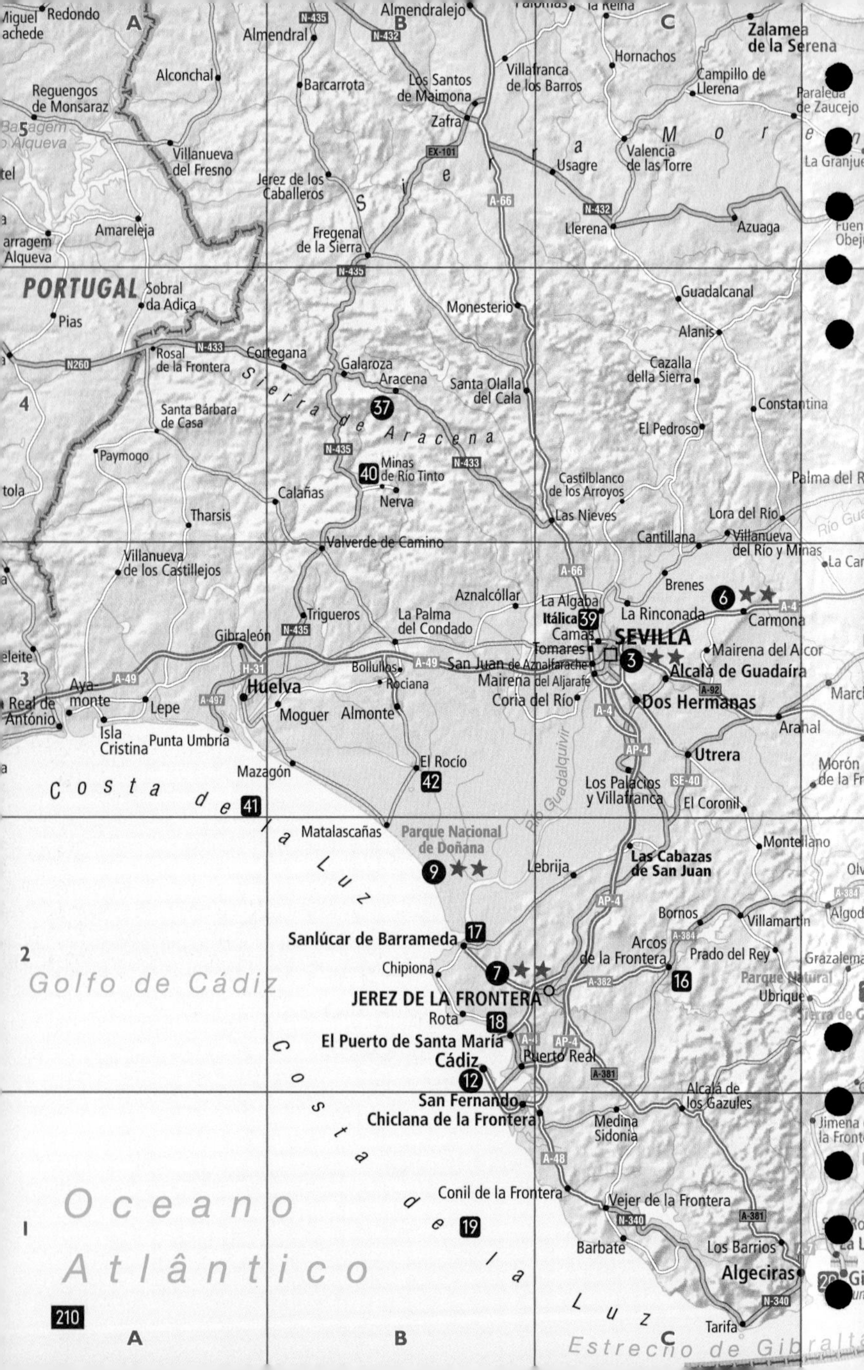

A
B
C
5
4
3
2
1
Miguel
achede
Redondo
Almendralejo
Almendral
N-435
N-432
Palomas
la Reina
Zalamea de la Serena
Hornachos
Alconchal
Reguengos de Monsaraz
Barcarrota
Los Santos de Maimona
Villafranca de los Barros
Campillo de Llerena
Paraleda de Zaucejo
Zafra
EX-101
Alqueva
Villanueva del Fresno
Usagre
Valencia de las Torre
La Granjue
Sierra Morena
Jerez de los Caballeros
A-66
Amareleja
Fregenal de la Sierra
Llerena
N-432
Azuaga
Fuen Obeju
arragem Alqueva
PORTUGAL
Sobral da Adiça
N-435
Guadalcanal
Pias
Monesterio
Alanis
N-433
N260
Rosal de la Frontera
Cortegana
Galaroza
Aracena
Cazalla della Sierra
Santa Olalla del Cala
Sierra de Aracena
37
Constantina
Santa Bárbara de Casa
El Pedroso
Paymogo
N-435
N-433
Minas de Río Tinto
40
Nerva
Castilblanco de los Arroyos
Palma del R
tola
Calañas
Tharsis
Las Nieves
Lora del Río
Cantillana
Villanueva del Río y Minas
Valverde de Camino
Villanueva de los Castillejos
A-66
La Car
Aznalcóllar
La Algaba
Brenes
6
Itálica
39
La Rinconada
Trigueros
La Palma del Condado
A-4
Carmona
N-435
Gibraleón
Camas
SEVILLA
Tomares
3
Mairena del Alcor
H-31
A-49
Bollullos
A-49
San Juan de Aznalfarache
Mairena del Aljarafe
Alcalá de Guadaíra
A-92
Ayamonte
Huelva
Rociana
Coria del Río
Real de António
A-497
Moguer
Almonte
A-4
Dos Hermanas
Marc
Lepe
Isla Cristina
Punta Umbría
Arahal
Río Guadalquivir
AP-4
Utrera
El Rocío
42
Mazagón
SE-40
Morón de la Fr
Los Palacios y Villafranca
Costa de la Luz
41
El Coronil
Matalascañas
Parque Nacional de Doñana
Montellano
9
Lebrija
Las Cabazas de San Juan
Olv
A-384
AP-4
Algod
Bornos
Villamartín
Sanlúcar de Barrameda
17
Arcos de la Frontera
A-384
Prado del Rey
Grazalema
Chipiona
7
Golfo de Cádiz
A-382
16
Parque Natural
JEREZ DE LA FRONTERA
Ubrique
Sierra de G
Rota
18
El Puerto de Santa María
A-4
AP-4
Puerto Real
Cádiz
12
A-381
Alcalá de los Gazules
San Fernando
Chiclana de la Frontera
Medina Sidonia
Jimena la Front
A-48
Oceano Atlântico
Conil de la Frontera
Vejer de la Frontera
19
N-340
A-381
Barbate
Los Barrios
Algeciras
N-340
Tarifa
Estrecho de Gibraltar

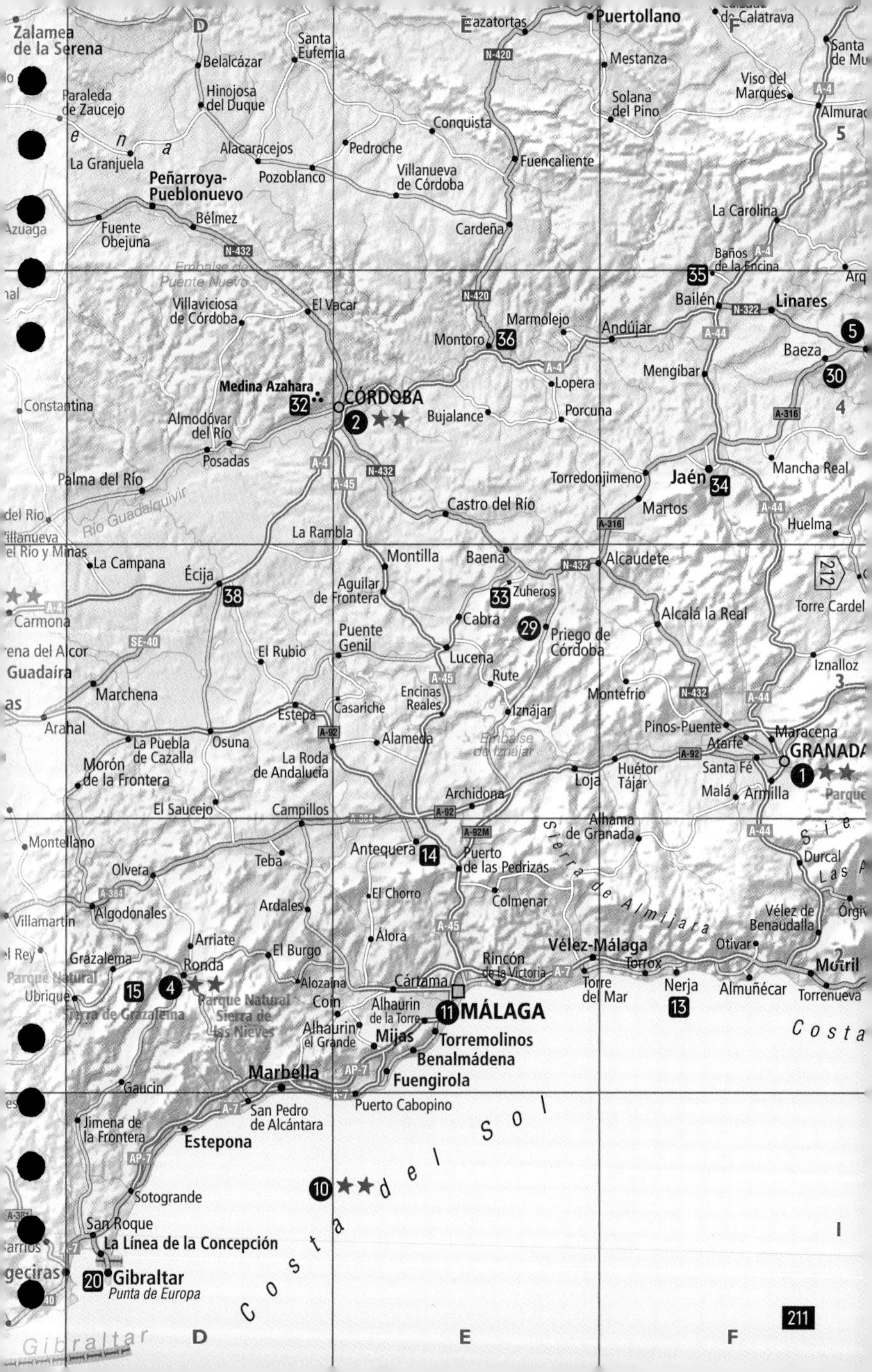
Zalamea de la Serena
D
Belalcázar
Santa Eufemia
Hinojosa del Duque
Paraleda de Zaucejo
Azatortas
E
N-420
Puertollano
Mestanza
Calzada de Calatrava
F
Solana del Pino
Viso del Marqués
Santa Cruz de Mudela
A-4
Almuradiel
5
Conquista
Pedroche
Alacaracejos
La Granjuela
Pozoblanco
Fuencaliente
Villanueva de Córdoba
Peñarroya-Pueblonuevo
Bélmez
Fuente Obejuna
Azuaga
N-432
Cardeña
La Carolina
Baños de la Encina
35
Arquillos
Embalse de Puente Nuevo
Villaviciosa de Córdoba
El Vacar
N-420
Marmolejo
Montoro
36
Andújar
Bailén
N-322
Linares
5
A-44
Baeza
Mengíbar
30
Lopera
A-4
Medina Azahara
32
CÓRDOBA
2
Bujalance
Porcuna
Constantina
Almodóvar del Río
Posadas
A-316
4
Palma del Río
A-4
N-432
A-45
Torredonjimeno
Jaén
34
Mancha Real
Martos
Río Guadalquivir
Castro del Río
A-44
Huelma
A-316
del Río
Villanueva del Río y Minas
La Rambla
Montilla
Baena
N-432
Alcaudete
212
La Campana
Écija
38
Aguilar de la Frontera
Zuheros
33
A-4
Carmona
Cabra
29
Priego de Córdoba
Alcalá la Real
Torre Cardela
SE-40
Puente Genil
El Rubio
Lucena
Iznalloz
Alcalá de Guadaíra
Rute
Marchena
A-45
Encinas Reales
Montefrío
N-432
3
Casariche
Estepa
Iznájar
A-44
Arahal
A-92
Pinos-Puente
Maracena
La Puebla de Cazalla
Osuna
Alameda
Embalse de Iznájar
Atarfe
GRANADA
Morón de la Frontera
La Roda de Andalucía
A-92
Huétor Tájar
Santa Fé
1
Loja
Malá
Armilla
Parque
Archidona
El Saucejo
Campillos
A-92
A-384
A-92M
Alhama de Granada
Sierra Nevada
A-44
Montellano
Sierra de Almijara
Teba
Antequera
14
Puerto de las Pedrizas
Durcal
Las Alpujarras
Olvera
A-384
El Chorro
Colmenar
Ardales
Algodonales
Vélez de Benaudalla
Órgiva
Villamartín
A-45
Álora
Arriate
Vélez-Málaga
Otívar
2
Grazalema
El Burgo
Rincón de la Victoria
Torrox
Motril
Parque Natural
Ronda
A-7
Ubrique
15
4
Alozaina
Cártama
Torre del Mar
Nerja
Almuñécar
Torrenueva
Parque Natural Sierra de Grazalema
Parque Natural Sierra de las Nieves
Coín
Alhaurín de la Torre
11
MÁLAGA
13
Costa
Alhaurín el Grande
Mijas
Torremolinos
Benalmádena
Marbella
AP-7
Fuengirola
Gaucín
A-7
Puerto Cabopino
A-7
San Pedro de Alcántara
Jimena de la Frontera
Estepona
AP-7
Costa del Sol
10
Sotogrande
San Roque
A-381
La Línea de la Concepción
A-7
Algeciras
20
Gibraltar
Punta de Europa
Gibraltar
D
E
F

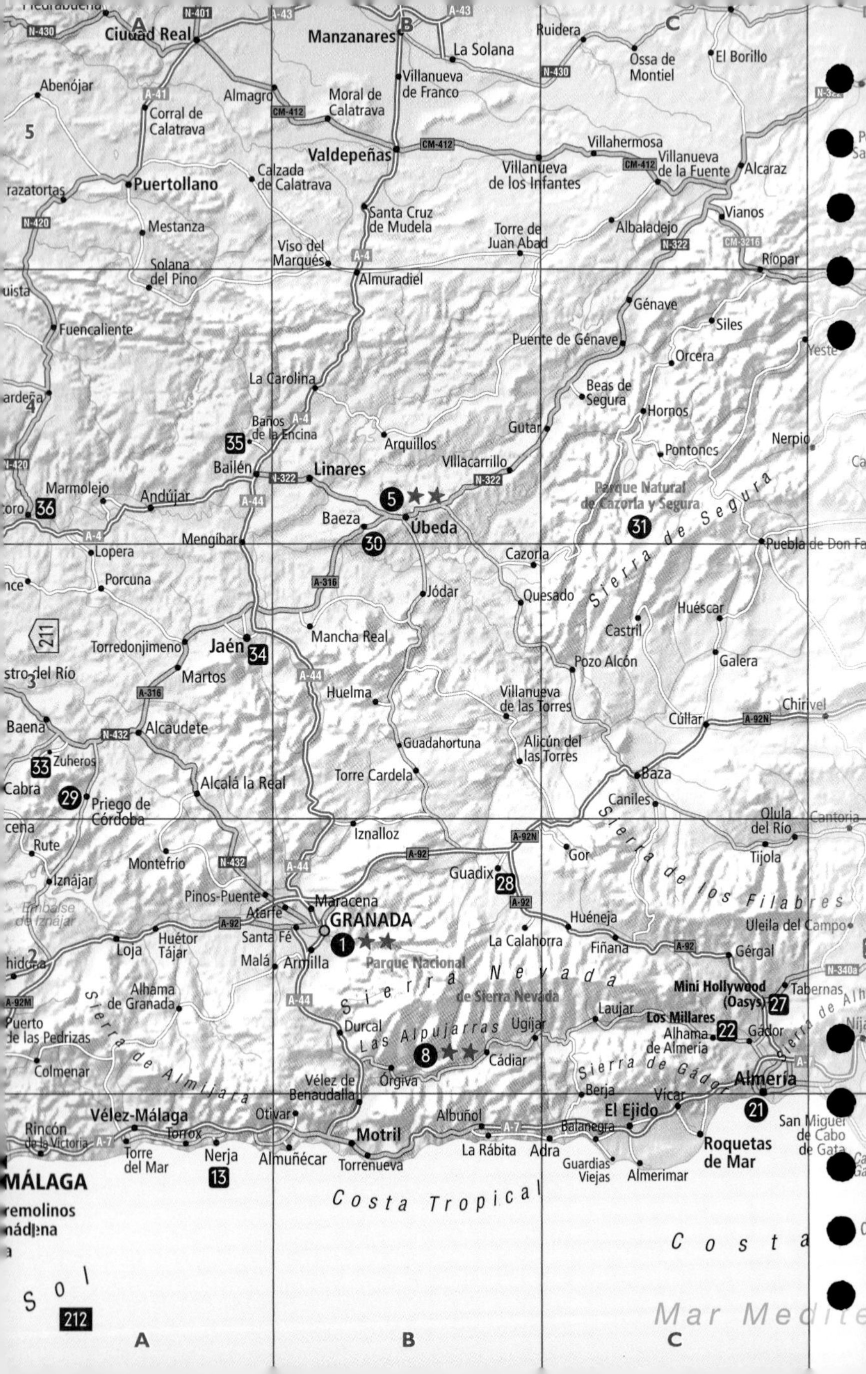
Ciudad Real
Manzanares
Ruidera
La Solana
Ossa de Montiel
El Borillo
Abenójar
Almagro
Villanueva de Franco
Moral de Calatrava
Corral de Calatrava
Valdepeñas
Villahermosa
Villanueva de la Fuente
Alcaraz
Calzada de Calatrava
Villanueva de los Infantes
Puertollano
Santa Cruz de Mudela
Vianos
Mestanza
Torre de Juan Abad
Albaladejo
Viso del Marqués
Riópar
Solana del Pino
Almuradiel
Génave
Fuencaliente
Siles
Puente de Génave
Orcera
Yeste
La Carolina
Beas de Segura
Hornos
Baños de la Encina
Gutar
Arquillos
Pontones
Nerpio
Bailén
Linares
Villacarrillo
Marmolejo
Andújar
Parque Natural de Cazorla y Segura
Baeza
Úbeda
Mengíbar
Cazorla
Puebla de Don Fa
Lopera
Sierra de Segura
Porcuna
Jódar
Quesado
Huéscar
Castril
Mancha Real
Torredonjimeno
Jaén
Martos
Pozo Alcón
Galera
Huelma
Villanueva de las Torres
Chirivel
Baena
Alcaudete
Cúllar
Guadahortuna
Alicún del las Torres
Zuheros
Cabra
Torre Cardela
Baza
Alcalá la Real
Priego de Córdoba
Caniles
Olula del Río
Cantoria
Rute
Iznalloz
Montefrío
Gor
Tíjola
Iznájar
Guadix
Sierra de los Filabres
Pinos-Puente
Maracena
Embalse de Iznájar
Atarfe
GRANADA
Huéneja
Uleila del Campo
Santa Fé
Huétor Tájar
Loja
Malá
Armilla
La Calahorra
Fiñana
Gérgal
Parque Nacional de Sierra Nevada
Sierra Nevada
Mini Hollywood (Oasys)
Tabernas
Alhama de Granada
Laujar
Los Millares
Sierra de Alhamilla
Puerto de las Pedrizas
Durcal
Las Alpujarras
Ugíjar
Alhama de Almería
Gádor
Sierra de Almijara
Cádiar
Colmenar
Sierra de Gádor
Almería
Vélez de Benaudalla
Órgiva
Berja
Vícar
Vélez-Málaga
Otívar
El Ejido
Albuñol
Rincón de la Victoria
Torrox
Motril
Balanegra
San Miguel de Cabo de Gata
Torre del Mar
Nerja
Almuñécar
Torrenueva
La Rábita
Adra
Guardias Viejas
Almerimar
Roquetas de Mar
MÁLAGA
Costa Tropical
Costa
Sol
Mar Medite
212
A
B
C
1
2
3
4
5
8
13
21
22
27
28
29
30
31
33
34
35
36
211
N-401
N-430
A-43
A-41
CM-412
N-420
A-4
N-322
CM-3216
A-44
A-316
N-432
A-92N
A-92
A-92M
A-7
N-340a

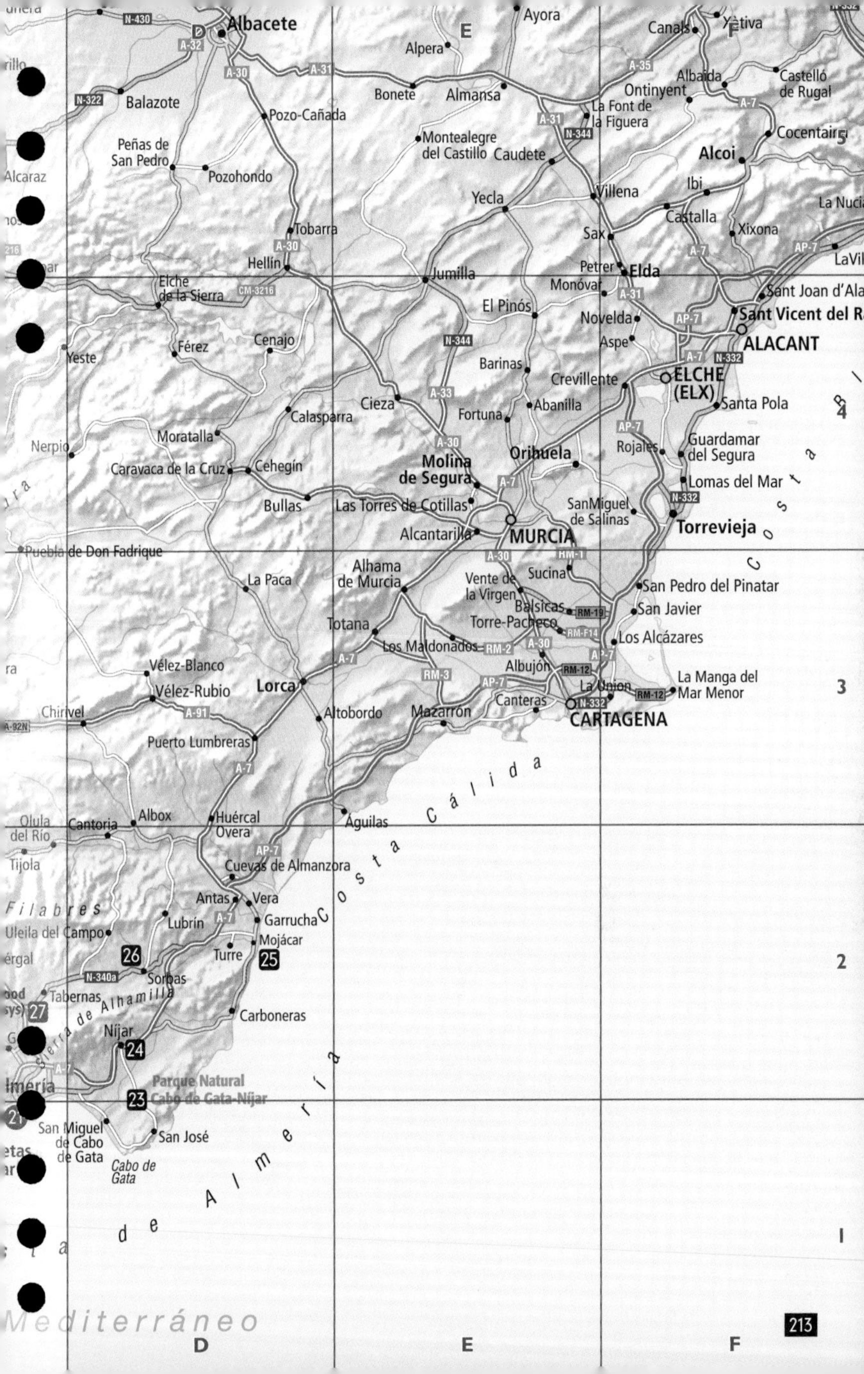

Albacete
Ayora
Canals
Xàtiva
Alpera
Balazote
Bonete
Almansa
Albaida
Castelló de Rugal
Ontinyent
La Font de la Figuera
Pozo-Cañada
Montealegre del Castillo
Caudete
Cocentaina
Peñas de San Pedro
Pozohondo
Alcoi
Alcaraz
Villena
Ibi
Yecla
La Nucia
Castalla
Xixona
Tobarra
Sax
Hellín
Petrer
Elda
Jumilla
Monóvar
Elche de la Sierra
El Pinós
Sant Joan d'Ala
Sant Vicent del Ra
Novelda
ALACANT
Cenajo
Yeste
Férez
Aspe
Barinas
Crevillente
ELCHE (ELX)
Cieza
Calasparra
Fortuna
Abanilla
Santa Pola
Moratalla
Nerpio
Rojales
Guardamar del Segura
Molina de Segura
Orihuela
Caravaca de la Cruz
Cehegín
Lomas del Mar
Bullas
Las Torres de Cotillas
SanMiguel de Salinas
Torrevieja
Alcantarilla
MURCIA
Puebla de Don Fadrique
Sucina
La Paca
Alhama de Murcia
Vente de la Virgen
San Pedro del Pinatar
Balsicas
San Javier
Totana
Torre-Pacheco
Los Alcázares
Los Maldonados
Vélez-Blanco
Albujón
La Manga del Mar Menor
Lorca
La Unión
Vélez-Rubio
Canteras
CARTAGENA
Chirivel
Altobordo
Mazarrón
Puerto Lumbreras
Costa Cálida
Olula del Río
Cantoria
Albox
Huércal Overa
Águilas
Tíjola
Cuevas de Almanzora
Filabres
Antas
Vera
Lubrín
Garrucha
Uleila del Campo
Mojácar
Turre
Sorbas
Tabernas
Sierra de Alhamilla
Carboneras
Níjar
Almería
Parque Natural Cabo de Gata-Níjar
San Miguel de Cabo de Gata
San José
Cabo de Gata
Costa de Almería
Mediterráneo
Costa Blanca
A-30
A-31
A-32
A-33
A-35
A-7
AP-7
A-91
N-430
N-322
N-344
N-332
N-340a
CM-3216
RM-1
RM-2
RM-3
RM-12
RM-19
RM-F14
E
F
D
1
2
3
4
5
23
24
25
26
27

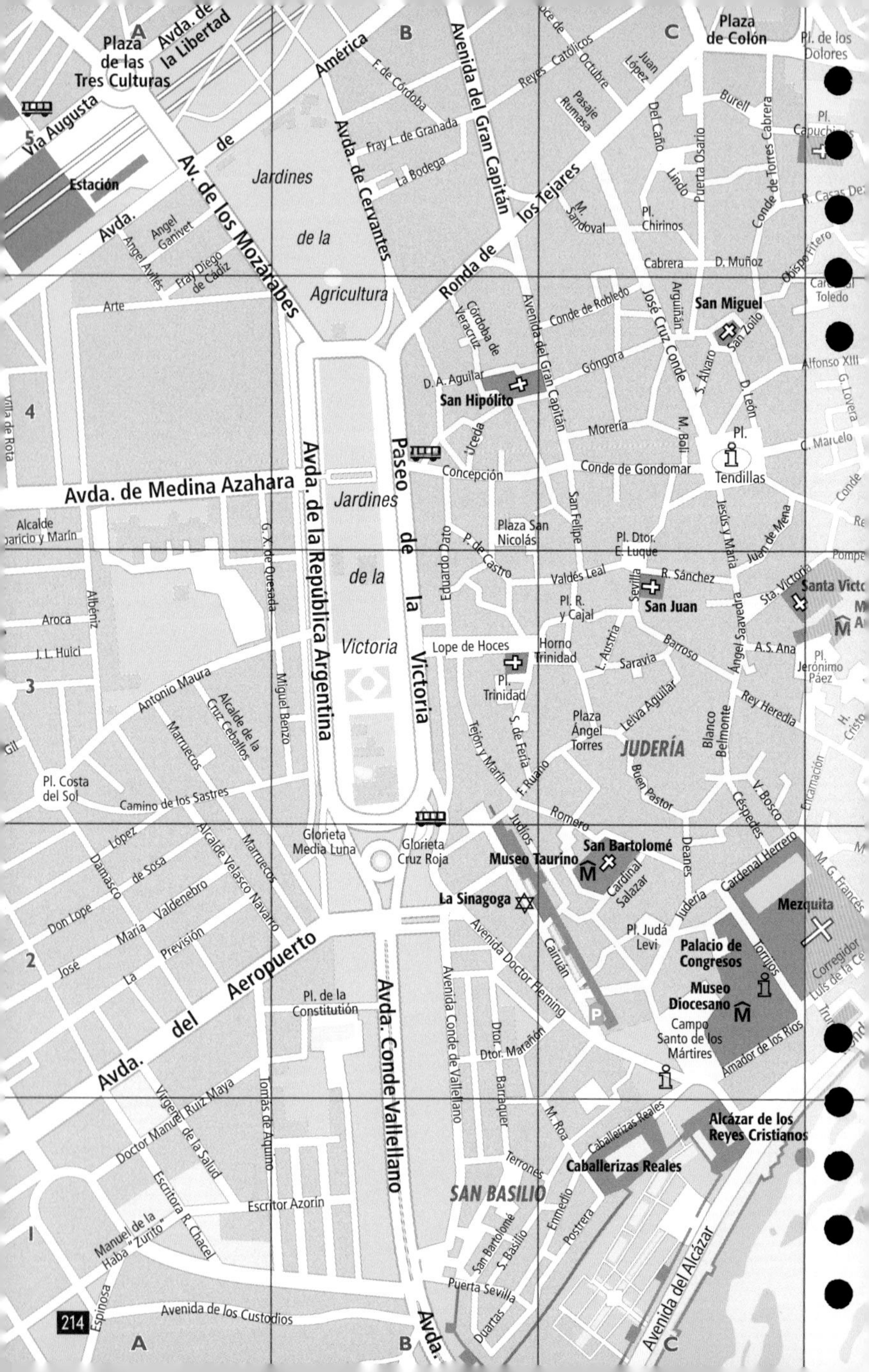

A
B
C
Plaza de las Tres Culturas
Avda. de la Libertad
América
Avenida del Gran Capitán
Plaza de Colón
Pl. de los Dolores
Vía Augusta
5
Estación
Av. de los Mozárabes
Avda. de
Jardines de la Agricultura
F. de Córdoba
Fray L. de Granada
La Bodega
Avda. de Cervantes
Reyes Católicos
Octubre
Juan López
Pasaje Rumasa
Burell
Del Caño
Puerta Osario
Conde de Torres Cabrera
Pl. Capuchinos
R. Casas Deza
Lindo
Ronda de los Tejares
M. Sandoval
Pl. Chirinos
Cabrera
D. Muñoz
Obispo Fitero
Angel Ganivet
Angel Avilés
Fray Diego de Cádiz
Arte
Córdoba de Veracruz
Conde de Robledo
José Cruz Conde
Arguiñán
San Miguel
San Zoilo
Cardenal Toledo
Alfonso XIII
Góngora
S. Álvaro
D. León
G. Lovera
D. A. Aguilar
San Hipólito
Villa de Rota
4
Uceda
Morería
M. Boil
Pl. Tendillas
C. Marcelo
Paseo de la Victoria
Concepción
Conde de Gondomar
Avda. de Medina Azahara
Avda. de la República Argentina
Jardines de la Victoria
Alcalde Aparicio y Marín
G. X. de Quesada
Eduardo Dato
P. de Castro
Plaza San Nicolás
San Felipe
Pl. Dtor. E. Luque
Jesús y María
Juan de Mena
Valdés Leal
Sevilla
R. Sánchez
Santa Victoria
Sta. Victoria
San Juan
Pl. R. y Cajal
Ángel Saavedra
Albéniz
Aroca
J. L. Huici
Lope de Hoces
Horno Trinidad
L. Austria
Barroso
A.S. Ana
Pl. Jerónimo Páez
Saravia
Pl. Trinidad
3
Antonio Maura
Alcalde de la Cruz Ceballos
Miguel Benzo
Marruecos
Tejón y Marín
S. de Feria
Leiva Aguilar
Plaza Ángel Torres
JUDERÍA
Blanco Belmonte
Rey Heredia
H. Cristo
Gil
Pl. Costa del Sol
Camino de los Sastres
F. Ruano
Buen Pastor
V. Bosco
Encarnación
Céspedes
Romero
Judíos
López
Damasco
de Sosa
Alcalde Velasco Navarro
Glorieta Media Luna
Glorieta Cruz Roja
San Bartolomé
Museo Taurino
Cardinal Salazar
Deanes
Cardenal Herrero
M. G. Francés
La Sinagoga
Judería
Mezquita
Don Lope
María
Valdenebro
Previsión
Avenida Doctor Fleming
Cairuán
Pl. Judá Levi
Palacio de Congresos
Torrijos
Corregidor Luis de la Cerda
2
José
La
Avda. del Aeropuerto
Pl. de la Constitución
Avda. Conde Vallellano
Avenida Conde de Vallellano
Museo Diocesano
Campo Santo de los Mártires
Amador de los Ríos
Dtor. Barraquer
Dtor. Marañón
Tomás de Aquino
Vigen de la Salud
Doctor Manuel Ruiz Maya
M. Roa
Caballerizas Reales
Alcázar de los Reyes Cristianos
Terrones
SAN BASILIO
Enmedio
Postrera
Escritor Azorín
Escritora R. Chacel
Manuel de la Haba "Zurito"
1
San Bartolomé
S. Basilio
Avenida del Alcázar
Puerta Sevilla
Avenida de los Custodios
Espinosa
Duartas
Avda.

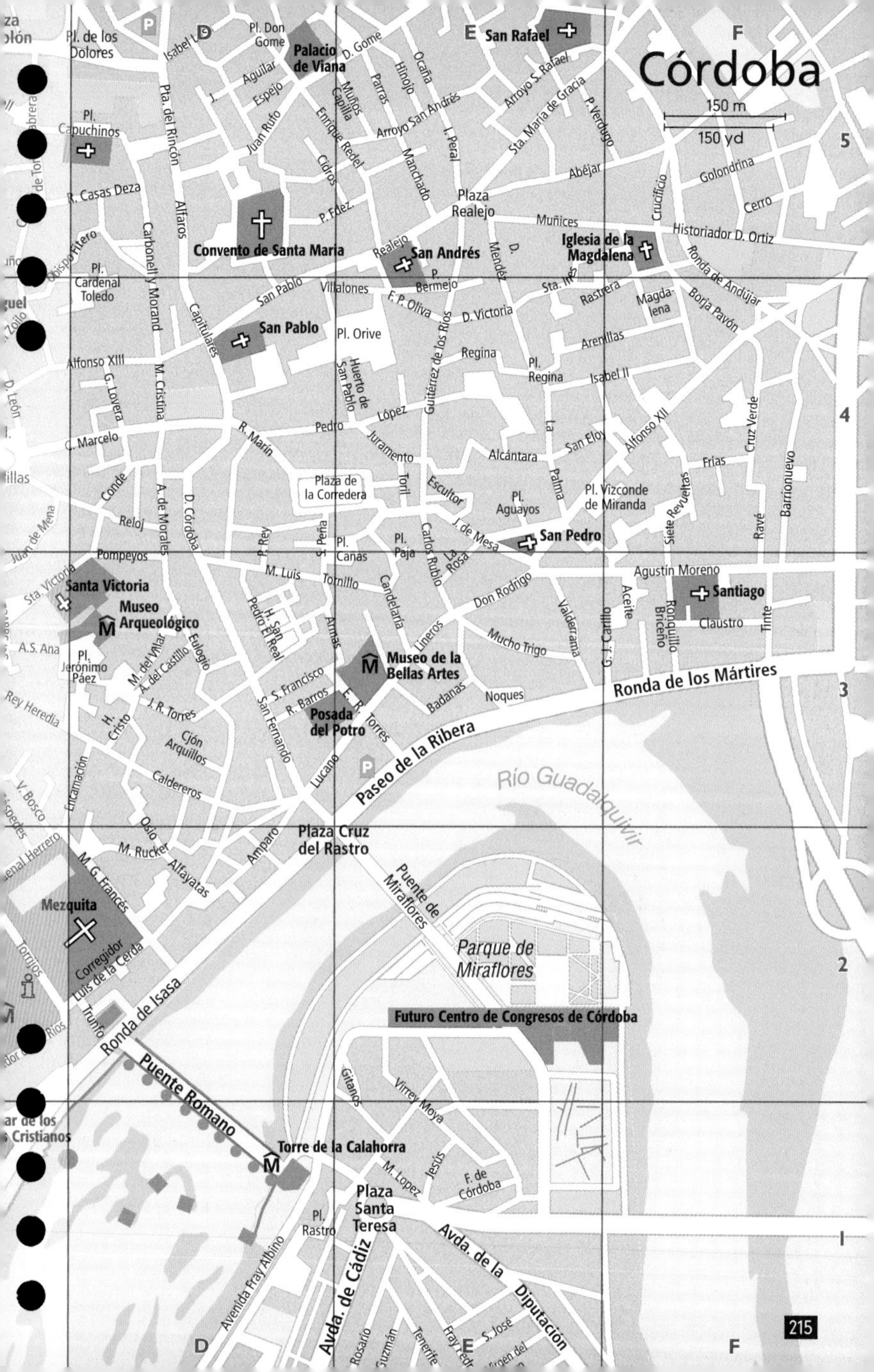
Córdoba
150 m
150 yd
D
E
F
5
4
3
2
1
Palacio de Viana
San Rafael
Pl. de los Dolores
Pl. Don Gome
Isabel II
Aguilar
Espejo
Juan Rufo
D. Gome
Muños Capilla
Parras
Hinojo
Ocaña
Arroyo S. Rafael
Sta. María de Gracia
P. Verdugo
Pl. Capuchinos
Pta. del Rincón
Enrique Redel
Arroyo San Andrés
I. Peral
Cidros
Manchado
Abéjar
Golondrina
Crucifício
R. Casas Deza
Alfaros
Carbonell y Morand
Convento de Santa María
P. Fdez.
Plaza Realejo
Muñices
Cerro
Historiador D. Ortiz
Iglesia de la Magdalena
Realejo
San Andrés
P. Bermejo
D. Méndez
Pl. Cardenal Toledo
Obispo Fitero
Ronda de Andújar
Sta. Inés
Rastrera
Magdalena
Borja Pavón
San Pablo
Villalones
F. P. Oliva
D. Victoria
Capitulares
San Pablo
Pl. Orive
Gutiérrez de los Ríos
Arenillas
Regina
Pl. Regina
Isabel II
Alfonso XIII
G. Lovera
M. Cristina
Huerto de San Pablo
López
Alfonso XII
Cruz Verde
Pedro
R. Marín
C. Marcelo
Juramento
La Palma
San Eloy
Alcántara
Frías
Barrionuevo
Plaza de la Corredera
Toril
Escultor
Pl. Aguayos
Pl. Vizconde de Miranda
Conde
A. de Morales
D. Córdoba
Reloj
Juan de Mena
P. Rey
S. Peña
Pl. Cañas
Pl. Paja
Carlos Rubio
La Rosa
J. de Mesa
San Pedro
Siete Revueltas
Ravé
Pompeyos
M. Luis
Tornillo
Agustín Moreno
Sta. Victoria
Santa Victoria
Museo Arqueológico
H. San Pedro El Real
Candelaría
Don Rodrigo
Valderrama
Aceite
Santiago
Ronquillo Briceño
Claustro
Tinte
A.S. Ana
Pl. Jerónimo Páez
M. del Villar
A. del Castillo
Eulogio
Armas
Lineros
Mucho Trigo
G. J. Carillo
Museo de la Bellas Artes
S. Francisco
Rey Heredia
J. R. Torres
H. Cristo
R. Barros
San Fernando
E. R. Torres
Badanas
Noques
Ronda de los Mártires
Posada del Potro
Cjón Arquillos
Paseo de la Ribera
Lucano
Río Guadalquivir
V. Bosco
Encarnación
Caldereros
Osio
M. Rucker
Amparo
Plaza Cruz del Rastro
Alfayatas
M. G. Francés
Puente de Miraflores
Mezquita
Torrijos
Corregidor Luis de la Cerda
Parque de Miraflores
Triunfo
Ronda de Isasa
Futuro Centro de Congresos de Córdoba
Puente Romano
Gitanos
Virrey Moya
Torre de la Calahorra
M. Lopez
Jesús
F. de Córdoba
Plaza Santa Teresa
Pl. Rastro
Avenida Fray Albino
Avda. de Cádiz
Avda. de la Diputación
Rosario
Guzmán
Tenerife
Fray Pedro
S. José
Alcázar de los Reyes Cristianos

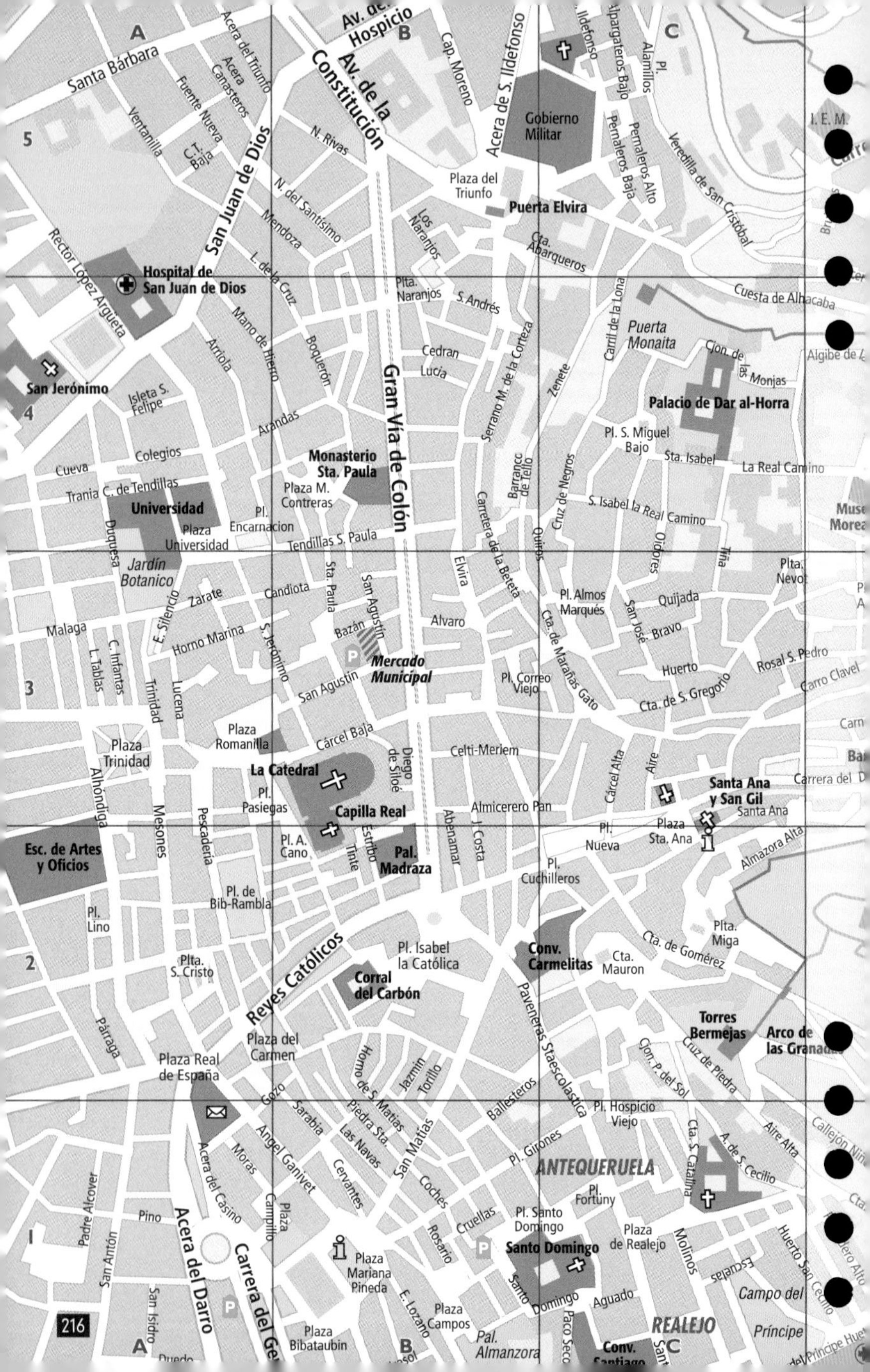
A
B
C
5
4
3
2
1
Santa Bárbara
Acera del Triunfo
Acera Canasteros
Fuente Nueva
Ventanilla
C.T. Baja
San Juan de Dios
Av. de Hospicio
Av. de la Constitución
Cap. Moreno
Acera de S. Ildefonso
Gobierno Militar
Alpargateros Bajo
Pl. Alamillos
Pernaleros Alto
Pernaleros Baja
I. E. M.
Veredilla de San Cristóbal
Plaza del Triunfo
Puerta Elvira
N. Rivas
N. del Santísimo
Mendoza
L. de la Cruz
Los Naranjos
Cta. Abarqueros
Rector López Argüeta
Hospital de San Juan de Dios
Plta. Naranjos
S. Andrés
Cuesta de Alhacaba
Carril de la Lona
Puerta Monaita
Cjon. de las Monjas
Algibe de
San Jerónimo
Mano de Hierro
Arriola
Boquerón
Gran Vía de Colón
Cedran
Lucia
Serrano M. de la Corteza
Zenete
Palacio de Dar al-Horra
Isleta S. Felipe
Arandas
Pl. S. Miguel Bajo
Sta. Isabel
La Real Camino
Colegios
Cueva
Monasterio Sta. Paula
Plaza M. Contreras
Barranco de Tello
Cruz de Negros
Trania C. de Tendillas
Universidad
Pl. Encarnacion
S. Isabel la Real Camino
Plaza Universidad
Tendillas S. Paula
Carretera de la Beteta
Quiros
Oidores
Tiña
Duquesa
Jardín Botanico
Zarate
Candiota
Sta. Paula
San Agustín
Elvira
Pl. Almos Marqués
Quijada
Plta. Nevot
E. Silencio
Malaga
Horno Marina
S. Jerónimo
Bazán
Alvaro
Cta. de Marañas Gato
San José
Bravo
L. Tablas
C. Infantas
Mercado Municipal
Huerto
Rosal S. Pedro
Carro Clavel
Trinidad
Lucena
San Agustín
Pl. Correo Viejo
Cta. de S. Gregorio
Plaza Romanilla
Cárcel Baja
Celti-Meriem
Plaza Trinidad
Diego de Siloé
Cárcel Alta
Aire
La Catedral
Santa Ana y San Gil
Carrera del
Alhóndiga
Pl. Pasiegas
Almicerero Pan
Capilla Real
Santa Ana
Mesones
Pescadería
Abenamar
J. Costa
Pl. Nueva
Plaza Sta. Ana
Esc. de Artes y Oficios
Pl. A. Cano
Estribo
Tinte
Pal. Madraza
Almazora Alta
Pl. Cuchilleros
Pl. de Bib-Rambla
Pl. Lino
Plta. Miga
Reyes Católicos
Pl. Isabel la Católica
Conv. Carmelitas
Cta. Mauron
Cta. de Gomérez
Plta. S. Cristo
Corral del Carbón
Párraga
Paveneras Staescolastica
Torres Bermejas
Arco de las Granadas
Plaza del Carmen
Horno de S. Matias
Jazmin
Tortillo
Cjon. P. del Sol
Cruz de Piedra
Plaza Real de España
Gozo
Sarabia
Piedra Sta.
Ballesteros
Pl. Hospicio Viejo
Aire Alta
Callejón Ni
Angel Ganivet
Las Navas
San Matias
Pl. Girones
Cta. S. Catalina
A. de S. Cecilio
Acera del Casino
Moras
Cervantes
ANTEQUERUELA
Padre Alcover
Pino
Acera del Darro
Campillo
Plaza
Coches
Cruellas
Pl. Fortuny
Pl. Santo Domingo
Plaza de Realejo
Molinos
Huerto Alto
San Antón
Carrera del Ge
Plaza Mariana Pineda
Rosario
Santo Domingo
Escuelas
Huerto San Cecilio
San Isidro
E. Lozano
Plaza Campos
Santo Domingo
Aguado
Campo del Príncipe
Paco Seco
Plaza Bibataubin
Pal. Almanzora
REALEJO
Príncipe
Conv. Santiago

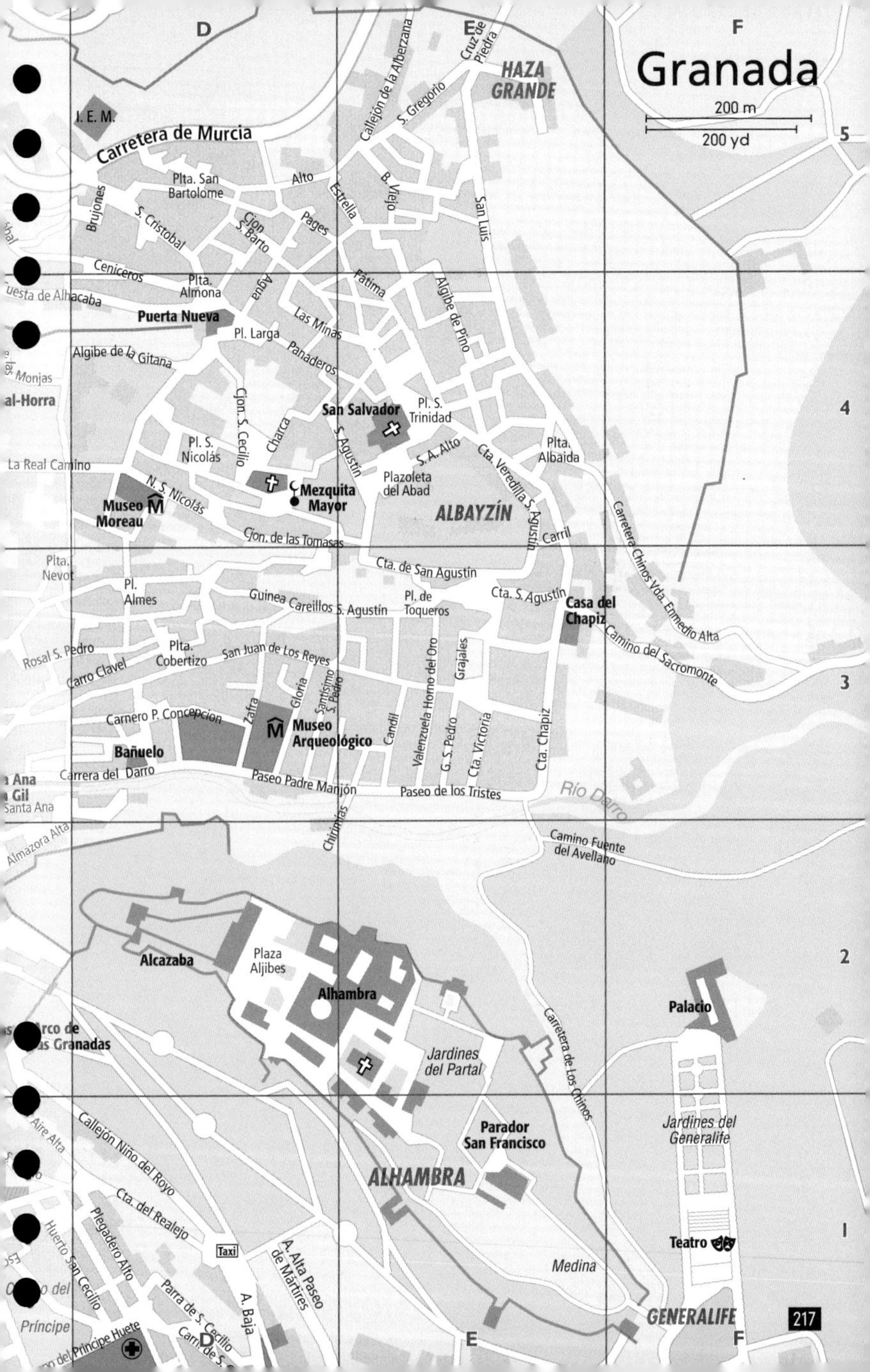
Granada
200 m
200 yd
D
E
F
5
4
3
2
1
HAZA GRANDE
Cruz de Piedra
Callejón de la Alberzana
S. Gregorio
I. E. M.
Carretera de Murcia
Plta. San Bartolome
Alto
Estrella
B. Viejo
San Luis
Brujones
S. Cristobal
Cjon S. Barto
Pages
Ceniceros
Plta. Almona
Cuesta de Alhacaba
Agua
Fátima
Algibe de Pino
Puerta Nueva
Las Minas
Pl. Larga
Panaderos
Algibe de la Gitana
las Monjas
al-Horra
Cjon. S. Cecilio
Charca
San Salvador
Pl. S. Trinidad
S. Agustín
Pl. S. Nicolás
S. A. Alto
Plta. Albaida
La Real Camino
Cta. Veredilla S. Agustín
Mezquita Mayor
Plazoleta del Abad
N. S. Nicolás
Museo Moreau
ALBAYZÍN
Carril
Cjon. de las Tomasas
Carretera Chinos Vda. Enmedio Alta
Plta. Nevot
Cta. de San Agustín
Pl. Almes
Guinea Careillos S. Agustín
Pl. de Toqueros
Cta. S. Agustín
Casa del Chapiz
Camino del Sacromonte
Rosal S. Pedro
Plta. Cobertizo
San Juan de Los Reyes
Carro Clavel
Grajales
Gloria
Santísimo S. Pedro
Carnero P. Concepcion
Zafra
Museo Arqueológico
Candil
Valenzuela Horno del Oro
G. S. Pedro
Cta. Victoria
Cta. Chapiz
Bañuelo
Ana Gil
Carrera del Darro
Paseo Padre Manjón
Paseo de los Tristes
Río Darro
Santa Ana
Chirimías
Almazora Alta
Camino Fuente del Avellano
Alcazaba
Plaza Aljibes
Alhambra
Palacio
Arco de las Granadas
Jardines del Partal
Carretera de Los Chinos
Aire Alta
Callejón Niño del Royo
Parador San Francisco
Jardines del Generalife
ALHAMBRA
Cta. del Realejo
Plegadero Alto
Huerto San Cecilio
Taxi
A. Alta Paseo de Mártires
Teatro
Parra de S. Cecilio
A. Baja
Medina
Príncipe
Príncipe Huete
GENERALIFE

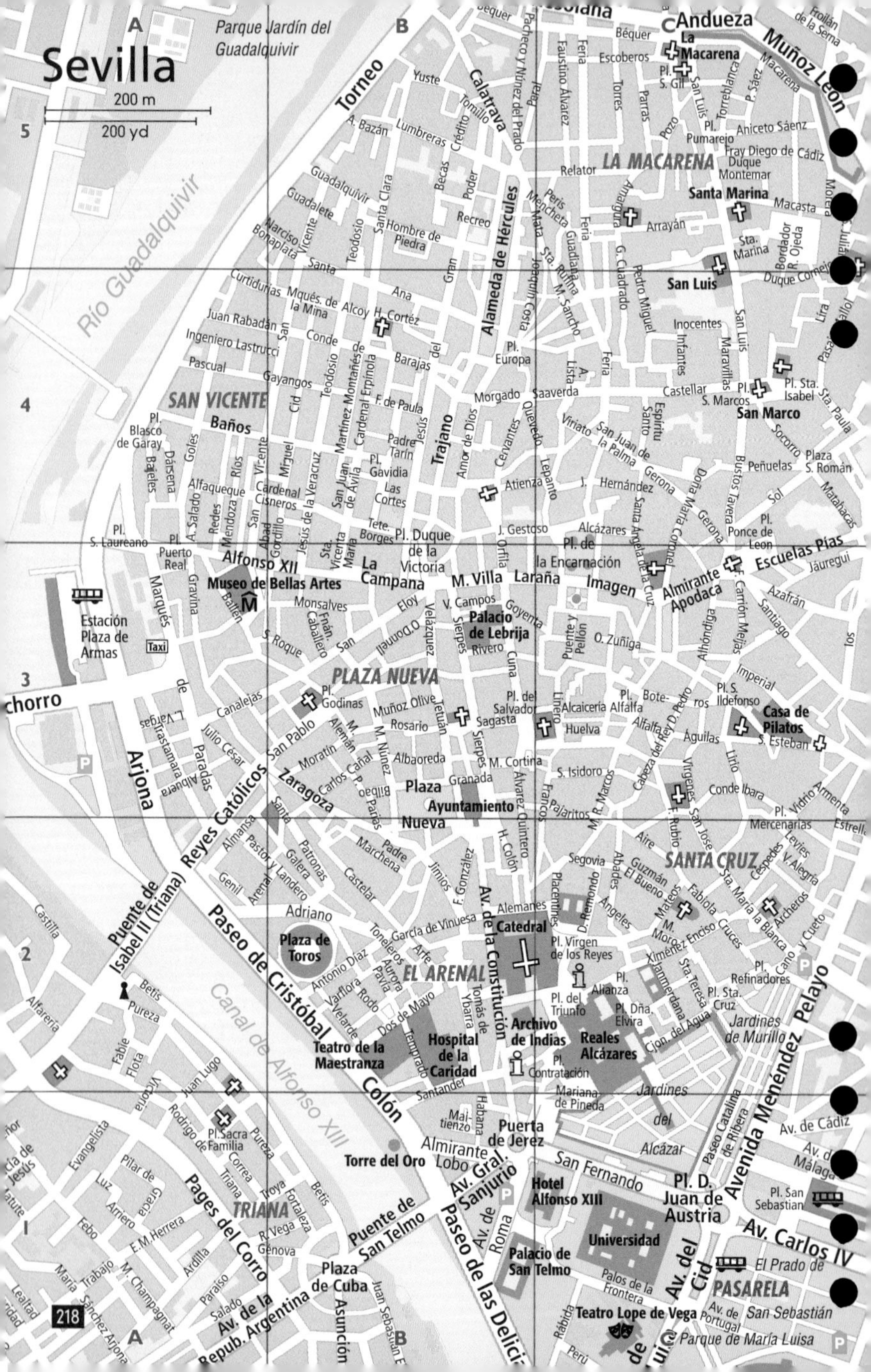

Sevilla
200 m
200 yd
A
B
C
5
4
3
2
1
Parque Jardín del Guadalquivir
Río Guadalquivir
Torneo
Calatrava
Andueza
La Macarena
Muñoz León
Pl. S. Gil
Froilán de la Serna
Béquer
Escoberos
Torres
Parras
Pozo
San Luis
Torreblanca
P. Sáez
Macarena
Feria
Faustino Álvarez
Pacheco y Núñez del Prado
Yuste
Tomillo
Crédito
A. Bazán
Lumbreras
Becas
Poder
Recreo
Guadalquivir
Guadalete
Santa Clara
Hombre de Piedra
Narciso Bonaplata
Vicente
Teodosio
Santa
Relator
LA MACARENA
Pl. Pumarejo
Aniceto Sáenz
Fray Diego de Cádiz
Duque Montemar
Santa Marina
Macasta
Arrayán
Sta. Marina
Bordador R. Ojeda
San Luis
Duque Cornejo
Peris Mencheta
Amargura
G. Cuadrado
Pedro Miguel
Alameda de Hércules
Joaquín Costa
M. Sancho
Guadiana
Sta. Rufina
Curtidurías
Mqués. de la Mina
Alcoy
Ana
H. Cortéz
Gran
Juan Rabadán
Ingeniero Lastrucci
Pascual
Conde
Gayangos
Barajas
del
San
Teodosio
Martínez Montañés
Cardenal Espínola
de
Pl. Europa
Lista
A.
Inocentes
Infantes
Maravillas
Lira
Pasaje Valvanera
SAN VICENTE
Baños
Pl. Blasco de Garay
F. de Paula
Jesús
Padre Tarín
Trajano
Morgado
Saaverda
Castellar
Pl. S. Marcos
Pl. Sta. Isabel
San Marco
Sta. Paula
Espíritu Santo
Viriato
San Juan de la Palma
Amor de Dios
Cervantes
Quevedo
Lepanto
Gerona
Socorro
Peñuelas
Plaza S. Román
Bustos Tavera
Doña María Coronel
Hernández
Sol
Matahacas
Goles
Dársena
Bajeles
Vírgen
Ríos
Miguel
Cid
Pl. Gavidia
Las Cortes
San Juan de Ávila
Jesús de la Veracruz
Alfaqueque
Cardenal Cisneros
Atienza
Salado
Redes
Mendoza
San
Abad Gordillo
Pl. S. Laureano
Pl. Puerto Real
Sta. Vicenta María
Tete. Borges
Pl. Duque de la Victoria
J. Gestoso
Alcázares
Santa Ángela de la Cruz
Pl. Ponce de León
Pl. de la Encarnación
Escuelas Pías
Jáuregui
Alfonso XII
Museo de Bellas Artes
La Campana
M. Villa
Laraña
Imagen
Almirante Apodaca
F. Carrión Mejías
Azafrán
Santiago
Estación Plaza de Armas
Marqués
Gravina
Bailén
Monsalves
Fnán. Caballero
Eloy
V. Campos
Palacio de Lebrija
Goyeneta
Puente y Pellón
Orfila
O. Zuñiga
Alhóndiga
Taxi
S. Roque
San
O'Donnell
Velázquez
Sierpes
Rivero
Cuna
los
PLAZA NUEVA
Imperial
Pl. S. Ildefonso
chorro
de
Canalejas
L. Vargas
Trastamara
Julio César
Paradas
Albuera
Arjona
Pl. Godinas
San Pablo
Muñoz Olive
Tetuán
Rosario
Pl. del Salvador
Sagasta
Lineros
Alcaicería
Huelva
Pl. Alfalfa
Alfalfa
Boteros
Cabeza del Rey D. Pedro
Águilas
Casa de Pilatos
S. Esteban
Lirio
Moratín
M. Alemán
M. Núñez
Albaoreda
Carlos Cañal
P. Bilbao
Parras
Plaza Nueva
Granada
Ayuntamiento
M. Cortina
S. Isidoro
Francos
M. R. Marcos
Pajaritos
Vírgenes
F. Rubio
San José
Conde Ibarra
Pl. Vidrio
Armenta
Mercenarias
Estrella
Levíes
V. Alegría
Céspedes
Reyes Católicos
Zaragoza
Santas
Almansa
Pastor y Landero
Galera
Patronas
Padre Marchena
Castelar
Jimios
F. González
Álvarez Quintero
H. Colón
Aire
Segovia
Abades
Guzmán El Bueno
SANTA CRUZ
Sta. María la Blanca
Genil
Arenal
Adriano
Puente de Isabel II (Triana)
Paseo de Cristóbal Colón
Castilla
Plaza de Toros
Toneleros
García de Vinuesa
Arfe
Antonio Díaz
Aurora
Pavía
EL ARENAL
Av. de la Constitución
Alemanes
Catedral
Placentines
D. Remondo
Ángeles
Mateos
M. Moro
Ximénez Enciso
Fabiola
Cruces
Archeros
Cano y Cueto
Pl. Virgen de los Reyes
Pl. Alianza
Pl. Refinadores
Pelayo
Betis
Pureza
Alfarería
Varflora
Rodo
Velarde
Dos de Mayo
Temprado
Tomás de Ybarra
Pl. del Triunfo
Pl. Dña. Elvira
Sta. Teresa
Pl. Sta. Cruz
Jardines de Murillo
Mesón del Moro
Fabie
Flota
Teatro de la Maestranza
Hospital de la Caridad
Archivo de Indias
Reales Alcázares
Cjon. del Agua
Pl. Contratación
Canal de Alfonso XIII
Victoria
Juan Lugo
Rodrigo de Triana
Pl. Sacra Familia
Pureza
Santander
Habana
Mariana de Pineda
Jardines del Alcázar
Paseo Catalina de Ribera
Avenida Menéndez Pelayo
Av. de Cádiz
Av. de Málaga
Evangelista
Pilar de Gracia
Correa
Mai-tienzo
Puerta de Jerez
Almirante Lobo
San Fernando
Pl. D. Juan de Austria
Pl. San Sebastián
Torre del Oro
Av. Gral. Sanjurio
Hotel Alfonso XIII
Av. Carlos IV
Luz
Arriero
Febo
E.M.Herrera
Troya
Fortaleza
Betis
R. Vega
Génova
TRIANA
Pages del Corro
Puente de San Telmo
Av. de Roma
Paseo de las Delicias
Universidad
Palacio de San Telmo
Av. del Cid
El Prado de San Sebastián
PASARELA
Palos de la Frontera
Av. de Portugal
Plaza de Cuba
Juan Sebastián Elcano
Asunción
Av. de la Repúb. Argentina
Trabajo
M. Champagnat
María Sánchez Arjona
Ardilla
Paraíso
Salado
Lealtad
Rábida
Perú
Teatro Lope de Vega
Parque de María Luisa
P

Index

Picture Credits

AA/Michelle Chaplow: 90, 136
AA/Jerry Edmanson: 29
AA/James A. Tims: 52
AA/Peter Wilson: 20, 166

akg-images: Bildarchiv Steffens 149 (top)

José Luis Alvarez: 26

DuMont Bildarchiv/Arthur F. Selbach: 5 (top), 6 (No 1, 3, 4, 5, 7, 9, 10), 10 (top), 12, 14, 15, 16, 24, 28, 32, 33, 41 (top), 45, 46, 49, 51, 53 (top), 55, 59, 60, 65, 70, 72/73, 80, 81, 86, 87, 91, 97 (left), 104, 108/109, 114 (left), 120, 122, 125, 126, 127, 131, 134, 135, 147 (right), 149 (bottom), 153, 158 (top), 159, 161, 162, 167, 171, 182, 186, 190/191

Fotolia: pepereyes 42, joserpizarro 43 (top), Ekaterina 53 (bottom), uckyo 67, Francisco Javier Gil 79 (left), Anibal Trejo 107,

Getty Images: 19, Daniel Perez Garcia-Santos 23, Carolyn Hubbard-Ford 82, Axiom Photographic Agency 82, Antonio Luis Martinez Cano 100, Foodcollection 113 (left), Lonely Planet 138, Moment Open/Inigo Fdz de Pinedo 140

huber-images: Reinhard Schmid 5 (bottom), Rellini Maurizio 40/41, Riccardo Spila 56, Günter Gräfenhain 121

laif: Redux/Nano Calvo 9, laif/hemis.fr/Frances Stephane 25, Gunnar Knechtel 41 (bottom), robertharding/Marco Simoni 64, Marc-Oliver Schulz 115 (bottom), laif/hemis.fr/Rene Mattes 132, Gernot Huber 172, Gunnar Knechtel 174, Monica Gumm 176

Lookphotos: Photononstop 6 (No 2), Kai Maeritz 6 (No 6), age fotostock/J. D. Dallet 6 (No 8), age fotostock 10 (bottom), Jürgen Richter 30 (bottom)d 34/35, age fotostock/San Rostro 69, Elan Feisher 89, age fotostock/J. D. Dallet 94, age fotostock 97 (right), 98, 101, 102, Photononstop 117, age fotostock 158 (bottom), Kai Maeritz 165, age fotostock 168, 170, Kai Maeritz 178/179, age fotostock/Thomas Dressler 188

mauritius images: Alamy/Ben Ramos 39 (top), age fotostock/Juan Carlos Munoz 39 (bottom), Alamy/Jerónimo Alba 42/43, Alamy/Jorge Tutor 43 (bottom), Alamy/Mikel Bilbao Gorostiaga Travels 77 (bottom), Alamy/Stuart Black 78/79, Alamy/Jerónimo Alba 79 (right), Alamy/Kevin Snelling 113 (right), 114/115, Alamy/Jerónimo Alba 128, Sabine Lubenow 142/143, Rene Mattes 148/149, Alamy/Felipe Rodriguez 151

picture-alliance: Global Travel Images 66, Carlo Morucchio 115 (top), Arco Images 139

Shutterstock: Gabor Kovacs Photography 62, Marcelina Zygula 77 (top), chrupka 78 (left), Alex Fonda 92, Tono Balaguer 147 (left), PHB.cz Richard Semik 148 (left)

On the cover: fhm/gettyimages (top); Monica Gumm/laif (bottom)
On the back cover: Matteo Colombo/gettyimages

Credits

2nd Edition 2020
Fully revised and redesigned

Worldwide Distribution: Marco Polo Travel Publishing Ltd
Pinewood, Chineham Business Park
Crockford Lane, Chineham
Basingstoke, Hampshire RG24 8AL, United Kingdom

Authors: Cordula Rabe, Des Hannigan, Josephine Quintero, Achim Bourmer
Editor: Annegret Gellweiler, Gerhard Junker, Michaela Salden, Sylvia Scheider-Schopf, Anja Schlatterer, Anette Vogt, Julia Wilhelm (red.sign, Stuttgart)
Revised editing and translation: Sarah Trenker, Lietzow
Design: CYCLUS · Visuelle Kommunikation, Stuttgart
Project manager: Dieter Luippold
Programme supervisor: Birgit Borowski
Chief editor: Rainer Eisenschmid

Cartography: © MAIRDUMONT GmbH & Co. KG, Ostfildern
3D illustrations: jangled nerves, Stuttgart

Printed in Poland

Despite all of our authors' thorough research, errors can creep in. The publishers do not accept any liability for this. Whether you want to praise us, alert us to errors or give us a personal tip – please don't hesitate to email or post:

MARCO POLO Travel Publishing Ltd
Pinewood, Chineham Business Park
Crockford Lane, Chineham
Basingstoke, Hampshire RG24 8AL
United Kingdom
Email: sales@marcopolouk.com

FSC
www.fsc.org
MIX
Paper from responsible sources
FSC® C018236

Andalucía

Travel with
Insider
Tips

www.marco-polo.com

How this Guide Works

Our guide introduces you to the sights in Andalucía in four chapters. The map below presents an overview of how the chapters are arranged. Each one has been allocated a special colour. In order to help you plan your trip, we have subdivided all the main points of interest in each chapter into three sections: the must-see sights are listed under the *TOP 10* and also highlighted in the book with two Baedeker stars. You'll find other important sites that didn't quite make our *Top 10* list in the *Don't Miss* section. A selection of other places worth seeing appears in the *At Your Leisure* section.

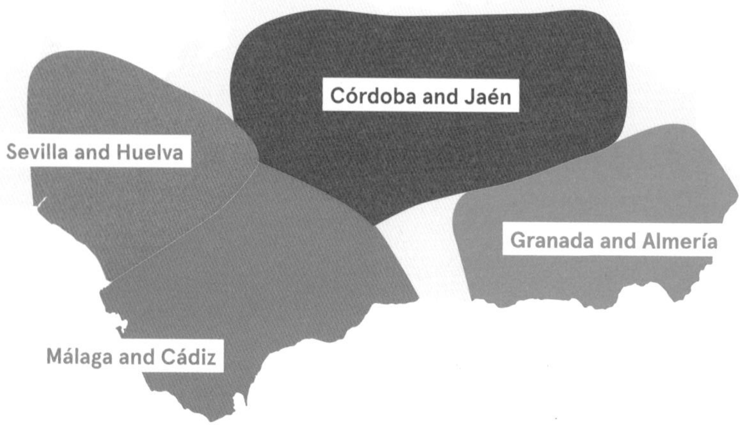